# VOICES FROM THE COUNCIL

edition 12222

# VOICES FROM THE COUNCIL

**EDITED BY Michael R. Prendergast AND M. D. Ridge**

PASTORAL PRESS
PORTLAND · OREGON

Voices from the Council

ISBN 1-57992-119-1

© 2004 Pastoral Press

Pastoral Press
An imprint of OCP Publications
5536 NE Hassalo
Portland, OR 97213
Phone 1-800-LITURGY (548-8749)
E-mail: liturgy@ocp.org
www.ocp.org

Editorial Assistance: Glenn CJ Byer, Bari Colombari, Geraldine Ethen, Nancy Wolf

The views and opinions expressed in the interviews and articles herein
are solely those of the authors and interviewees, and not necessarily
those of OCP, its publisher, and/or the editors.

Publisher: John J. Limb
Editorial Director: Paulette McCoy
Book Design: Judy Urben
Cover Design: Le Vu
Art Director: Jean Germano
Cover Art: Jean Germano
    (The images of Pius XII, John XXIII, Paul VI, and John Paul II
    were inspired by Vatican postage stamps. Ms. Germano lived in Rome 1964–1978,
    including some time in the employ of the North American College.)

# TABLE OF CONTENTS

## PART 1: COUNCIL FATHERS

## PART 2: PERITUS AND STAFF

## PART 3: THEOLOGIANS

# PART 4: MEDIA/OBSERVERS

# PART 5 APPENDIX

# Introduction

The vigor and courage of the Catholic Church can be traced in the records of twenty Ecumenical Councils, as well as countless provincial and regional councils throughout the centuries. Growth and maturity have not come about without conflict, which has made these councils momentous occasions in the life of the institutional church.

As he set in motion the Second Vatican Council (the 21st Ecumenical Council), Pope John XXIII rejected the prophets of doom who forecast disaster for the church. His enthusiasm and his personal commitment to the Council led him to open his arms to welcome, for the first time, participation by non-Catholic parties. He was so positive about the need for new direction and "fresh air" in the church that he invited all people of good will to join the church in "welcoming the good tidings of salvation more favorably."

This call for unity issued by both Council popes, John XXIII and Paul VI, is a common thread in the interviews and reflections that make up *Voices from the Council*. These people—one woman and thirty-two men—were present in person at St. Peter's in Rome or were responsible immediately following the Council for implementing the directives of this historic event held from 1962–1965. They were there as Council fathers, *periti* (experts), theologians, members of the media or observers. They were the Council's architects and participants.

In *Voices from the Council*, Oregon Catholic Press has taken a unique opportunity to celebrate the 40th anniversary of this momentous gathering—in particular, the publication of the Constitution on the Sacred Liturgy *(Sacrosanctum concilium)*. The *Voices* project started as a series of articles for the quarterly liturgical/music-planning journal *Today's Liturgy*. Realizing that many Council participants had died and others were now in their eighties or nineties, we expanded the project to include even more of those who were engaged four decades ago in an earthshaking movement to open the church to new ideas. Many see these people as the prophets of our age. They are the ones who were trained before the Council was conceived, the ones who carried out its directives, argued for its approach, taught students and parishioners the concepts, and incorporated into their personal and spiritual lives the directives emanating from the Council. We wanted to learn from these Council participants, who now could look back on its momentous and courageous statements and share their vivid memories and their insight for the present and future church.

The challenge that Pope John XXIII stated in his opening address—"to work actively so that there may be fulfilled the great mystery of that unity"—has been met willingly by the people we have interviewed. In this book they have preached, written, inspired, comforted and challenged their fellow believers. They have been forever changed because of their participation in this Council. The Council's challenge is still a goal today, "unity through truth." These interviews remind us yet again of its importance.

We are deeply grateful to the interviewers and translators who undertook the enormous task of interviewing people from thirteen countries and six continents. We hope that those readers who remember the Council will find their enthusiasm rekindled, and that those too young to have experienced it will find in these interviews a lively, thought-provoking, inside look at a remarkable event in history.

Michael R. Prendergast
M.D. Ridge

# Foreword

Forty years ago, the fathers of the Second Vatican Council set out to accomplish four goals:

- to impart an ever-increasing vigor to the Christian life of the faithful;

- to adapt more suitably to the needs of our own times those institutions that are subject to change;

- to foster whatever can promote union among all who believe in Christ;

- to strengthen whatever can help to call the whole of humanity into the household of the church.

These opening words of *Sacrosanctum concilium* have been the cause, the hope, and the guide for the renewal which has so graced our church over the past forty years. That renewal has borne great fruit in the life of the church, instilling an enthusiasm for the faith, which is the driving force of the new evangelization. In other ways, however, the Council has been misunderstood or even misrepresented, resulting in a misapplication of the intent of the Council fathers.

In recent years, particularly in regard to the liturgical renewal, a conscientious attempt has been made to return to the original intent of those bishops from throughout the world who witnessed the promulgation of their first conciliar document some forty years ago. Such a work requires a careful study of the original words of the Council fathers, sometimes even a retranslation of their thoughts for a new generation of Catholics seeking to understand the movement of the Holy Spirit in those first days of the conciliar renewal of the church.

The present volume is helpful in this regard as we listen to the voices of those who were present for the birth of the Council, which was to define the work of the church in our times. While the constitutions and other documents of the Council will always be the authentic voice of Vatican II, the voices of those who were present for those momentous days provide a wonderful stimulus to a renewed study of what the Council fathers said and did. In his homily opening the Second Vatican Council on October 11, 1962, Pope John XXIII spoke of the Council as "an occasion for the celebration once again of the unity between

Christ and the church," and proclaimed that the primary concern of the Council was "that the sacred and central truths of our Christian faith should be guarded and taught more effectively."

The interviews contained in this volume help to tell the story of how well or how inadequately we have embraced that vision. May God grant us the grace to continue the work so well begun.

Msgr. James P. Moroney
Executive Director
Secretariat for Liturgy (BCL)
United States Conference of Catholic Bishops

# Opening Address of Pope John XXIII
## October 11, 1962

Mother Church rejoices that, by the singular gift of Divine Providence, the longed-for day has finally dawned when—under the auspices of the Virgin Mother of God, whose maternal dignity is commemorated on this feast—the Second Vatican Ecumenical Council is being solemnly opened here beside St. Peter's tomb.

### The Ecumenical Councils of the Church

The Councils—both the twenty ecumenical ones and the numberless others, also important, of a provincial or regional character which have been held down through the years—all prove clearly the vigor of the Catholic Church and are recorded as shining lights in her annals.

In calling the vast assembly of bishops, the latest and humble successor of the Prince of the Apostles who is addressing you intended to assert once again the Church's magisterium (teaching authority), which is unfailing and endures until the end of time, in order that this magisterium, taking into account the errors, the requirements and the opportunities of our time, might be presented in exceptional form to all men throughout the world.

It is but natural that in opening this universal council we should like to look to the past and to listen to its voices, whose echo we like to hear in the memories and the merits of the more recent and ancient pontiffs, our predecessors. These are solemn and venerable voices, throughout the East and the West, from the fourth century to the Middle Ages, and from there to modern times, which have handed down their witness to those Councils. They are voices which proclaim in perennial fervor the triumph of that divine and human institution, the Church of Christ, which from Jesus takes its name, its grace and its meaning.

Side by side with these motives for spiritual joy, however, there has also been for more than nineteen centuries a cloud of sorrows and of trials. Not without reason did the ancient Simeon announce to Mary, the Mother of Jesus, that prophecy which has been and still is true: Behold this child is sent for the fall and the resurrection of many in Israel, and for a sign which shall be contradicted (Luke 2:34). And Jesus Himself, when He grew up, clearly outlined the manner in which the world would treat His person down through the succeeding centuries with the mysterious words: He who hears you, hears me (Luke 10:16), and with those others that the same Evangelist relates: He who is not with me is against me and he who does not gather with me scatters (Luke 11:23).

The great problem confronting the world after almost two thousand years remains unchanged. Christ is ever resplendent as the center of history and of life. Men are either with Him and His Church, and then they enjoy light, goodness, order and peace. Or else they are without Him, or against Him, and deliberately opposed to His Church, and then they give rise to confusion, to bitterness in human relations, and to the constant danger of fratricidal wars.

Ecumenical Councils, whenever they are assembled, are a solemn celebration of the union of Christ and His church and hence lead to the universal radiation of truth, to the proper guidance of individuals in domestic and social life, to the strengthening of spiritual energies for a perennial uplift toward real and everlasting goodness.

The testimony of this extraordinary magisterium of the Church in the succeeding epochs of these twnety centuries of Christian history stands before us collected in numerous and imposing volumes, which are the sacred patrimony of our ecclesiastical archives, here in Rome and in the more noted libraries of the entire world.

### The Origin and Reason of the Second Vatican Ecumenical Council

As regards the initiative for the great event which gathers us here, it will suffice to repeat as historical documentation our personal account of the first sudden bringing up in our heart and lips of the simple words, "Ecumenical Council." We uttered those words in the presence of the Sacred College of Cardinals on that memorable January 25, 1959, the feast of the conversion of St. Paul, in the basilica dedicated to him. It was completely unexpected, like a flash of heavenly light, shedding sweetness in eyes and hearts. And at the same time it gave rise to a great fervor throughout the world in expectation of the holding of the Council.

There have elapsed three years of laborious preparation, during which a wide and profound examination was made regarding modern conditions of faith and religious practice, and of Christian and especially Catholic vitality. These years have seemed to us a first sign, an initial gift of celestial grace.

Illuminated by the light of this Council, the Church—we confidently trust—will become greater in spiritual riches and, gaining the strength of new energies therefrom, she will look upon the future without fear. In fact, by bringing herself up-to-date where required, and by the wise organization of mutual cooperation, the Church will make men, families and peoples really turn their minds to heavenly things.

And thus the holding of the Council becomes a motive for wholehearted thanksgiving to the Giver of every good gift, in order to celebrate with joyous canticles the glory of Christ our Lord, the glorious and immortal King of ages and of peoples.

## Opportunities of Holding the Council

There is, moreover, venerable brothers, another subject which it is useful to propose for your consideration. Namely, in order to render our joy more complete, we wish to narrate before this great assembly our assessment of the happy circumstances under which the Ecumenical Council commences.

In the daily exercise of our pastoral office, we sometimes have to listen, much to our regret, to voices of persons who, though burning with zeal, are not endowed with too much sense of discretion or measure. In these modern times they can see nothing but prevarication and ruin. They say that our era, in comparison with past eras, is getting worse and they behave as though they had learned nothing from history, which is, none the less, the teacher of life. They behave as though at the time of former Councils everything was a full triumph for the Christian idea and life and for proper religious liberty.

We feel we must disagree with those prophets of gloom, who are always forecasting disaster, as though the end of the world was at hand. In the present order of things, Divine Providence is leading us to a new order of human relations which, by men's own efforts and even beyond their very expectations, are directed toward the fulfillment of God's superior and inscrutable designs. And everything, even human differences, leads to the greater good of the Church.

It is easy to discern this reality if we consider attentively the world of today, which is so busy with politics and controversies in the economic order that it does not find time to attend to the care of spiritual reality, with which the Church's magisterium is concerned. Such a way of acting is certainly not right, and must justly be disapproved. It cannot be denied, however, that these new conditions of modern life have at least the advantage of having eliminated those innumerable obstacles by which at one time the sons of this world impeded the free action of the Church. In fact, it suffices to leaf even cursorily through the pages of ecclesiastical history to note clearly how the Ecumenical Councils themselves, while constituting a series of true glories for the Catholic Church, were often held to the accompaniment of most serious difficulties and sufferings because of the undue interference of civil authorities. The princes of this world, indeed, sometimes in all sincerity, intended thus to protect the Church. But more frequently this occurred not without spiritual damage and danger, since their interest therein was guided by the views of a selfish and perilous policy.

In this regard, we confess to you that we feel most poignant sorrow over the fact that very many bishops, so dear to us, are noticeable here today by their absence, because they are imprisoned for their faithfulness to Christ, or impeded by other restraints. The thought of them impels us to raise most fervent prayer to God. Nevertheless, we see today, not without great hopes and to our immense consolation, that the Church, finally freed from so many obstacles of a profane nature such as trammeled her in the past, can from this Vatican Basilica, as if from a second apostolic cenacle, and through your intermediary, raise her voice resonant with majesty and greatness.

### Principle Duty of the Council: The Defense and Advancement of Truth

The greatest concern of the Ecumenical Council is this: that the sacred deposit of Christian doctrine should be guarded and taught more efficaciously. That doctrine embraces the whole of man, composed as he is of body and soul. And, since he is a pilgrim on this earth, it commands him to tend always toward heaven.

This demonstrates how our mortal life is to be ordered in such a way as to fulfill our duties as citizens of earth and of heaven and thus to attain the aim of life as established by God. That is, all men, whether taken singly or as united in society, today have the duty of tending ceaselessly during their lifetime toward the attainment of heavenly things and to use only for this purpose the earthly goods, the employment of which must not prejudice their eternal happiness.

The Lord has said: "Seek first the kingdom of God and his justice" (Matthew 6:33). The word "first" expresses the direction in which our thoughts and energies must move. We must not, however, neglect the other words of this exhortation of Our Lord, namely: "And all these things shall be given you besides" (Matthew). In reality, there always have been in the Church, and there are still today, those who, while seeking the practice of evangelical perfection with all their might, do not fail to make themselves useful to society. Indeed, it is from their constant example of life and their charitable undertakings that all that is highest and noblest in human society takes its strength and growth.

In order, however, that this doctrine may influence the numerous fields of human activity, with reference to individuals, to families and to social life, it is necessary first of all that the Church should never depart from the sacred patrimony of truth received from the Fathers. But at the same time she must ever look to the present, to the new conditions and new forms of life introduced into the modern world which have opened new avenues to the Catholic apostolate.

For this reason the Church has not watched inertly the marvelous progress of the discoveries of human genius and has not been backward in evaluating them rightly. But, while following these developments, she does not neglect to admonish men so that, over and above sense-perceived things, they may raise their eyes to God, the Source of all wisdom and all beauty. And may they never forget the most serious command: "The Lord thy God shalt thou worship, and Him only shalt thou serve" (Matt. 4:10; Luke 4:8), so that it may not happen that the fleeting fascination of visible things should impede true progress.

### Manner in which Sacred Doctrine Is Spread

Their having been established, it becomes clear how much is expected from the council in regard to doctrine. That is, the Twenty-first Ecumenical Council, which will draw upon the effective and important wealth of juridical, liturgical, apostolic and administrative experiences, wishes to transmit the doctrine, pure and integral, without any attenuation or distortion, which throughout twenty centuries, notwithstanding difficulties and contrasts, has become the common patrimony of men. It is a patrimony not well received by all, but always a rich treasure available to men of good will.

Our duty is not only to guard this precious treasure, as if we were concerned only with antiquity, but to dedicate ourselves with an earnest will and without fear to that work which our era demands of us, pursuing thus the path which the Church has followed for twenty centuries.

The salient point of this Council is not, therefore, a discussion of one article or another of the fundamental doctrine of the Church which has repeatedly been taught by the Fathers and by ancient and modern theologians, and which is presumed to be well known and familiar to all.

For this a Council was not necessary. But from the renewed, serene and tranquil adherence to all the teaching of the Church in its entirety and preciseness, as it still shines forth in the acts of the Council of Trent and First Vatican Council, the Christian, Catholic and apostolic spirit of the whole world expects a step forward toward a doctrinal penetration and a formation of consciences in faithful and perfect conformity to the authentic doctrine which, however, should be studied and expounded through the methods of research and through the literary forms of modern thought. The substance of the ancient doctrine of the deposit of faith is one thing, and the way in which it is presented is another. And it is the latter that must be taken into great consideration with patience if necessary, everything being measured in the forms and proportions of a magisterium which is predominantly pastoral in character.

*How to Repress Errors*

At the outset of the Second Vatican Council, it is evident, as always, that the truth of the Lord will remain forever. We see, in fact, as one age succeeds another, that the opinions of men follow one another and exclude each other. And often errors vanish as quickly as they arise, like fog before the sun.

The Church has always opposed these errors. Frequently she has condemned them with the greatest severity. Nowadays, however, the spouse of Christ prefers to make use of the medicine of mercy rather than that of severity. She considers that she meets the needs of the present day by demonstrating the validity of her teaching rather than by condemnations. Not, certainly, that there is a lack of fallacious teaching, opinions and dangerous concepts to be guarded against and dissipated. But these are so obviously in contrast with the right norm of honesty, and have produced such lethal fruits, that by now it would seem that men of themselves are inclined to condemn them, particularly those ways of life which despise God and His law or place excessive confidence in technical progress and a well-being based exclusively on the comforts of life. They are ever more deeply convinced of the paramount dignity of the human person and of his perfection as well as of the duties which that implies. Even more important, experience has taught men that violence inflicted on others, the might of arms and political domination, are of no help at all in finding a happy solution to the grave problems which afflict them.

That being so, the Catholic Church, raising the torch of religious truth by means of this Ecumenical Council, desires to show herself to be the loving mother of all, benign, patient, full of mercy and goodness toward the children separated from her. To the human race, oppressed by so many difficulties, she says like Peter of old to the poor man who begged alms from him: "Silver and gold I have none; but what I have, that I give thee. In the name of Jesus Christ of Nazareth, arise and walk" (Acts 3:6). In other words, this Church does not offer to the men of today riches that pass, nor does she promise then a merely earthly happiness. But she distributes to them the goods of divine grace which, raising men to the dignity of sons of God, are the most efficacious safeguards and aids toward a more human life. She opens the fountain of her life-giving doctrine which allows men, enlightened by the light of Christ, to understand well what they really are, what their lofty dignity and their purpose are, and, through her children she spreads everywhere the fullness of Christian charity, than which nothing is more effective in eradicating the seeds of discord, nothing more efficacious in promoting concord, just peace and the brotherly unity of all.

### The Unity of the Christian and Human Family Must Be Promoted

The Church's solicitude to promote and defend truth derives from the fact that, according to the plan of God, who wills all men to be saved and to come to the knowledge of the truth (1 Timothy 2:4), men without the assistance of the whole of revealed doctrine cannot reach a complete and firm unity of minds, with which are associated true peace and eternal salvation.

Unfortunately, the entire Christian family has not yet fully attained to this visible unity in truth.

The Catholic Church, therefore, considers it her duty to work actively so that there may be fulfilled the great mystery of that unity, which Jesus Christ invoked with fervent prayer from His heavenly Father on the eve of His sacrifice. She rejoices in peace, knowing well that she is intimately associated with that prayer, and then exults greatly at seeing that invocation extend its efficacy with salutary fruit even among those who are outside her fold.

Indeed, if one considers well this same unity which Christ implored for His Church, it seems to shine, as it were, with a triple ray of beneficent supernal light: namely, the unity of Catholics among themselves, which must always be kept exemplary and most firm; the unity of prayers and ardent desires with which those Christians, separated from this Apostolic See, aspire to be united with us;

and the unity in esteem and respect for the Catholic Church which animates those who follow non-Christian religions.

In this regard, it is a source of considerable sorrow to see that the greater part of the human race—although all men who are born were redeemed by the blood of Christ—does not yet participate in those sources of divine grace which exist in the Catholic Church. Hence the Church, whose light illumines all, whose strength of supernatural unity redounds to the advantage of all humanity, is rightly described in these beautiful words of St. Cyprian:

> The Church, surrounded by divine light, spreads her rays over the entire earth. This light, however, is one and unique, and shines everywhere without causing any separation in the unity of the body. She extends her branches over the whole world by her fruitfulness; she sends ever farther afield her rivulets. Nevertheless, the head is always one, the origin one for she is the one mother, abundantly fruitful. We are born of her, are nourished by her milk, we live of her spirit (*De Catholicae Ecclesiae Unitate*, 5).

Venerable brothers, such is the aim of the Second Vatican Ecumenical Council, which, while bringing together the Church's best energies and striving to have men welcome more favorably the good tidings of salvation, prepares, as it were, and consolidates the path toward that unity of mankind which is required as a necessary foundation in order that the earthly city may be brought to the resemblance of that heavenly city where truth reigns, charity is the law, and whose extent is eternity (cf. St. Augustine, Epistle 138, 3).

*Conclusion*

Now, "our voice is directed to you" (2 Cornithians 6:11), venerable brothers in the episcopate. Behold we are gathered together in this Vatican Basilica, upon which hinges the history of the Church where heaven and earth are closely joined, here near the tomb of Peter and near so many of the tombs of our holy predecessors whose ashes in this solemn hour seem to thrill in mystic exultation.

The Council now beginning rises in the Church like daybreak, a forerunner of most splendid light. It is now only dawn and already, at this first announcement of the rising day, how much sweetness fills our heart. Everything here breathes sanctity and arouses great joy. Let us contemplate the stars, which with their brightness augment the majesty of this temple. These stars, according to the testimony of the Apostle John (Revelation 1:20), are you, and with you we see shining around the tomb of the Prince of the Apostles, the golden candelabra, that is, the church is confided to you (Revelation).

We see here with you important personalities, present in an attitude of great respect and cordial expectation, having come together in Rome from the five continents to represent the nations of the world.

We might say that heaven and earth are united in the holding of the Council—the saints of heaven to protect our work, the faithful of the earth continuing in prayer to the Lord, and you, seconding the inspiration of the Holy Spirit in order that the work of all may correspond to the modern expectations and needs of the various peoples of the world.

This requires of you serenity of mind, brotherly concord, moderation in proposals, dignity in discussion and wisdom of deliberation.

God grant that your labors and your work, toward which the eyes of all peoples and the hopes of the entire world are turned, may abundantly fulfill the aspirations of all.

Almighty God! In Thee we place all our confidence, not trusting in our own strength. Look down benignly upon these pastors of Thy Church. May the light of Thy supernal grace aid us in taking decisions and in making laws. Graciously hear the prayers which we pour forth to Thee in unanimity of faith, of voice and of mind.

O Mary, Help of Christians, Help of Bishops, of whose love we have recently had particular proof in thy temple of Loreto, where we venerated the mystery of the Incarnation, dispose all things for a happy and propitious outcome and, with thy spouse, St. Joseph, the Holy Apostles Peter and Paul, St. John the Baptist and St. John the Evangelist, intercede for us to God.

To Jesus Christ, our most amiable Redeemer, immortal King of peoples and of times, be love, power and glory forever and ever. Amen.

Reprinted with permission from the *Council Daybook, Vatican II*, published by National Catholic Welfare Conference, 1312 Massachusetts Ave., N.W., Washington, D.C. 20005, © 1965, all rights reserved.

# Gather and Remember
## *Pope John XXIII Hymn*

FINLANDIA, 11 10 11 10 11 10
Jean Sibelius (1865–1957)
Arranged by Peter Quint

Owen Alstott

1. Now is the time to gath-er and re-mem-ber
2. This was our call, so clear and so in-vit-ing:
3. And so a-rose from ev-'ry town and vil-lage
4. Al-might-y God, re-vis-it your cre-a-tion.

1. Our si-lent past, in church a voice-less throng,
2. "Come and cre-ate a new and liv-ing voice.
3. Wom-en and men in won-drous har-mo-ny
4. In-still new life in hearts both old and young.

1. Fro-zen in time as in a cold De-cem-ber,
2. Be not a-fraid! God's spir-it is en-light-'ning
3. Sing-ing the song with long-lost hope and cour-age,
4. O Je-sus Christ, re-new in us the vis-ion:

1. Un-til that won-drous shep-herd came a-long,
2. All that you do, your ev-'ry fal-t'ring choice.
3. Rais-ing a-gain the cross for all to see,
4. A world where peace and jus-tice can be-long.

1. Who said, "A-rise! Come, fan the dy-ing em-ber
2. Your song will be trans-form-ing and u-nit-ing.
3. Sign of new hope, new life and new be-gin-nings,
4. O Spir-it Blest, fill ev-'ry land and na-tion.

1. And bring to life my peo-ple's prayer and song!"
2. You are God's gift— in you we all re-joice!"
3. Sign of the Christ who came to set us free.
4. Come, re-cre-ate in us God's liv-ing song!

# Glossary

***acheiropita/acheropita***—a Greek term, literally, made without hands. An image of Jesus or the Madonna; for example, the image of Jesus as shown on the veil of Veronica or the shroud of Turin.

***acta concilii***—the acts of the Council; the record of the work of the Second Vatican Council.

***ad experimentum***—a provisional approval of a rite that is to be tested for a set length of time.

***ad limina***—literally meaning at the doorway, this term refers to the visits that bishops from all over the world make (every five years) to Rome to visit the pope and various Roman congregations.

***aggiornamento***—bringing up to date, updating to the present day (*giorno*); a term used by John XXIII as one of his reasons for calling the Second Vatican Council.

***anamnesis***—refers to a type of remembering so powerful as to make present the reality being recalled.

***anathema***—used in dogmatic definitions to exclude those who do not agree with the teaching of the church.

***aula***—in general, a room or auditorium; in the case of the Second Vatican Council, the *aula* was St. Peter's basilica.

**Biblicum**—the Pontifical Biblical Institute in Rome, run by the Society of Jesus (Jesuits).

**Catholic Action**—a group of Catholics organized to further social causes in the world.

**Chaldean Rite**—a rite and community of the Catholic Church originating in what is now Iraq.

***Cherubicon/Cherubikon***—an ancient hymn of the Byzantine liturgy which begins with a reference to the cherubim (angels), "Let us who mystically represent the cherubim and sing the thrice-holy hymn to the life-giving Trinity...."

***circumstantes***—literally, those standing about, those who participate in the liturgy.

***coetus***—a gathering of any kind, but often used for the liturgical assembly or for a group studying a church document.

**conciliar**—pertaining to the Council.

***Concilium***—the group assigned the task of preparing the Council, as well as a periodical that discusses its implementation.

***Concilium ad Exquendum Constitutionem de Sacra Liturgia***—the Council assigned the task of the proper implementation of the Constitution on the Sacred Liturgy.

**constitution**—formal teaching of an Ecumenical Council. The Second Vatican Council issued four documents called constitutions: the Constitution on the Sacred Liturgy; two dogmatic constitutions (the Dogmatic Constitution on the Church and the Dogmatic Constitution on Divine Revelation), and the Pastoral Constitution on the Church in the Modern World. Constitutions usually describe or define doctrinal matters but, as the term "pastoral" suggests in the Pastoral Constitution on the Church (*Gaudium et spes*), they can also reflect on how doctrinal teachings and moral issues apply to certain situations.

**Curia**—departments in Rome that perform their duties in the name of the pope and with his authority for the good of the churches and in the service of bishops.

***decennium/decennia***—a period of ten years; decade.

**declaration**—document that summarizes and articulates (often showing significant development) the church's current teaching. The Second Vatican Council issued three declarations: on Christian Education, on the Relation of the Church to Non-Christian Religions, and on Religious Liberty.

**decrees**—Similar to constitutions, these documents can contain doctrinal matter. Similar to declarations, they contain more specific observations and recommendations for reform in the church. The Second Vatican Council issued nine decrees: on the Catholic Churches of the Eastern Rite; on Ecumenism; on the Apostolate of the Laity; on the Missionary Activity of the Church; on the

Adaptation and Renewal of Religious Life; on the Media of Social Communications; on the Pastoral Office of Bishops; on the Ministry and Life of Priests, and on the Priestly Training.

*Divino afflante spiritu*—an encyclical of Pope Pius XII on promoting biblical studies (1943).

*dixi*—the perfect form of the verb to speak or say, meaning, "I have said."

*dramatis persona(e)*—those who are playing a role, acting in a certain function.

*ecclesia ad extra/ecclesia ad intra*—refers to the audience to which a document is addressed: either the church speaking to the world (*ad extra*) or to itself (*ad intra*).

*Ecclesia semper reformanda est*—an old church saying (dictum) that in English means "The church is always being reformed." The longer form says that the church is *simul sancta et semper reformanda* (at the same time holy and being reformed).

*Ecclesiam suam*—encyclical of Pope Paul VI on the Church (1964).

*Ekphonesis*—Words of a prayer spoken aloud or sung.

**encyclical**—Latin term for "curricular letter," a formal letter, written by the Holy Father, which addresses doctrinal, moral and/or disciplinary matters.

*et omnes*—"and all" or "and everyone."

*flabella*—a fan used in papal ceremonies.

**Holy Office**—now the Congregation for the Doctrine of the Faith, formerly the Inquisition.

*Humani generis*—an encyclical of Pope Pius XII, concerning some false opinions threatening to undermine the foundations of Catholic doctrine (1950).

*in possessione*—from the Latin "*possessio,*" possessing or occupying.

**indult**—a special permission granted to deviate from a disciplinary document.

*Intégristes*—those who opposed any changes to the Roman rite or to the language of the liturgy.

*Kalenda*—a section of the Roman Martyrology for December 25, which details the birth of Christ in terms of the history of the world.

*L'Arche*—a community founded by Jean Vanier, dedicated to ministry with the mentally challenged.

*Laborem exercens*—an encyclical of John Paul II on human work (1981), on the ninetieth anniversary of *Rerum novarum.*

*legomenon*—a saying or form of speech. For example, an *hapax legomenon* is a word form that occurs only once in the Scriptures.

**magisterium**—the teaching ministry of the church vested in Rome.

*Monitio*—a formal admonition.

*Motu proprio*—a document decreed by the pope on his own authority.

*Mystici Corporis*—an encyclical on the liturgy by Pope Pius XII (1943).

**Nuncio**—an ambassador for the Holy See.

*Osservatore Romano*—the official newspaper of the Holy See, first published in 1861.

*Pacem in Terris*—a document on peace in the world by John XXIII (1963).

*pallium*—a circular white woolen band with pendants front and back featuring six black crosses, given by the pope to archbishops as a symbol of their authority and fidelity to the Roman pontiff.

*Patres conciliares*—Council fathers; the bishops of the world gathered in an Ecumenical Council.

*pensione*—a form of accommodation; usually small, family-run and inexpensive.

*Perichoresis*—the doctrine of *Circuminsession*, signifying the relationship among the three Persons of the Trinity.

*peritus/periti*—an expert or consultant to the Council. At the Second Vatican Council, bishops were able to appoint their own theological advisers.

*persona non grata/personae non gratae*—a person or persons who are so ostracized that their very existence is not recognized.

*Populorum progressio*—an encyclical of Paul VI on the progress of peoples (1967).

*Populorum progressio*—an encyclical of Paul VI on the progress of peoples (1967).

*Praenotanda*—the introductory section to a ritual which defines the theology of the sacrament or rite and outlines the correct form of celebration.

*Primus inter pares*—one of the ways the role of the pope was understood, as the "first among equals."

*Rapporteur*—a reporter to the commissions or Council.

*renovaris*—from the Latin *renovo, renovare*: to renew; renewal.

*Resurrexit*—from the Latin, "He is risen"; a liturgical custom of Easter morning, in which statues of Jesus and Mary meet and Jesus reveals himself as risen.

*salvific*—having the power, or intending, to bring about salvation.

*San Anselmo*—the Pontifical Liturgical Institute in Rome, run by the Benedictine Order.

*schema/schemata*—an outline or draft of a council document.

secretariat—a resource and clearinghouse for a topic related to the Council. Some secretariats originated as preparatory groups (Promoting Christian Unity and Social Communications), others (Dialogue with Non-Believers and Dialogue with Non-Christians) came about as an inspiration from the Council. Following the Second Vatican Council some of these secretariats became offices of the Roman Curia.

Secretary General—a church official whose role was to prepare and organize the work for the Council. Pope John XXIII appointed Archbishop Pericle Felici to serve in this role for the Second Vatican Council.

*sedia gestatoria*—the chair in which the pope was carried aloft in solemn processions.

*semper idem*—from the Latin, "always the same."

*Servus Servorum Dei*—from the Latin, "the servant of the servants of God," one of the titles of the pope, as servant (minister) of the bishops who serve (minister to) the whole people of God.

**Theological Commission**—one of the Second Vatican Council's ten prepatory commissions. This commission was headed by Cardinal Alfredo Ottaviani and closely tied to the Holy Office. This commission saw its role as the guardian and defender of orthodoxy throughout the Council.

*Universa Laus*—from the Latin, "universal praise." International study group for liturgical vocal and instrumental music, formally constituted at Lugano, Switzerland, in 1966, based on a group of European liturgists and musicians who began meeting in 1962.

**Vatican I (1869–1870)**—the twentieth Ecumenical Council of the church, held on Vatican territory, known especially for its Constitution on the Church and the definition of papal infallibility.

**Vernacular Society**—an organization once devoted to changing the language of the Roman rite to the common language of the worshipping community.

**vernacularist**—anyone who was in favor of changing the language of the Roman rite to the common language of the worshipping community.

**zucchetto**—the small round skullcap worn by clerics, especially abbots, bishops, cardinals and the pope.

# Documents of the
# Second Vatican Council

Constitution on the Sacred Liturgy (*Sacrosanctum concilium*), December 4, 1963.

Decree on the Media of Social Communications (*Inter mirifica*), December 4, 1963.

Dogmatic Constitution on the Church (*Lumen gentium*), November 21, 1964.

Decree on Ecumenism (*Unitatis redintegratio*), November 21, 1964.

Decree on the Catholic Churches of the Eastern Rite (*Orientalium ecclesiarum*), November 21, 1964.

Decree concerning the Pastoral Office of Bishops in the Church (*Christus dominus*), October 28, 1965.

Decree on Priestly Training (*Optatam totius*), October 28, 1965.

Decree on the Adaptation and Renewal of Religious Life (*Perfectae caritatis*), October 28, 1965.

Declaration on the Relation of the Church to Non-Christian Religions (*Nostra aetate*), October 28, 1965.

Declaration on Christian Education (*Gravissimum educationis*), October 28, 1965.

Decree on the Apostolate of the Laity (*Apostolicam actuositatem*), November 18,1965.

Dogmatic Constitution on Divine Revelation (*Dei verbum*), November 18, 1965.

Pastoral Constitution on the Church in the Modern World (*Gaudium et spes*), December 7, 1965.

Decree on the Ministry and Life of Priests (*Presbyterorum ordinis*), December 7, 1965.

Declaration on Religious Liberty (*Dignitatis humanae*), December 7, 1965.

Decree on Missionary Activity of the Church (*Ad gentes divinitus*), December 7, 1965.

For further reference and study:
The documents of the Second Vatican Council are available on the Vatican's Internet website. There is the option of choosing each document in a variety of languages:
www.vatican.va/archive/hist_councils/ii_vatican_council/index.htm

For a printed volume:
*The Sixteen Documents of Vatican Council II: Constitutions, Decrees, Declarations,* Austin Flannery, OP, ed. (Northport, NY: Costello Publishing Co.) 1996.

# PART 1

# Council Fathers

# Cardinal Francis Arinze

## Interviewer: Aurelio Porfiri

Transcribed by Lam Shuk Yin

**What was your capacity at the Council?**

I was a Council father, a council member in the last session of Vatican II, which means September to December 1965, because I myself was ordained bishop August 29, 1965, just two weeks before the last session. At the last session of Vatican II, as a member of the Council, I was probably the youngest bishop. I was 32 years old at that time.

**Then you attended one session of the Council?**

I attended only the last session in 1965; I did not attend any of the other sessions. The first, second and third, I did not attend.

**What was the most significant moment at the Council for you?**

For me, of course, the most significant moment was December 8, 1965, when Pope Paul VI finally closed the Council. The day before, many final documents were given solemn approval. But that was the day, we can say, the Council said to the world: "Behold! We have worked, now accept the fruit of our work," and the Council delivered seven messages read by seven cardinals on that day.

## Of all the documents of the Council, which one is most significant for you and why?

I think it is *Lumen gentium* (Dogmatic Constitution on the Church) for me, because *Lumen gentium* is where the Council says what the church thinks of herself: the church's self-identity. The church really said: This is who I am; this is how I see myself, how I see my mandate from Christ. I think that therefore it is the most important—and most significant—because you can call it the foundation for the other documents. Only one who understands *Lumen gentium* will see where divine revelation fits in, where the sacred liturgy fits in that church, where that church dialogues with the whole world (*Gaudium et spes*—Pastoral Constitution on the Church in the Modern World), or how that church dialogues with other Christians through ecumenical dialogues with other believers (*Nostra aetate*—Declaration on the Relations of the Churches to Non-Christian Religions), or what that church is saying to its bishops, priest, seminarians, religious and lay faithful: this is what we require you to do. All of them come into focus in the context of *Lumen gentium*.

## What is the most important teaching that came out of the Council?

Everybody will have his own opinion. I think the most important teaching is where the church sees herself as instrument of union of people with God and of unity between peoples. In the first paragraph of *Lumen gentium* the church sees herself as sent by God to be the instrument that unites people to God and also the instrument which unites peoples. That is very dynamic in many senses of that word.

## Whom do you feel was the most significant figure at the Council?

The most significant figure was invisible, and that is the Holy Spirit. We did not see it without the eyes of faith, but its activity was obviously the most important in that Council. Then, obviously, the Holy Spirit—through Pope John XXIII, now Blessed, and Pope Paul VI—directed that Council, called it, directed it, concluded it. All of us are instruments of the Lord. Of course, we can speak of the bishop members, the cardinals, the theologians. I shall not go into all that.

## What was the most significant statement from the Council and why?

I would liken this to the question on the most important teaching. A very significant statement is that the church is sent by Christ as instrument—as an instrument used by God to unite people with himself and also to unite people with one another. That inspires the entire apostolate of the church, whether the apostolic mission *ad gentes* for those who do not yet believe in Christ, or the mission within the Christian community: the efforts to regain the unity of Christians, to engage other believers, or simply engage with the world. That statement remains very significant indeed: the church as instrument, the union of people with God and the unity among peoples.

## What has happened that you never imagined would happen?

I did not imagine that some people inside the church would contest what the church teaches—some of them theologians, some not, but they do not accept all that the church teaches. They accept some and reject other areas of faith and moral teaching of the church. Another thing that I did not imagine would happen is people's carelessness in liturgical matters, their lack of respect for the liturgical tradition of the church. They have their own opinion; they insist on what they think, on what they want. Another thing is that so many who had been ordained priests abandoned their sacred ministry, and so many who were professed as religious brothers, sisters, monks and nuns abandoned their consecrated life; I did not imagine that that would happen. People allowed themselves to be carried away by a secular mentality in matters touching the family and God's will about chastity; many allowed themselves to be carried away by a spirit that is not the spirit of the Gospel. I did not imagine that would happen, especially to the extent that it did.

## And what hasn't happened?

I expected increased reverence toward the sacred, especially toward the Holy Eucharist. I think, of course, many people are very respectful, but there are also some who are not respectful, and many people are worried about diminution of faith on matters touching the Holy Eucharist. I also expected an increase in reverence in general in sacred matters: reverence about the church building, reverence toward the priest, reverence toward sacred things. That has not grown as much as I expected. Also, what has not happened yet is Christian unity: the Second Vatican Council desired very much the reunion of Christians. Progress has been made, but the reunion has not yet happened, and we must continue to pray and work for it.

# Is there any issue you regret that the Council did not address?

Well, no Council can address every issue, but I think that Vatican II addressed very many issues and set up structures that help us. So it was in the light of Vatican II that Pope Paul VI instituted the Synod of Bishops. Vatican II encouraged Bishops' Conferences and also encouraged the meeting of religious in consecrated life and of the lay faithful and the activity of the lay faithful. With these, then, we have the structures to face all new challenges, because there will always be challenges. Therefore, there is not one topic that I regret the Council did not address; rather, I think the Council set up enough structures to face the future.

# What has been the most significant liturgical achievement and what do we yet need to do to implement full, conscious and active participation, also regarding liturgical music?

Well, a very significant liturgical achievement is what you have just said—the active participation of the lay faithful. When we celebrate Mass today, compared to how we celebrated fifty years ago, a person will notice that it is more a thing of all of us. It is not a new doctrine, but a rearrangement of the form of celebration has encouraged that, and that is very positive. Also very significant is the attention to the Bible. It is not new, but it is now read more abundantly than before: at Mass, at baptism, at confirmation, and all the other celebrations. There is a greater attention to liturgical roles: this is the part for the priest, this is the part for the deacon, this is the part for the choir, this is the part for the lector— and no one person does all of them, which is very good, and very significant.

Still to be implemented is the attention to what the Council said, and what the church has said in these forty years, because the church does not stand still. The church is not from the Vatican museum; the church is not from a refrigerator. The church is alive. So Vatican II is not the end of the world. The church is alive in every age. Therefore we need to listen to that same church in the last forty years.

For example, the Holy Father issued an encyclical letter on the Holy Eucharist, *Ecclesia de eucharistia*, [April 17, 2003] telling us what the church teaches us today about this holy sacrament and sacrifice. Attention to all that is very important, going along with Holy Mother Church. I say that because some people decide to stop; they do not want to continue moving with Holy Mother Church. They decide on the year they want. Some decided on 1962, and in that year they stopped, and they do not move with the church any more since 1962. Perhaps they might have decided 1570 or 1600. What I have to say to them is that the Holy Spirit was with the church on the day of Pentecost, and also at the Council of Jerusalem in the year 50, and also at the Council of Trent in the year 1545, and also at the Second Vatican Council 1962–1965. The Holy Spirit is always with the church. Christ promised this, and the promise of Christ remains firm forever. So we believe not only in God the Father, the Son and the Holy Spirit, we believe in the holy Catholic Church also.

### In your opinion, should there be a third Vatican Council, and what topic would you bring to the table?

Well, the third Vatican Council will happen whenever the pope calls it. But, if you ask me do I think it should be called now, I answer no. I do not think it should be called now because we have not yet done many of the things the Second Vatican Council asked us to do. Some of the things we have begun, but we must continue. A Council does not immediately get down to the roots in the parishes and in the villages within forty years. More time is needed, unless there is an emergency. Moreover, the church, since the Council, has developed the Synod of Bishops. There have now been ten ordinary synods (these are continental synods); there are even some specific area synods, like the synod for Lebanon, synod for Holland. So there are structures. Bishops' conferences are encouraged at both the national and regional levels. In Africa we have nine regional bishops' conferences, and we have bishops' conference associations at the continental level: Asia, Europe, Latin America, Africa, the Pacific. So we are not lacking in structures. We are not lacking meetings today, and exercises of collegiality. What we need to do is to make them as fruitful as possible.

### Is there any special historical or cultural significance that Vatican II occurred in the 1960s? Could it have happened earlier, later, in your opinion?

God's providence governs history, human events and, therefore, also church history. To God, everything is clear. To us humans, everything is not clear: we see only a little. Looking back, it seems to me providential that the Second Vatican Council took place at that time. It was a time of great flowering in the mass media, radio, press, television and their derivatives. It was a time of a breakout of communications—the jet airplane, so you can get to Australia in twenty-four hours—it was the decade of the commercial jet. It was also the decade of independence for many countries that were previously colonies; there were many new members of the United Nations. It was also a time known for tension between the power blocs:

East, West. So divine providence perhaps favored the church and the world with the Second Vatican Council to face our times and prepare both the church and society for the third millennium. But in the final analysis, God knows best.

Cardinal Francis Arinze was born in Eziowelle in the archdiocese of Onitsha, Nigeria, in 1932. He was educated in the Seminary of Nuewi, Nuewi, Nigeria; Seminary of Enugu, Enugu, Nigeria; Pontifical Urbanian University, Rome; and the University of London, London, England.

He was appointed coadjutor of Onitsha on July 6, 1965 and promoted to the metropolitan see of Onitsha June 26, 1967. He attended the final session of the Second Vatican Council in 1965. Pope John Paul II created him a cardinal on May 25, 1985. From 1984–2002 he was president of the Pontifical Council for Interreligious Dialogue. He became the Prefect of the Congregation for Divine Worship and the Discipline of the Sacraments October 1, 2002.

# Bishop Charles A. Buswell

*Bishop Charles Buswell, Bishop of Pueblo, Colorado, became too ill to complete an interview for this book. The following remarks are adapted from his privately printed autobiography,* Peace and Love Always *[Des Moines, Iowa: Big Red Quick Print, 2002]. Used with permission Diocese of Pueblo, CO.*

The Second Vatican Council was about to begin. I received a paper blizzard, giving indications and directions for the Council as well as topics and *schemas* for each session. Being rather busy as a new bishop, I did not pay too much attention to the material; much of it appeared to be a rerun of the material we had been given in seminary.

During the three years before the beginning of the Council, I regularly attended the annual meeting of the bishops of the United States, then called the National Catholic Welfare Conference (NCWC). The president was always the ranking prelate of the United States—at that time, Cardinal [Francis] Spellman [1889–1967], Archbishop of New York, who presided over the bishops' sessions with a spirit of authority. There was not much discussion, and I think the cardinal felt he was responsible only to God. Some of the bishops of the West said NCWC meant not the National Catholic Welfare Conference, but Nothing Counts West of Chicago. Often the cardinal would propose a question, have no discussion of it, and proclaim that the conference issue had been moved, seconded and carried, all in one breath. There was never any discussion.

In contrast, however, the Second Vatican Council held public discussion on all sorts of matters given for our consideration. There was freedom and encouragement to open topics for discernment. This freedom was especially apparent when the first speaker—Cardinal [Achille] Liénart [1884–1974], Cardinal Archbishop of Lille, France—was presented at the Council. (The speakers were chosen in order of seniority.) The general secretary had Archbishop [Pericle] Felici [1911–1982], announce that the Roman Curia had assigned those who would be members of the conciliar Committee and would be entrusted with the responsibility of moving the material of the Council. Cardinal Liénart took exception to this curial decision, and said the bishops themselves should name this committee since the Council was to be a council of bishops and not a council of the Roman Curia. The second speaker, Cardinal [Joseph] Frings [1887–1978], Archbishop of Cologne, Germany, seconded Liénart's suggestion, saying the bishops should be given the responsibility for moving the prepared material of the Council. At that point, Archbishop Felici terminated the discussion and went to the Board of Five Presidents that the Holy Father had named for resolution of the issue; they determined that indeed the committee should be made up of the bishops themselves. Archbishop Felici then announced that this working session would be terminated and the bishops, not the Roman Curia, would be free to name the members of the committee as well as be responsible for the workings of the Council. This was an important breakthrough at the beginning of the Council.

There was one meeting of the general assembly of the Council prior to the first working session; this was the celebration of the liturgy of the Eucharist presided over by Pope John XXIII. At this Mass he gave a very impressive homily, which set the tone for the entire Council. He said the Council would not condemn or excommunicate. There would be freedom of discussion, and the purpose of the Council would be to give new light to the world. The church was not to be a static remnant of past glory but a dynamic organism to penetrate the world with a spirit of truth and light. The church would open windows to let in fresh air and bring in a new vision.

There were to be four sessions of the Council, each dominated by the spirit that John XXIII indicated at the first liturgy: a spirit of freedom and common understanding, a spirit of openness to other religions and the world. The Council would provide an opportunity for the church to exercise a real influence toward good for all, and to help in the cause of peace for all nations.

The first session centered on a discussion of the liturgy of the church. I think the initial plan was to discuss first the nature of the church, but it was determined that the documentation for this grave and important matter was not sufficiently in tune with the spirit of Pope John XXIII. In fact, all prepared material was subjected to careful scrutiny because it had been built upon the past spirit of the church, and Pope John XXIII wanted to infuse the church with a new spirit.

One document had been prepared not by the Roman Curia but by an international group of theological and liturgical scholars. In this group were two United States experts in modern liturgy: Father Frederick McManus [b. 1923], later named a monsignor, and Benedictine Father Godfrey Diekmann, of Collegeville, Minnesota, who played an important part in the commission's activities. They had been especially prominent in the National Liturgical Conference; and from them I had received a new awareness and education on the importance of the liturgy in the formation of the church.

I was very impressed and convinced that new forms for the liturgy would be proposed at the Council. Because of the freshness of the material provided by the preparatory commission, the liturgy became the first item chosen to begin the Council's activities. As a matter of fact, the entire first session was given over to the topic of the liturgy. Certain indications were to be important for the entire work of the Council. For instance, one of the most important parts of the liturgical reform was the call for the full and active participation of the faithful in carrying out the liturgy of the church. Formerly, bishops and priests had been solely responsible for carrying out the liturgy; now, while they would still be responsible for it, the liturgy must include the full, conscious and active participation of all baptized persons in the worship of the church. This could be interpreted to mean that ordained and unordained would be responsible for the church, because we *are* the church.

The Second Vatican Council, then, is the "Council on the Church." It considered first of all the church within itself and then the church in its relations with those outside itself. The church within itself had too long been considered a clerical church—the pope's church, the bishops' church and the priests' church. The Council reminded us that the church is the church of *all baptized* people; and the faithful, both men and women, have a responsibility for the welfare of the church. All should be considered as equal to one another through baptism and the outpouring of the Spirit; all are one in Christ. Lay people are to be considered in full equality with the ordained, though they have different responsibilities.

The church also recognized responsibility to those "outside" the church, i.e., not members of the Roman Catholic church, and those not baptized. So, with a new ecumenical spirit, the Council reconsidered its relationship with unbaptized persons. It gave us a new outlook on the church as an organization, as an organism, and as part of the human family, seeing all people as an important part of the human family with whom to interrelate and learn.

In the liturgy of the church, as we had seen in the discussion of the document on the liturgy, the Word of God was to play a very important part. Not only were the Scriptures to be presented more fully over a three-year period of time, but also be brought to bear on daily life. Scripture proclaims that God is really present and speaks to us directly through the Word. In the Council documents that followed, then, we were reminded of the necessity to apply the Word to ourselves in order to understand the importance of working towards justice and peace. This not only applies to the organized membership of Roman Catholics, but also must be extended to baptized members of other faiths or others who may not be baptized. Through the Word of God, we are to become men and women of justice and peace. The Word of God *is* the word of peace. This Word of God prohibits *all* discrimination within and outside the church. There is to be *no* discrimination because of sex, color of skin or any other factor, and the dignity of every person is to be respected.

The Vatican Council roused a great deal of enthusiasm for developing an ecumenical spirit to work hand in hand with other denominations. On my return from the first session of the Council, I was asked to meet with two members of the Knights of Columbus [council] #557 in Pueblo; they said that since the Council had called for a better spirit of ecumenism, they would like to have a Mass celebrated the following Columbus Day (1963) at the fairgrounds with the Episcopal Bishop of Colorado, Bishop [Joseph L.] Minnis, as homilist. I thought that was a very good idea and gave permission. It was a moving experience, and everyone was excited that Roman Catholics and Episcopalians could come together in worship. (I was unable to attend since I was in Rome attending the second session of the Vatican Council.) *Time* magazine was said to have designated this occasion as one of two of the most significant events of the year in the Western Hemisphere.

After the first session of the Second Vatican Council, I received a letter from Archbishop [Egidio] Vagnozzi [1906–1980], the Apostolic Delegate, who had read in the diocesan paper that I was present at an interfaith meeting held in St. Therese Chapel of St. Mary Corwin Hospital in Pueblo, Colorado. He wrote that he would like to have a report on this meeting so that he in turn could report to the Supreme Sacred Congregation of the Holy Office. In due time I responded: "Dear Archbishop Vagnozzi, There was a general interfaith meeting held in the St. Therese Chapel of St. Mary Corwin Hospital at the time and date you indicated. I was present at that meeting. The meeting was so bland that I'm sure the Sacred Congregation of the Holy Office would not be interested in the slightest degree. If, however, you wish further information on this matter, I would be pleased to advise. Sincerely yours, Charles A. Buswell, Bishop of Pueblo."

The Ecumenical Council gave impetus to a number of different events in the diocese of Pueblo and elsewhere. One example was to have evening Masses on Saturday. It was decided that perhaps an extension of this practice could apply to funerals. Somehow the media received word of the matter, and it was publicized all over the United States that the Diocese of Pueblo was authorizing evening funerals. I received a number of letters, generally in favor of this practice. One letter of opposition came from a woman in Pittsburgh, Pennsylvania, who wrote, "Dear Bishop Buswell, I understand that Monsignor Delaney has obtained permission for evening funerals in your diocese. What is the matter with Monsignor Delaney anyway? We have the best funerals in the morning. Catholic funerals are always in the morning. Protestant funerals are in the afternoon, and Jewish funerals are in the evening. Are you located among a lot of Jews out there? Ever since Pope John XXIII has come to office, everything seems to be happening. Thousands of people come to the plaza of St. Peter's to hear the pope speak, but not any of them go to Mass."

I mention this incident to you to cite the wide discrepancy of thinking between the past and present that existed at this time among Catholics.

During one of the sessions of the Second Vatican Council, I was at dinner at the North American College where all the bishops were present. As I was leaving, I passed by the table where Bishop [William Patrick] O'Connor [1886–1973] of Madison was seated. I said, "Oh, bishop, I have good news for you. We have a wonderful person from your diocese as a volunteer in our diocese. Her name is Jean Troy." He replied, "Oh yes, I know her and I don't want you to marry her in evening services either." I said, "I don't want to marry anyone. I promised I wouldn't do that." "Well," he said, "that stuff might fly in Pueblo, Colorado, but you're a scandal to the church in the rest of the country." He was, of course, referring to my approval of having marriages in the evening, a very popular practice for many in the diocese.

Because of the spirit of the Council, we established a program called the Ministry of Christian Service to prepare the faithful for leadership in the diocese. Women and men from various parishes in the diocese were invited to be trained in leadership, with the hope that some day they might be ordained to the diaconate. At that time, permission had been given for women to be readers and ministers of the Eucharist in the parish, roles that used to be minor orders in preparation for ordination. It was my thought that at the end of three years the church would grant permission for both men and women to be ordained in the diaconate program. However, instead of being allowed to ordain women as deacons, the church decided to eliminate all the minor orders and re-establish two orders only, the order of the acolyte and the order of reader, as ministries rather than as orders. But women were forbidden to serve officially in these capacities, even though they actually did serve as eucharistic ministers and acolytes. Since we were not able to ordain women to the diaconate, we decided in our diocese to ordain neither men nor women [as deacons] and chose other forms of ministering. Nevertheless, the program of the Ministry of Christian Service was an excellent program for ministry training for both men and women, and was one of the first in the U.S. to be recognized as such.

Women were officially welcomed to the proceedings of the third session of Vatican II. They were not permitted to vote but were welcomed at all the activities of the Council and had a great influence behind the scenes.

An especially poignant experience regarding the role of women in the church happened in 1976. Cardinal [John Francis] Dearden [1907–1988] of Detroit, then President of the National Conference of Catholic Bishops, called the first Call to Action Conference, which was sponsored by the bishops. Several committees were formed at this meeting. I served on the Committee for Justice, which had decided it was important to consider the ordination of women as a justice issue. We submitted a proposal to Rome calling for the theological study of women's ordination as well as for approval of the ordination of women to the diaconate. I presented this proposal on behalf of the committee. There was much discussion about this proposal around the country; I attended one of these discussions in Baltimore. I was the only United States bishop to attend the second Call to Action Conference.

I was always faithful in participating in the national bishops' meetings and joining in the concelebration of the liturgy on the closing day. Once I arrived back at the bishops' meeting too late to vest and concelebrate, so I sat in the pew. The experience of that day ended up making a big impression on me. The parade of 250 bishops did not convey to me a sense of simplicity or a sense of the pilgrim church as a people of God, which we had talked about at Vatican II. Cardinal [John Joseph] Krol's [1910–1996, Archbishop of Philadelphia] miter seemed to stand as tall as the Empire State Building. Then, at the time of the proclamation of the Word, Elizabeth McAllister stood up in the assembly, approached the front of the church and stood in the ambo. She insisted that we should be a church of the poor, not of an elite. Two priests in vestments came up and literally dragged her out of the ambo and into the sanctuary. I could not go to Communion that day. Indeed, the voices of women must be heard or the church will simply not come into its full potential.

Those days then were very exciting. There were new forms of worship, a new sense of thinking, and a desire to have full participation by everyone in the life and thought of the church.

We continued in our efforts to be faithful to the spirit of openness, freedom and justice, which was so much a part of building a Vatican II church in the Diocese of Pueblo. Always, I strove to be a bishop of love and peace and reverence toward all.

Bishop Charles A. Buswell was ordained to the priesthood on July 9, 1939, for the diocese of Oklahoma City. Pope John XXIII called Monsignor Buswell to the episcopate at the age of 45 on August 8,1959. At his installation Mass he gave part of his homily in Spanish, as a salute to the Spanish-Americans of the diocese. The symbolic action was to be the first of many steps dedicated to confirming the dignity of minorities throughout his years as bishop.

Three months after becoming bishop, he established the Diocesan Liturgical Commission. He wrote his first pastoral letter on the liturgy, addressing it to the people of his diocese, on January 1, 1960. That same year he was elected to the Board of Directors of the North American Liturgical Conference and for more than a decade influenced the direction of programs and policies for that national organization during the years of preparation for the Second Vatican Council, and the years following the Council that focused on implementing the conciliar norms.

Bishop Buswell was a participant in all four sessions of the Second Vatican Council. He especially welcomed the Constitution on the Sacred Liturgy (*Sacrosanctum concilium*) and returned to his diocese to proceed immediately with its implementation. He served for twenty-one years as the second bishop of Pueblo, Colorado, and resigned as bishop in 1979.

# Bishop Frank Marcus Fernando

## Interviewer: Nihal Abeyasingha, CSsR

### What was your capacity at the Council?

I was an auxiliary bishop taking part in the Council. In fact, I was one of the youngest, being hardly 34 years of age. I attended only the last session, which began September 14 and ended December 8, 1965. I must say it was the most fruitful session, considering the fact that eleven documents were completed and promulgated during that period.

### What was the most significant moment at the Council for you?

I can only speak of the last session—and there were a few significant moments in it. October 28, 1965, was important. Six documents were promulgated that day:

Decree on the Pastoral Office of Bishops in the Church (*Christus dominus*);
Decree on the Training of Priests (*Optatam totius*);
Decree on the Ministry and Life of Priests (*Presbyterorum ordinis*);
Decree on the Adaptation and Renewal of Religious Life (*Perfectae caritatis*);
Declaration on the Relation of the Church to Non-Christian Religions
(*Nostra aetate*);
Declaration on Christian Education (*Gravissimun educationis*).

December 7, too—the last event in St. Peter's Basilica—was memorable. On that day the Pastoral Constitution on the Church in the Modern World (*Gaudium et spes*) was promulgated, as well as Decree on the Ministry and Life of Priests (*Presbyterorum ordinis*), Decree on the Church's Missionary Activity (*Ad gentes divinitus*) and Declaration on Religious Liberty (*Dignitatis humanae*).

And, of course, I cannot forget the magnificent closing ceremony on December 8, 1965, at St. Peter's Square. It was a sunny and bright day. A very touching moment was the handing over of special messages by the Holy Father to representatives of different groups, intellectuals, sick and infirm, and so forth. I remember the representative of the disabled, a blind man, led by his dog, coming up to the pope. Paul VI spoke a few words to the man and handed over the message. Then he tied a red ribbon and bow around the neck of the dog. Television cameras were flashing the whole thing. Those Italians conduct their ceremonies rather well.

## Of all the documents of the Council, which is the most significant for you and why?

For me the most significant was the document on the church's missionary activity—*Ad gentes divinitus*—passed on December 7, 1965.

I had the feeling that we were forgetting to obey the clear mandate given by Jesus Christ: Go and preach! By and large, we were becoming a maintenance church. There is no doubt dialogue and religious freedom and relations with non-Christian religions are important. But somehow the Lord's command to preach the Gospel seemed sidetracked. There was too much talk about the "little flock" theory of the church. The enormous missionary effort of the church throughout the centuries seemed to be undermined. At such a time, the document on the missions brought into sharp focus this essential imperative on the part of the church. Article two of that document emphasized that the church is missionary in nature. Not only those who chose the missionary life but all the baptized are in some way sent *ad gentes*.

## What is the most important teaching that came out of the Council?

To me, it was the biblical teaching on the church as the people of God. We had got used to thinking of the church as an institution—in fact, as a rather monolithic institute.

The "people of God" concept introduced a new dynamic. It was almost a paradigm shift. The call of Vatican II was essentially a call to holiness, not a call for new structures. The grace of God flows into the hearts of men and women, into the people of God: it does not flow into structures. I believe that the post-Vatican II confusion was, in good measure, due to this misunderstanding. Everybody spoke of new structures. The need for inner reform was forgotten.

## Whom do you feel was the most significant figure at the Council?

I know you expect me to name a person, but let me first state that the Holy Spirit's presence was always there. It was almost palpable. You will remember in the earlier stages of the Council, there were strong differences of opinion. There was polarization. It was a field day for the media. As time went on, we found a certain sobriety and clarity setting in. It was the work of the Holy Spirit.

At that time I was auxiliary to the late Cardinal Thomas Benjamin Cooray, OMI [1901–1988], of the Archdiocese of Colombo. He took part in the entire Council. I remember seeing him poring over the draft documents and taking notes. He made some important interventions, too, during the Council.

Cardinal Cooray shared with me some of his experiences in the Council. In the earlier stages of the Council, the fashionable thing was to attack the Curia and various other bodies. Cardinal Cooray said that, when his turn came, he prayed a great deal and prepared his speech. The point he brought out on the Council floor was this: In the church we have a particular way of doing things, a certain sense of decorum and respect for authority. If we hold important church institutions to ridicule, everybody would stand to lose, and nothing constructive would be done. In making that speech, the Cardinal was going against the current prevailing at that moment. He said he could hear a pin drop in the *aula* when he spoke. That intervention had a profound impact on the assembly.

The speeches following his became more sober and constructive. I mention this incident to indicate the presence of the Holy Spirit.

Pope Paul VI was always present in the background. We know he had a bad press. He was deeply respected by the Council fathers.

A very visible presence was that of Archbishop Pericle Felici [1911–1982], the General Secretary of the Second Vatican Council, a very taxing and responsible task. In warm and fluent Latin, he made the daily announcements. The archbishop also had to read some important documents; for example, he read the papal brief declaring the Council completed on December 8, 1965.

## What was the most significant statement from the Council and why?

I would say that the sixteen documents themselves, taken together, constituted the main achievement of the Council. There were also statements at various stages emanating from the Council—not directly forming part of the sixteen documents. The sixteen documents, too, contain some wonderful passages. I find it difficult, now, to put my finger on one thing and say, "This was it! This was the most significant statement."

## What has happened that you never imagined would happen?

From a historical perspective I can hardly think of anything as impossible to happen in the church. God can make very luminous things to happen in the church. He can also allow unhappy things to happen in the church, and yet save his church. There have been the Borgia popes long ago; and there has been the year with three wonderful popes in our own times. Our present Holy Father has broken many records. In that sense, there was nothing I imagined would never happen. Vatican II now belongs to history.

It seems to me that with the media explosion we have, and the worldwide travels of the pope, a good deal of that sense of mystery and awe will disappear from the church. A good deal of demythologizing will take place.

## What hasn't happened?

Many people predicted doom when John XXIII announced the Council. They said it was not the time; they said it would rock the boat too much. We know all that. Now we know Vatican II was one of the best things that happened for the church. It prepared the church to face unparalleled challenges in our times. I remember a remark made by a Buddhist judge speaking privately with me. He said, "Bishop, I consider myself a good Buddhist. There is one thing in your church I appreciate very much. You all have built-in structures to correct mistakes and adapt yourselves to the needs of the times. Unfortunately, we do not have it." He said that. I think that's what Pope John XXIII wanted when he spoke of "*aggiornamento.*"

## Is there any issue you regret that the Council did not address?

Even Ecumenical Councils are children of their times; they took up questions that were relevant for those particular periods. Looking back after forty or fifty years, we might be tempted to say, "Why didn't the Vatican Council treat this, and this other subject?"

Some of the problems came later—the morality of preemptive war, for instance, important bio-ethical questions and so forth. The church will go on. There will be Roncalli popes in the future, too.

## What has been the most significant liturgical achievement, and what do we yet need to do to implement full, conscious and active participation?

To my mind, the use of the indigenous languages in the liturgy was the major breakthrough. We have to admit that some of the old things we used to treasure had to give way—the sense of mystery, for instance, and the Gregorian chant. We can't have it both ways.

Some of the present rites are perhaps a bit too rigid. A little more leeway could be given to charismatic elements of prayer—even in the liturgy. A little more openness toward adaptations in the best sense of the word—while always remaining faithful to the spirit of the liturgy—might be helpful. I know this is not easy. In some countries where the line of separation between local culture and non-Christian religions is not very clear, adaptation can lead us into unpleasant situations. I would rather have a rigid liturgy than an ambiguous one, which would mislead the faithful.

## In your opinion should there be a third Vatican Council, and what topic(s) would you bring to the table?

To those who would propose having a third Vatican Council now, I would say, "Don't!"

## What Council teaching was most difficult to implement in the local churches?

Whatever the Council taught, finally, was highly nuanced. They kept the door open for a degree of adaptation. The need to take local initiative was generally accepted. That being the case, I can't pinpoint and say, "This, and this, were difficult to implement." Failure to implement is, it seems to me, a result of hesitation and lethargy rather than difficulty.

**Is there any special historical or cultural significance that Vatican II occurred in the 1960s? Could it have happened earlier, later, in your opinion?**

It was not long after the end of World War II. The Cold War was on. Many colonies had regained independence. Various revolutions in the behavior patterns of men and women were taking place. There was new theological reflection going on. From hindsight, we now feel it had been the correct time to hold Vatican II.

**Vatican I [1869–1870] is remembered for the definition of papal infallibility, even though that was not the only thing it did. Would you say that the two documents—*Lumen gentium* and *Gaudium et spes*—will be things that Vatican II will be remembered for?**

There is no doubt that the Constitution on the Church (*Lumen gentium*) was the lapidary document of Vatican II. It laid a solid theological foundation for other documents. But, however rich that document is, if the Council had dwelt only on the dogmatic aspect of the church, Vatican II would probably have gone down in history as merely self-analyzing, perhaps a trifle introverted, and not sufficiently reaching out to the world at large.

The bishops saw this point—and the idea of the "Church in the Modern World" took shape. On the other hand, if only the Pastoral Constitution on the Church in the Modern World had come out of the Council, that too would have given only a partial view of the church—as something pragmatic, as something insufficiently anchored. Thus, these two documents complement each other. *Lumen gentium* was, in a sense, seminal, containing many truths in embryo. *Gaudium et spes* drew out those elements and helped to make the church more relevant to our times. These two documents will be remembered for a long time to come.

**In your long experience as bishop, have you seen a deepening of the spirit of Vatican II among the clergy and religious? Or have you seen a return to the pre-Vatican II mentality in the name of not disturbing the faith of the ordinary faithful?**

You seem to be asking whether we are going back on the intuitions of Vatican II. Are we having second thoughts? Is there a worry that the opening of windows has resulted in some venerable statues being thrown down, and some golden tapestries being torn apart?

What shall I say? You remember the old philosopher who said that you cannot step into the same river twice. What you stepped into before is gone; it is perhaps now in the sea. The church is in the world and the world itself is moving at a terrific speed. The world of today is not the world of the sixties. In a sense, that is true of the church, too. So this question of moving away from Vatican II or moving toward it can be confusing. Being "conservative" or "progressive" is often a relative term. I know people who are quite conservative in some aspects and highly progressive in other aspects.

It is just possible that some of the Vatican II champions of change gradually began to worry and feel disillusioned and began to say, "My God! We didn't expect all this!" Even people with heroic courage and openness can at times feel uneasy. I would hesitate to say that they are reneging on their earlier commitment. Life is never black or white. It is gray.

When we studied at Propaganda Fide College in Rome in the early fifties, the rector of our college was Monsignor Felice Cenci. He was rector for nearly twenty-five years. He used to speak a great deal about "auto-formation," self-formation. He knew he was being criticized by the authorities in other colleges as being too liberal, too progressive. We of course were perfectly happy with him; he was a very holy man. Monsignor Cenci died a deeply disappointed man. After the Vatican Council he was accused of being too old-fashioned, and there were problems connected with discipline in the college.

In Matthew 13:52, Jesus spoke of the householder who brings out of his treasure house things new and old. We can apply those words to our context. The wisdom and experience of the preconciliar church—even the ambiguous part of it—are not to be simply jettisoned. Vatican II sheds new light on a host of things. We have to make use of these past experiences and fresh insights. I personally think that this is what the church has been doing in these post-Vatican times. Jesus Christ is the Lord of history. Let us not be beguiled into error. It may be that the best is yet to be.

## Is there anything you would like to note in a lighter vein?

Well, I might relate a couple of things. There were two bars or cafes right in St. Peter's Basilica. The bishops jokingly named them "Bar Jonas" and "Bar Abbas." They served orange juice, *dolce Italiana* and, of course, excellent cappuccino. I remember there were boards there saying "*vietato fumare* (smoking prohibited)." Unfortunately, those signs could not be clearly read, as there was too much smoke from cigars and cigarettes. All this, of course, was during the interval.

I also remember the general sessions attended by the pope. The whole nave at St. Peter's Basilica was lit for television cameras. It was rather warm. We had to come in our official dress; we also had to wear the miter when seated. Naturally, some of us were nodding. I enjoyed myself watching the tall miters of bishops floating in all directions.

One day Archbishop Felice announced that the pope was going to present to each bishop a golden ring. Some bishops remarked, "A golden ring? When we are asked to live lives of poverty? Besides, how are they going to take the measurements? There's no time!"

The next day they brought more than 2,000 small red boxes to the *aula*. Rome is clever! The ring consisted of a flat piece of metal—obviously gold. All you had to do was to press it from the two edges and make a ring according to the size you wanted and slip it on to your finger.

Now that simple ring became a model. The precious stones [that had previously been common in bishops' rings] disappeared a good deal. I know many bishops, who were appointed after the Vatican Council ended, made their rings on that model. Pope Paul VI would have rejoiced!

Frank Marcus Fernando, bishop of Chilaw, Sri Lanka, was born October 19, 1931. After completing his secular studies in Colombo, he studied philosophy and theology in Rome at the Propaganda Fide College (1951–1957). He was ordained a priest on December 22, 1956. His companions at Propaganda Fide College included Archbishop Daniel Pilarczyk of Cincinnati, and Archbishop Leobard D'Sousa, Bishop Emeritus of Nagpur, India, who also took part in the Second Vatican Council.

Bishop Fernando, who originally belonged to the Archdiocese of Colombo, at the age of 33 was appointed auxiliary to Cardinal Thomas Benjamin Cooray, O.M.I., Archbishop of Colombo, and attended the final session of Vatican II. In 1968, he became coadjutor of the Diocese of Chilaw and, on the retirement of his predecessor, Bishop of Chilaw in 1972. Prior to his ordination as bishop, he had been a schoolteacher, editor of a Catholic weekly and rector of the minor seminary in Colombo.

Bishop Fernando, a graduate of the University of London, has written a number of books in Sinhala, the chief language of Sri Lanka; he is a well-known writer and speaker, and has been president of the Catholic Bishops' Conference in Sri Lanka for ten years.

# Archbishop James M. Hayes

## Interviewer: Bernadette Gasslein

**What was your capacity at the Council?**

I was at the Council for the first session and for the final session. At the first session I went with Archbishop [Joseph Gerard] Berry [1902–1967], the archbishop of Halifax; I was there more as an observer than anything. I associated with the bishops who were there; we all stayed at the same lodgings, so I heard what was going and heard their impressions and attitudes, and had an idea of just how things were going. In addition, they had theologians and experts come and speak to them quite frequently during the Council; I was able to participate in many of those sessions as well, so I was there, following the Council, in a non-official way.

**When you were there as an observer, were you able to sit in on the sessions?**

I was there for some sessions but not for all. I had a press card from the local newspaper, so I was able to join the journalists sometimes, and hear some of the debate, at least. That wasn't very satisfactory because it was rather difficult to follow; it was easier to read the reports afterwards. The archbishop made available to me all the documentation that he had.

## Did Archbishop Berry die during the Council?

No, he died in 1967. I was made bishop in April 1965; I went to the Council in 1965 as a Council father. I was auxiliary bishop of Halifax, but later I was appointed administrator of the diocese; in effect I was the bishop representing the diocese at the time.

## What kinds of shifts in thinking did you witness?

There were big changes in thinking right from the second week of the first session, when they had to discuss the liturgy. Even before they began to discuss liturgy, they were going to appoint chairpersons for commissions, bishops who would listen to the debates and then work on the amendments that might be made to the documents that were presented. The bishops discovered that it was frankly a foregone conclusion that the heads of the Vatican departments would just be chosen and that would be it. The archbishop of Lille [Cardinal Achille Liénart, 1884–1974] and the archbishop of Cologne [Joseph Frings, 1887–1978]—they objected and said, "Now, all the bishops are here; most of them of the same nationality are living in the same lodgings or nearby; they could easily get together and nominate their own persons to head these commissions." I suppose that certainly went back to the central commissions and to the Holy Father; but the result of it, as I recall, was that the debates were suspended for a couple of days over a weekend and nominations or proposals were submitted, and that was the basis for the leadership of these commissions.

In effect, that meant that the bishops were given some responsibility for the agenda. That recognized the principle of collegiality, too. It would in a way also determine the membership on the commissions, as they were formed. They [the commissions] were very important because the way the Council worked is that the bishops were given *schemas*—proposals, working papers—which were to be studied. They were studied at home; the bishops could discuss the documentation with theologians or other experts; then they would be debated at the Council. The debate didn't end with a yes or no vote to accept the documentation; it ended with a vote to cease the debate and then submit all the original documents and all the proposals for amendments. What was debated during the Council were the amendments that were made, so the amendments that were accepted would be added to the documents or introduced into the documents or rejected. Someone had to give a reason as to why they were accepted or not accepted, so the documents sometimes went through several drafts before the final document was placed before the whole Council for a vote. It was really a complicated process, but it's something like the draft legislation that comes to Parliament, after all.

**In a sense, the process would seem to offer people who wanted to get into the debate and voice their opinion on something a lot of opportunity to do so.**

Yes, that's right. They had to submit a request to speak; they were accepted and placed on a roster. Sometimes it came to the point when the assembly considered that the matter had been sufficiently discussed and no further debate was necessary, so we would take a vote on that. Then we would go on to something else. But if they didn't have a chance to speak, they could still present written interventions.

**What in your own way of thinking changed? What did you see change in yourself during this period?**

I think I went there with the hope that the bishops from different parts of the world would bring something to the Council and that we would be able to hear from the Council some pastoral directives that would change our way of dealing with people and celebrating the worship of the church, especially even our understanding of the church. You know, the Council didn't just come out of the blue. We had the liturgical movement, the biblical movement, the ecumenical movement—all these things were flourishing in the 1950s, not to mention Young Catholic Workers, Young Catholic Students, Catholic Action, and so many lay organizations like that. The kinds of attitudes toward the church that were developed there were really the perfect basis for the Council to begin.

**So the basis for the Council was actually in the lay people already?**

Oh yes! The lay people weren't asking for a Council, but lay people were doing things that observant leaders could see were the manifestation of the gifts of the Spirit. That's one way to say it. The liturgical movement and the biblical movement, for example, were the work of experts and scholars in the beginning; but as they were put into effect, they became an activity of the church as well. I think of [Annibale] Bugnini [1912–1982], the man who was secretary of the Council for implementing the Constitution on the Sacred Liturgy (*Sacrosanctum concilium*). When I was a student in Rome in the early fifties, 1954–1957, there was no mention of a Council at all. He was editing a little booklet that came out every week to encourage lay participation in the liturgy. I used to get it because I was interested in seeing how they were trying to promote lay participation in the liturgy in Italy and I had no idea of who he was; and then all of a sudden he appears as the secretary for the Council for implementing the Constitution. You had men like that who were real scholars, but not simply involved in research.

### They were scholars, but also pastors?

That's right. The ideal pastor of all was Pope John XXIII, you know. He made that so clear in his opening speech at the Council: this was to be a pastoral Council. I'm sure that you've read that opening address yourself a few times; it was so encouraging, you know. (see page x in this edition)

### Do you think we've lost sight of that pastoral vision of the Council?

I don't think that we've lost sight of it. I think that we've settled for having done enough for now. I don't believe that that's true; I think that we have to try to continue the thrust that the Council gave us. But that's part of the difficulty we're having now, I suppose, in promoting full, active, and conscious participation in the celebration of the Eucharist, especially.

### Say a little bit more about that. What do you think the difficulty is right now? Where do we need to go with that?

I think the difficulty comes right from the beginning of the Council. The bishops at the Council had a wonderful experience of the power and presence of the Holy Spirit in the Council sessions, and even the ones who weren't very interested suddenly became absolutely inspired. They looked forward to coming back home and bringing this wonderful experience to the people of the diocese. When they got back, the people weren't prepared for that and it didn't happen to the extent that so many people expected. I think that those of us who have been working on liturgical renewal have had the same idea: we see what things mean, and how things ought to work, and we've never been able to explain that to the people. Some of us have tried to do it and even became discouraged, or tired of saying the same thing over, and finding that the fire isn't catching on the way we would like.

### There's certainly a certain spirit of discouragement right now.

That's right. The discouragement leads people to go back to other things, but I don't see that as a solution at all. And I'm certain that wasn't the spirit of Pope

John at the opening of the Council. I have his address at the opening of the Council, and the kind of things that he says, like "It wasn't necessary for us to have a Council just to repeat the traditional authentic teaching of the church." He goes on to say:

> The substance of the ancient doctrine of the deposit of faith is one thing, and the way in which it is presented is another. And this latter must be taken into great consideration, everything being measured in the forms and proportions of a teaching office which is predominantly pastoral in character.

I think that we were all steeped in the idea that we got the teaching from the church, and then we just presented it to the people, who took it and followed it like that. But we're dealing with a different kind of people now, just as the bishops discovered that they were a different sort of group as well when they decided that they wanted to have a more direct share in the management of the Council.

**Are you suggesting that part of the difficulty that we have right now is that the lay people in the church have lost this sense of who they are, for instance, a sense that came out of the liturgical movement, that came out of the Young Christian Workers, all of those kinds of movements?**

I wouldn't say they've lost the sense, but I would say that it's not as sharp. You know, when you come up with something new, people are inquisitive. They watch, they look, they ask, they find out what it's all about and then they say, "Oh yeah, that's what it is," and that's it. Well, we can't keep up that enthusiasm for this new event forever. But the substance behind it, the teaching behind it, has to go on.

**I would imagine that the same principle that Pope John articulated at the beginning—about the substance being one thing and the presentation of that substance as another—has to be taken as kind of a perennial principle.**

That's exactly what I'm saying: the way it's presented. This suggests that in 2003 we can't even use the ways to communicate that were effective in 1963 or 1965. That entire social upset of the sixties and seventies has produced, at least in the Western world, a whole different people with whom we're trying to deal and communicate, and whom we're trying to teach.

## A very different kind of people.

Absolutely. Who would have thought in 1965 that one of our most serious concerns would be how we're going to understand Moslems and how we're going to be able to deal with them, communicate with them, dialogue with them, appreciate what they have to offer? That's the fact right now. You don't have to be in a big city where there are a dozen mosques to be aware of that and have a need to face the situation.

But these things didn't happen because of the Council. They happened because of social change. This brings us back to what Pope John was saying. We have to find new ways to communicate. What's really essential? What do we have to hold on to, to be clear that we're not giving up everything? We really need the gifts of the Spirit again.

## Then people begin to argue about theological approaches. Is the language of scholasticism the only theology that can be used?

That's certainly not the case. Even at the Council that was made clear. The kind of glaring example of it was the revision of the ordination rites. Rites that had been used in the church for centuries, maybe more than 1,000 years, were rejected and replaced because they no longer said what ordination means. It was only the Dogmatic Constitution on the Church (*Lumen gentium*) that really settled the question that the ordination of a bishop is a sacrament.

Before the Council the sacrament of orders was conferred on the subdeacon, deacon and priest. The bishop was consecrated; he was just a priest. You couldn't give a priest anything more than the power to make the body and blood of Christ present. The bishop was just given authority, but not sacramental power. The clarification of the office of bishop as a sacrament comes from the Constitution on the Church (*Lumen gentium*). It was the most significant document of the Council.

## Why would you say that?

Because the whole purpose of the Council was to help us to realize and understand what the church really is. All the other things—what we find in the church and through the church, what the church thinks and teaches—we had to have the basis for that. That's given to us in the Constitution on the Church.

If we all had the same understanding of the church, our life would be much simpler. If we all had the understanding of the church that we find in the

Council, everyone would want to participate in the liturgy. Everyone would feel that they were being cheated if they couldn't be involved in what's going on in the parish, in the diocese.

**I think that, many times, we end up fighting about things that we think are liturgical or theological but are actually ecclesiological.**

That's right.

**What was the most significant moment at the Council for you?**

Well, the significant moment for me was the opening with Pope John and the speech that he gave there, and what I was able to learn from it afterwards. It really wasn't possible to follow this long speech in Latin, and get the import. On the same day, in the evening, after the official opening was all over, Pope John had told his secretary that he wouldn't do anything more public that day, that the opening of the Council was enough for the day and for the whole world; but so many people came to St. Peter's Square and were calling out and cheering, and asking for him to come and speak to them, that finally he opened the window and leaned out the window and spoke to the people in the crowd. He talked to them like a father and like a pastor. Then the thing that I found most striking of all: When they were leaving and he gave them his blessing, he said, "Go home and give your kids a hug and tell them that it's from the Holy Father." Now I'd been in Rome during the last years of Pope Pius XII. I couldn't imagine that a pope could talk like that! Before that it was all solemn and staged. Pius XII, his health wasn't very good; there was nothing joyful or personal in the way he related to people. I was really touched by the way Pope John spoke.

The other significant moment was at the closing of the Council. A representative of the Patriarch of Constantinople came. He and Paul VI did more than absolve; they eliminated completely all the interdicts and excommunications that the Orthodox and Latin churches had issued against one another. At the close of the Council, the Patriarch came up and embraced Paul VI at the altar in St. Peter's. He was a very impressive man. He had this beautiful purple cope, I remember. Everybody in the place could just feel that the air was charged with charity and reconciliation and all the things that the Council had been talking about for four years.

Then just shortly after the close of the Council, there was an ecumenical celebration in St. Paul's, where the Council had first been announced. Paul VI spoke at that. It was just a beautiful call to ecumenical dialogue and cooperation. I remember that at the end we sang "Now Thank We All Our God"—it was being sung in at least half a dozen languages, maybe more. It was the same hymn going up from this whole crowd. That was a very moving scene. Those are the things that I always remember as having an emotional impact on me at the Council.

**To imagine people getting together, singing a German chorale—Catholics, Protestants, Anglicans…**

Yes, everyone who wanted to be there—it was wide open. All the observers from the other churches who were at the Council, they were there. Some of them had parts in the celebration. It was a kind of Liturgy of the Word.

**And that would have probably been the first of that kind of service ever.**

I'm sure it was the first. That was a kind of lesson that I came back from the Council with. That was more powerful than reading the decree on ecumenism, for example.

**When we think of those first moments, that's pretty overwhelming. We need more first moments like that to capture the Council.**

That's the situation we're facing with the liturgy. How do we create other occasions like that? I don't know. Those things that I mentioned really weren't staged. That was the impact that they had.

**How do we create other occasions that capture the essence in gesture and word, that embody the experience of what the documents were really talking about? Some of my friends who have daughters in their early twenties ask the same question, but from the perspective of women's issues. They say, "My daughters don't understand any more what it was like to be a woman when I was growing up. They just take for granted all of the progress that women have made in the last thirty years. They think it was always like this. They don't realize there was a huge change."**

That's why I can't make comparisons any more between what it was like before the Council and what it's like now. The ones I'm talking to don't have any experience of it.

## Would you say the ecclesiological theme was the most important to come out of the Council?

The nature of what is the church—that was the most important thing. There was another change in direction at that stage, too, when we began to debate the Constitution on the Church. The debate started out with this working paper that had come from the Congregation for the Doctrine of the Faith. As soon as it was presented, as soon as the one who was presenting it completed his talk, Cardinal Liénart got up again and said, "This is totally inadequate; it's only about the institution. There's no mention of the church as mystery." Those who had prepared the working paper didn't view the church as a mystery.

They continued the debate for a couple of days; other people came in on it. Cardinal [Leo Joseph] Suenens [1904–1996, archbishop of Mechelen and Brussels] was one of those who spoke the same way; Cardinal [Paul-Emile] Léger [1905–1991, archbishop of Montreal, Canada] was one of those who said that the Constitution on the Church was key to the Council. Cardinal [Giovanni Battista] Montini, Archbishop of Milan, made such an appealing presentation that the debate was discontinued, but it was discontinued with a message from the Holy Father that a completely new draft would be presented at the next session of the Council. (This was just in the last week of the first session, which ended on December 8, 1962.) And that is in fact what happened. Now we have this Constitution on the Church, which begins with the people of God, and tells us what the mystery of the church is, and how it is described in sacred Scripture. After that, it gets into some of the institutional aspects of being church, because this mysterious community can't exist unless it has a kind of framework, a setup to hold it together and make it recognizable. So that was a very powerful moment in the Council.

## When you came back from the Council, how did you implement that kind of teaching, that kind of vision?

People were so open to hearing that they were the people of God, it was almost as if they were waiting for it. It became the way people were thinking of themselves. That helped with ecumenism, for they realized that other Christians, everyone who's baptized, is part of what we call the church, the people of God.

## I imagine it helped for liturgy, too.

Yes, another crossover between the Constitution on the Liturgy and the Constitution on the Church is that both documents say that the church is a sacrament, a

33

sacrament of Christ. Both documents say that the Eucharist is the summit and source of the church's life. The two things work together. I think that if the bishops had tried to start with the church first, it wouldn't have come about the way it did. The fact that they started with the liturgy—everyone knew a little bit about liturgy, and they were comfortable about that and able to talk about it—meant that the debates weren't interrupted or discontinued as with some of the other documents. When they came back to the Council's second session and had this new draft document that had been prepared and studied at home before they came, they were in a different mindset. I think that, as a result, it's the finest thing that the Council produced.

**They started from something that was relatively non-threatening.**

Everybody felt they could be at home here—as celebrants of the liturgy. After all, this was the way they saw this church. They were told that, at the Council, the bishops with the pope speak on behalf of the church. Many of them, when they came to the Council, thought, "Well, we'll be given these things. We'll check them over, and maybe touch them up a little bit and be able to go home." Nobody thought the Council was going to go on for four years.

**What was the general consensus about how long the Council would last?**

I think some people thought it would be over in one session, or that they'd have to have a second one. Nobody thought it would go on as long as it did.

**Of the people behind the scenes at the Council—theologians like [Karl] Rahner, [Yves] Congar, [Marie-Dominique] Chenu, [Joseph] Ratzinger— whom would you say was the most significant?**

I was always impressed with Yves Congar [1904–1995], mainly because he was an ecclesiologist and his input and impact on the Constitution on the Church was very significant. Karl Rahner [1904–1984] is certainly the one who produced the most theological writing, and I think that he's had a huge impact on theologians everywhere. Those would be the two figures whom I'd remember.

**You've mentioned Cardinal Liénart, Cardinal Suenens, Cardinal Frings. Whom did you think was the most significant figure at the Council?**

Of all of them, I'd have to say Pope John and then Pope Paul VI. If you go back to the cardinals, I'd have to say that Suenens was probably the one who impressed me most. I thought he had what everyone was looking for: how to communicate to the people, and what is it that the church needs to do and say. He and Montini together made that proposal about the church being a mystery, first of all, and then being a mystery that exists in the world and has to have some visible structure that can be recognized. The other thing is that he was certainly the one who pushed most strongly for the document on the Church in the Modern World.

Whenever I mention that document, I always point out to people that it's the church *in* the world, because there are other documents that speak of the church *and* the world. A World Council of Churches document from the same time was entitled *The Church and the World.* It was Suenens, and the people who gathered with him, who made it clear that this was to be the church *in* the world that they wanted to speak about or present.

I think that we all had the idea that our own personal society was divided into two spheres: We were members of the church, religious people, and we also had a secular responsibility. To say "the church *in* the world" is to say that we can't make that separation. It takes us out of the ghetto mentality. It's not the church *and* the world; it's the church *in* the world. As the church *in* the world, if we want to say something, we're saying it *as* the church, and we're saying it *to* the church, but we want the world to hear what we're saying, too.

We want the world to hear what we're saying because since the 1960s, the 1970s, the thing that we've lost is a kind of public conscience, a social sense of morality, what's right and wrong. That was the aim of the document on the Church in the Modern World: to help people develop a sense of values, to provide the basis to help people form that social conscience. Now if everybody says what they feel, first of all, and what they want, and then what they think they have a right to, we don't have any kind of public values any more. Individuals can gather people together to change public policy in ways that are not always beneficial to the whole of society.

## Are you saying that we have lost the sense of a common good?

Yes, absolutely. That's exactly what I'm talking about. But how are we to define the common good? The document on the Church in the Modern World was an attempt to give people some insight so that they could discern what was the common good, and allow that to influence their thinking and choose what was right and good, and what ought to be done.

**Sometimes people blame a document such as *Gaudium et spes* for that loss, whereas it's probably more of a social change, a change in culture, that has taken place.**

The loss of the sense of common good is something that has happened in society. The whole teaching of Vatican II was to help people realize the common good, for instance, religious freedom as a right for everybody. When you say that the church recognizes religious freedom, that means that the conscience or the religious practices of other people have to be accepted, and that they have the right to do these things. The Vatican Council said that, but that's not what's caused the loss of a sense of public morality.

We can only hold together as a society if we have common goals, if we really understand what is right and good, if we want to work together for that, if we want to respect one another in doing that and we don't want to deny anybody their own rights. At the same time we have to have some agreement on values—what it is that society needs, or what is the right thing for society to do. This whole war in Iraq [2003] made it clear that there is a vast division of opinion on what's right and good, what nations have the right to do. We have the same thing, of course, in family matters and everywhere else. I don't have any simple solution to that. We have this document on the Church in the Modern World, but when you read it you just get tired because it is so long and so detailed. I wonder how we can break this open, make the message clearer, put the message into effect, because that just hasn't happened. It's a wonderful document, but it hasn't had the impact at all that it ought to have had.

**We've talked about the most significant document, the most significant figures. What about the most significant statement? Is there any single one?**

Paragraph 41 of the Constitution on the Liturgy, which said that the most significant manifestation of the church is the celebration of the Eucharist by the bishop surrounded by his priests and his ministers, and with the full, active participation of the faithful. I think that is the most significant statement.

I think that the purpose of the Council was to tell us what the church is. You want to see what the church is? Here's the way it shows itself, and that from this manifestation of the church, this icon, this vision of the church, we should be able to find out all the other things we're going to need.

The most significant teaching or fresh presentation would be on the paschal mystery. I think of years of going to retreats when the resurrection was never mentioned—you probably had the same experience—but we can't do that since the Council because the resurrection is everywhere. The teaching on the paschal mystery was really the most significant teaching that came from the Council, for me.

## How do we keep that vision of liturgy in CSL 41 from deteriorating into the institutional view that the Council was trying to overcome?

You can't have a celebration of the liturgy without institution.

## But you can have a celebration of the liturgy in which the institution takes over the celebration.

Not if you have the full, active and conscious participation of all the faithful. It presents the vision of the church: When everybody is there, and everyone is fully involved, that's the way the church ought to be. That's the ideal of the church.

## This is, in essence, the antidote to clericalism.

Of course it is. It's not just the presence of the church in that spot, but also the presence of the church throughout the world. The realization of the universal church is right there.

## What happened at the Council that you never imagined would happen?

Positive: the hundreds and hundreds of lay people who are sacramental ministers here in the diocese. I would never have thought of that—not only that they go out from the celebration of the Eucharist to bring Communion to the faithful, but that they feel they have something to bring *to* the celebration as well.

## What about things that aren't so positive?

In 1965 Pope Paul VI announced the formation of the synod of bishops. All the people that were around me at the time, the bishops who were around me at the time were saying, "Isn't this wonderful! We're going to be able to continue this marvelous experience of the power and presence of the Spirit, our ability to make a contribution to the life of the church is going to go on; it won't be the same but even after we go home, the spirit of the Council will still be able to survive."

So we've had I don't know how many synods—more than fifteen, I think—but they haven't really been the synod of bishops. They've been gatherings of people who came and expressed opinions; but then we got a document afterwards that sometimes didn't relate very positively to what was brought from different parts of the world. It just hasn't worked out the way it ought to.

The idea of the synod then was that people would go home and consult with their own people; the bishops of the country would gather together some kind of common proposals, bring these to the synod; the proposals would be debated or compared or whatever; and finally, the synod itself would bring out some teaching or some pastoral directives. But that's not what happened.

I remember being a delegate to the synod for the laity in 1987; we had a huge intense consultation of lay people all across the country. We had local meetings in different dioceses, and provincial meetings, and the bishops' conference [sponsored meetings]. We really had a great store of information, and that was put into the submissions that were made at the synod. But then these things went into the pot, and everybody went home. We were just told that the Holy Father would issue a synod document when all things had been considered. And so we'd get a document from the Holy Father: It's a beautiful document as I recall, a beautiful homily on the Scriptures and so forth, but it's hard to find the concerns or recommendations, proposals, and so on, that came from different people from different parts of the world. It's hard to find that there, and that's been the experience of the other synods. You've heard that. To me it's the big disappointment, especially having been there when the announcement was made. I was so thrilled to think that somehow this experience of the power and presence of the Spirit was going to be continued.

**When you put this description and critique of the synodal process into the context of Vatican II, it makes me think perhaps one of the problems we're facing is that synodal process hasn't worked as a way of continuing to implement Vatican II.**

The synodal process hasn't worked because it isn't a process that was anticipated. Archbishop Maxim Hermaniuk CSsR [1911–1968], the late Metropolitan of the Ukrainian Church in Canada, was a delegate to almost every synod and was on the central committee for a while. He spoke on this every single time.

**He was very strong on that, wasn't he?**

Yes he was, because he came from a synodal background in the Ukrainian church; but it never got into print in the final documents from any synod.

**This process was so totally different from the process of Vatican II?**

So different from what Pope John XXIII was saying: We have to express it in the methods that are current at the time. That's not how other statements are reached by groups. We want to communicate the teaching of the church as people communicate now.

**Sometimes when I look at these huge documents that still come out of Rome, I think of how communication bytes are getting smaller and smaller, and communication is much more visual. I wonder why they're still sending us 30,000-word documents.**

That's part of the difficulty for implementing the Council right now. We have all these documents, but we don't even have time to read them. So we have to find some way to distill what's there. I look at all the paper that I have here in my house, and all the hundreds and hundreds of talks that I gave on these subjects. We still have to extract not only the meaning, but also the spirit, from all the documentation.

**Should we have a Vatican III?**

No—because Vatican II is not over yet.

**Will Vatican II ever be over?**

Yes, it will be over. Every Council has a phase of reception. Maybe some of the things that are not happening are telling us, "This is not the sense of the people." We do these things, or say these things, or believe these things—and certainly we have to try to hear what the people are saying about family life—so I think that right now we are still going through this phase of reception.

Think of the Council of Trent. One of the decrees of the Council of Trent was that there were to be seminaries and education for the clergy in dioceses and regions; everyone thought that was a good idea, but the ones who made it happen weren't born until about thirty or thirty-five years after Trent. So when I celebrate infant baptisms, I say, "Maybe you'll be the one who will do the things that we were trying to envision in the 1960s."

I'm not giving up on Vatican II. I think we have to keep on trying; we have to find other ways of communicating the message. We have to try to break open the Constitution on the Church, and we have to look at the document on religious liberty that really was so contested at the Council—there was such a debate over it. Right now it's very apropos. It talks about religious liberty for all, and we have another document about the relationship between church and other religions. Both those things have been put on the shelf, but we have to bring them out and find some way to teach the message. The Declaration on Religious Liberty and the one on the relation of the church to non-Christian religions also has an added document that came from the Council, but wasn't called a separate Council document—the document on our special relationship with the Jews. Especially with all the things that are going on in the Middle East these days, we should be hearing more about the Catholic teaching on these things.

But the main thing I want to say is that I still think that the implementation of the Council is something that's still going on. Take the area that we're both most familiar with: the liturgy. Think of some of the things that were done right after the Council when people didn't understand what they were doing. We say, "Thank God that's over with." That was an attempt to implement something, and it has died out, it's disappeared, because it wasn't the right thing to do.

**We grew beyond it, we figured it out.**

Sure, exactly. And we had to have those things to let people see what was sensible and what was misguided.

**What's the most difficult part to implement in the local church?**

Trying to have all the councils and commissions that were mandated by the Council. The hardest thing was to get individual parishes to approach that with the right attitude. Sometimes pastors didn't agree with the idea; sometimes the people on the councils thought it was just a way to get together and approve of what was done. It's still difficult. Even having a diocesan pastoral council—for them to have some sense of what their responsibility is, and giving them the freedom and authority to exercise that—those were difficult situations. They're changing. I don't know whether they're becoming easier; that varies a lot from place to place.

**If you had one thing you wanted to say to a new bishop in terms of passing on what you received from the Council, what would you say?**

I'd tell him to have the greatest respect, and have an open ear, an open eye, and an open heart to what the people in his diocese are saying and thinking, and what their needs are. That has to determine what he's going to do.

## That hearkens back to Pope John's principle, right?

It does, and it comes back to the thing that is made so clear in the Constitution on the Church: The bishop or the pastoral leader is the servant of the community. That's really the way it's expressed most frequently and forcefully at the Council.

## If you had one thing that you would say to a twenty-year-old, somebody who has not experienced the world that you grew up in, what would you pass on to them from the Council?

I'd tell them to love the church. And I'd tell them, "You love your grandfather, but he frustrates you sometimes. And you love your parents, but behind their backs maybe you laugh at them. It's okay to feel that way about the church. It doesn't mean you don't love the church."

## What would you say to people who are really discouraged about Vatican II?

I keep telling them that the Holy Spirit was present at Vatican II, and we did the right thing. It may not have happened yet, but it will come about. Some things we tried seem to have disappeared, but I say, "I'm going to wait a little while; I think that some of those things are going to be revived again. They're going to come back to life again. Maybe it's fall right now; but there's going to be a new springtime again." They won't come back in the same way, but what's behind them will still be important. I think that's particularly true about ecumenical efforts.

## What would you say about what's happening right now in terms of liturgy?

I think I'd have to ask people some questions first and find out what is it they're trying to do when they decide on one thing or another. Whenever I went to a parish, I would always try to greet the people before Mass, talk to them, see if I could find out if they had anything they wanted to tell me, or that the parish needed to know about. Now it seems that some places have fifteen minutes of absolute quiet before Mass, and say the rosary. I don't think that's the way you gather people into community to be fully active and participatory in what we're going to do. Why they do some things, why they don't do other things that are recommended and seem to be reasonable ways of doing things—that's what I'd like to find out.

## Is there any issue that you regret that the Council didn't address?

I think that, at the time of the Council, every issue that was appropriate was addressed in some way. Those things were sifted out very well when the initial documentation was changed around. What I spoke of not happening with the synods did happen with regard to the Council. You think of some things happening now, and wonder why the Council didn't address it. That was simply because it wasn't an issue then. But I think that the Council addressed the issues that were current at the time.

The bishops were certainly in charge of the agenda, so whatever the bishops wanted the Council to deal with was dealt with.

Since the Council, my sense of the pastoral ministry of the bishop has been enhanced and broadened by the principles and attitudes that were part of the Council's gift to me personally. And they have continued to bear fruit for the past ten years since my retirement, in my involvement in pastoral ministry to the sick in an ecumenical setting.

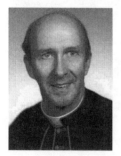

Archbishop emeritus James M. Hayes was ordained a presbyter of the Archdiocese of Halifax, Canada, in 1947, ordained a bishop in 1965, and was Archbishop of Halifax from 1967–1990. He has served as president of the Canadian Bishops' Liturgical Commission and on the Episcopal Board of ICEL. He was present at the first session of Vatican II and returned as a Council father for the final session in 1965.

# Archbishop Raymond G. Hunthausen

From a speech delivered at Seattle University October 11, 2002, "We Need A Miracle—Expect One: Reminiscences on Vatican II and My Life as a Bishop." Reprinted with permission of the editor of the *School of Theology and Ministry Review*, Seattle University, Volume 3, 2003.

The beginning for me was 1959 when John XXIII was visiting with some of the cardinals and was troubled a bit about what was happening in the world and what the church ought to be about. The word "council" was mentioned, and it spread like wildfire. For almost four years, preparatory commissions put the documentation together. There was consultation with the bishops of the world: What ought we to be addressing if we come together in Rome?

In those days Bishop Joseph Michael Gilmore [1893–1962] was the bishop of Helena, Montana, and a good friend; he looked forward to the Second Vatican Council with great anticipation but in April he died suddenly. On July 11 [1962], I was named bishop of Helena. I was frightened to death, of course, frightened to death! I was ordained August 30. I really was the youngest bishop from the United States, the last bishop ordained that summer.

There had been a flurry of ordinations—I think a dozen or so—that summer; they were trying to get us all over to the Council. At the annual meeting of the bishops we would have our own table, and we would celebrate the fact that, in our minds at least, we were a special group. There aren't many of us left. I'd like someone to research that. How many of us bishops are there in this country who attended all four sessions of the Council? We are a vanishing breed and an endangered species—kind of like that spotted owl, I think. Even legislation won't keep us in existence. So one gets older and now, I suppose, I am one of the oldest of the Council fathers.

I remember getting the documentation. It came in big bundles and I had little or no time to look at it. I was overwhelmed. The other bishops in the country and across the world had received this documentation months in advance.

But when we got to Rome, most of that documentation was set aside. I wondered whether 90 percent of the bishops knew what was going on. You see, the documentation had been received but, in the opinion of some bishops, not one of those documents was worthy to begin a discussion. The bishops were of the mind that [since this material had been prepared by the Curia] the bishops themselves should be in more command of what the documents contained. The bishops themselves should be in the position to appoint members of the commissions and the rest of it. So the opening day of the Council, I think we were in session for less than an hour. It was a very short time, at least, and a great deal of wonder went on about what would happen.

I went to the Council with Bishop [Bernard] Topel [1903–1986] of Spokane and Bishop [Sylvester] Treinen [1917–1996], who had been ordained the bishop of Boise just a month before me; he was from North Dakota, and I had gone over for his ordination. It was the first time I had met him, but somehow we agreed that we would all stay at the same place, and Bishop Topel arranged for this. Wouldn't you know, he got us into a convent three miles away from St. Peter's. When we got there, the question was "How in the world are we going to get to St. Peter's?" Now there were buses, as you remember from those days—all of the pictures of bishops in buses, dressed in their red regalia, all over town and crowding the piazza at St. Peter's. We, of course, didn't have any bus service.

I checked around and found a graduate student, a graduate priest from the United States who had a Volkswagen bug he wanted to sell. I remember buying it for $1,300. Besides Topel and Treinen, there was also a Bishop Hilary Hacker [1913–1990] from Bismarck. They said, "That's great, as long as you do the driving!"

So I did all the driving for that first session. (That's right—you think Seattle's bad!) Now imagine this: Bishop Hacker about 6'2", Bishop Topel a little over six feet and Bishop Treinen about my size—the four of us in a VW bug, in these red cassocks!

The Council hadn't been in session very long when I was driving to the piazza of St. Peter's. We were right in front of what they used to call the Holy

Office; we could see the colonnades of the square ahead of us—busy, busy intersection. The policeman out front was waving traffic through. I was the last one to be waved through, and I was sort of sticking out. The bug was sticking out into the intersection more than I would like, so I edged up to the car in front of me and I touched the bumper.

Holy smoke! The door of the car in front of me opened up, and this fellow came dashing out and he looked down at the car and his hands were waving like this, and all of a sudden he looked into the Volkswagen. He just could not believe it. (I can't gesture the way the Italians do; I can't do justice to it.) With a kind of helpless gesture, he got back into his car and drove away.

About that Volkswagen—we had it only the first session because we changed residences for the second and following sessions. I tried to sell that car at the end of the first session and couldn't; the student priest had purchased it up in Germany, and it was now down in Italy, and the paperwork was more than any dealer wanted to mess with. Finally I went up to Via Veneto to an American car dealer. He said, "If I were you, I'd send it back to the States." I said, "How in the world do I do that?" I can't recall the particulars but we had it shipped. A friend of mine picked it up; I said sell it. I made 300 bucks. That's a fact. Bishop Topel said, "I wish I had bought it instead of you!"

Well, back to that procession of the Council. I was so far down the list that quite frankly, my seat was not in the main body of the basilica of St. Peter's. I was in the balcony along the sides, the first one up on the left side as you look down the length of the basilica from the rear (there were theologians or observers in these balconies). Recently appointed bishops and I had the seats in the front row on the left hand corner. Now all of the bishops behind me, they could hardly see anything of what was going on down below because they just weren't close enough. But I was right over the cardinals—right over the cardinals. In the first sessions particularly, the cardinals could do almost anything they wanted. The first thing in the morning, as we would begin the sessions, all they had to do was raise their hand and they could speak. Most others had to present a written intervention in order to be called to the microphone.

And Cardinal [Alfredo] Ottaviani [1890–1979]—most of us remember his name—I don't think it was deserved, but he was identified as the villain. He was the man who was trying to pressure and push for all the Curia positions; he would get up to make an intervention, and the secretary would very politely tell him that his ten minutes were up and he had to sit down. He would still be ranting and raving as he walked back up the aisle and talking to his fellow cardinals—

always with a smile on his face. I came to like that man, and really felt this was a man with a cause, and he was giving it his best shot. I know over time we read that he felt defeated by what happened in the Council because so much that he had proposed and expected to be rubber-stamped was simply sent back.

I mentioned Cardinal Ottaviani and his ability to speak Latin. I was at the opposite end of the spectrum: I had a very difficult time following the interventions. As a matter of fact, if a French bishop were to stand up and read off his intervention in Latin, it sounded to me like French. I could understand and follow a good bit those from the United States and English-speaking countries, but much of it was lost by me and (if they admitted it) by a good number of other bishops in the hall. They were not that expert in conversational Latin. So much of it was missed.

You may remember reading about Cardinal [Richard] Cushing [1895–1970] of Boston and his willingness to underwrite the cost of translation—you know, instantaneous translation. I remember when the engineers and communications people were wandering through the hall and experimenting with the possibility of equipping all of us with microphones so that we could get our translation. This effort didn't last very long, though, because the technicians discovered that there was no way they could keep the conversations in the hall; the press would be privy to them outside. I don't know if it was the Holy Father or the bishops as a body, but they simply didn't want that. I think it would have added a great deal to the experience of the Council to be able to follow word for word and not have to go home at night and pick up the written interventions. They were always available to us, no problem about that; but it would have been good to be able to hear the inflection and the rest of it in the hall itself.

Let me move on to the second session of the Council. Notice that I'm not telling you anything about the documents. There was no document published during the first session, but at least there was an awful lot of work done and put back into committee so that much work would be done in second and third sessions.

Between the first and second sessions I spent at least a month at the Mayo Clinic in Rochester; I had a back operation. While I was there recouping, I was privileged to attend the ordination ceremony of Bishop George Speltz [1912–2004], who was ordained as the auxiliary bishop of Winona, Minnesota. He was a good friend of Bishop Treinen's; at the next session, we did an awful lot of walking around together and he eventually came to live with us. It was a new place, Madre Pie Pensione, which was walking distance to St. Peter's Square. In our red regalia, rain or otherwise, we walked back and forth to the sessions of the

Council. George Speltz is a wonderful guy, but shy and retiring in a lot of ways. He had his mind made up that he was going to record the opening talk by Paul VI, but he wondered how he might do this. "Just take the tape recorder," we said. "Well," he said, "mine is a brand new one, and I have never really used it." We encouraged him. "Just put it in your briefcase and take it in." "Won't the Swiss Guard stop me?" "No, they won't pay any attention to you at all."

There we were at the opening session in our miters and our copes, and George had his briefcase. We hadn't yet gotten seat assignments in the second session, so we were all sitting together about midway down on the bleachers way up high. When it came time for the Holy Father to speak, George reached down inside his briefcase. There are two buttons that you have to push in order to record, and he hit only the play button. He had a demonstration tape in there, and out came a John Philip Sousa march. Everybody within earshot all turned around and, of course, I looked in the other direction. It must have been a year or two before George Speltz was even willing to look at a tape recorder again.

During the second session, I went up to Florence with Bishop Topel to visit Gonzaga in Florence. [Gonzaga University is in Spokane, Washington.] These were some of his people and he wanted to visit the Jesuit fathers and others on faculty and see some of the students. We had barely arrived in town when we began to hear the rumors that John Kennedy had been assassinated. Information wasn't all that complete yet, but I remember getting to Gonzaga in Florence and having dinner, and the kids listening to the radio and coming back with updates. Within an hour it was confirmed that John F. Kennedy had been assassinated. That, of course, is branded in my memory. But what I also remember is this: the next day in the square as we were admiring Michelangelo's *David,* a little Italian gentleman came up behind us and tapped me on the shoulder. I turned around and he had tears in his eyes; his only remark was, "We have lost our two Johns." John XXIII had died; I think it was in June that year. These two men touched the world and touched the hearts of so many people, and this elderly Italian gentleman was expressing that.

I remember coming back to the third session of the Council. A cabbie would take you anywhere for a John F. Kennedy fifty-cent piece.

The Council was an ideal training ground for someone who had just been appointed a bishop. These sessions were overwhelming, but wonderfully instructive and exciting. You remember about the theologians and all of the so-called experts who were in Rome. One could go almost anywhere any afternoon, any evening and find one of these theologians—[Edward] Schillebeeckx, [Hans] Küng or [Karl] Rahner, or maybe some of the observers, or Robert McAfee Brown—and they would all be commenting on what was going on right there and then in the Council. It was immediate; it was reinforcing what was happening. You could go to a press conference every afternoon where several of the bishops who had made an intervention that day would give you some background on why they said what they said, and what the implication was for them, for the church and for the document under discussion. Bishop Treinen, Bishop Speltz and I, we solved all the problems of the world in those days. We would wander the neighborhood in which we were living, getting some exercise or stopping and sitting on the steps of a church building in the evenings or nights and just discussing.

I do remember the lengthy discussion we had on the document On the Church in the Modern World (*Gaudium et spes*). Maybe that is where some of the thoughts and impressions about nuclear warfare entered my mind.

It was a great time for the bishops of the world—I think any Council would be, but certainly for the bishops of the United States. We got to know one another as we could never have gotten to know one another any other way. We saw one another frequently, not only in Council halls, but in special gatherings arranged to bring us together. That lingered, with a beneficial effect for us bishops after the Council was over. Cardinal John Dearden [1907–1988] of Detroit was our chairperson for the United States Conference of Catholic bishops—I think we elected him for two rounds—a marvelous gentleman, who certainly was touched deeply by the Council. Because we knew one another, in those first years after the Council, the discussion and the agenda were vital and lively. The agenda of the bishops these days pales, compared to what we were talking about in those days.

I heard at the Council a good bit of ecumenism, and it resonated with my own experience as a Christian. I grew up in Anaconda, Montana, which many people refer to as a Catholic city. Not really; it might be 40 percent Catholic and the rest Protestant. I do believe in that Montana community there was a great respect for church by all. We grew up with young people not of our own church, but when we'd get to talk about churches and our freedom to go to a church or a wedding or to a funeral, I still remember that caution, "Oh no, you can't go to a Protestant church." I just used to think, "It doesn't make sense! After all, I play ball with that fellow whose mother was getting married." I don't think it came so much from my family, but it was a kind of a sense. It worked both ways.

Well, listening to the Council and reflecting on it, I was liberated—absolutely liberated. When I came home from the Council, I remember being invited by the Montana Council of the Churches in Boulder, Montana, to kind of a hotel and spa there. I was frightened to death. "I'm completely comfortable with people of other churches," I was saying to myself. "I'm going to have to go as a bishop. I'm going to have to go there and defend the faith!" But I went. It was one of the greatest experiences of my life. I came to know men and women in a way that was so supportive of my own ministry. We were all looking for ways to get to God and to understand what was happening in our lives.

When I came here to Seattle and I received an invitation to go to the 7:00 a.m. meeting every Thursday morning with the [interdenominational church executive group made up of the major Christian denominations, including the executive director of the Church Council of Greater Seattle and the executive director of the Washington Associations of Churches], the same thing happened. I became so close to these men and women that quite frankly I would share anything with them. It was just a great starting point. Whenever we might have something to discuss, whether it might be controversial or whatever, we didn't have to go through all this business of getting to know one another; we could simply take off in the right direction. I don't hesitate to say that I probably would have been more comfortable sharing some of my most intimate problems with some of those people, maybe more readily than with some of my bishop friends. We need in our world to come to a deeper respect for one another—and that's not easy, is it?

A good number of people have said, "Until the Christian people can find a way to come together and reconcile and be one, what more can we expect of peace in our world?" There are a lot of peoples of different religions and persuasions, and we don't work at it hard enough. We can have bilateral discussions all we want—and they are important and they need to be had—but I think that before that, we need to put emphasis on simply getting to know one another. Respecting one another, loving one another—it is what Jesus said, you know. He wants us to be one as he and the Father are one, but he also said, "Love one another as I have loved you," and it applies across the board. I didn't intend to say all that. But ecumenism was one of the things that was foremost in my mind when I came back from the Council.

The other major impact of the Council on my life as a bishop was shared responsibility. The Second Vatican Council helped us take real responsibility for our lives and our decision making. It was not enough simply to do what we were told. Before the Council, something or somebody out there had to take the responsibility; someone else had to take the blame for what might go wrong in our lives.

That's not enough, nor is it sufficient to say, "I'll do whatever I want to do." That is totally contrary to what the Gospel is about and what Jesus has come to teach us. The harder way is to make an effort in prayer to examine what the church is saying on an issue, if it be a church issue—to open ourselves to the Spirit, to discern the Spirit and then, even though it might be difficult, to arrive at a decision that is truly ours. I guess what the Council tried to help us do was to help us grow up—to become mature Christians aware of what is going on in our life and what is going on in our church: "Why am I doing that?" To examine our motivation and to do that under the influence of the Spirit—always, always the Spirit. Today we need to pray for the Spirit in our life, in our church and in our world.

Anthony DeMello, in his book *Contact with God* [Image Books], makes the observation: the church of our time is in crisis. That is not always a bad thing. Crisis is an opportunity to say, "Yeah, it's OK to grow, to grow up and become mature and examine one's life, to work at it, to become better people." There is chaos only if the Spirit isn't hovering over it.

So what we really need in our church and our world today is an in-pouring of the Spirit, to become people of the Spirit and to recognize, as did the first disciples, that the Spirit is always there in our lives—that, as Jesus told the disciples, we need to wait for the coming of the Spirit.

We have a hard time waiting. The Spirit is gift. We cannot make the Spirit happen, but we need to have a sense of anticipation. We need a miracle. Expect one. Be people of hope always, because God is in our midst. There isn't any question about that. Over and over again we continue to pray, as honestly and as profoundly as we can, that the Spirit will touch our lives and touch our world. The Father will surely give the Spirit more readily to those who ask for the Spirit.

Ask yourself, "When last did I ask for the Spirit in my life and in my work and in the church?" It is there, more than ever before, to help us all to understand what Vatican II was about—because I have no doubt in my mind that Vatican II has a lot yet to be lived.

God be with you all.

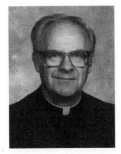

Raymond G. Hunthausen was born in Anaconda, Montana in 1921 and was president of Carroll College from 1957–1962. His episcopacy coincided with the Second Vatican Council and was marked with great change both within the diocese and within the church itself. He served as bishop of the Helena diocese from 1962–1975.

In the early Montana church, Native American missions played an important role. In 1963, a new mission was established by the diocese in the Central American country of Guatemala under the leadership of Father Jim Hazelton. In a cooperative agreement with the Diocese of Solola, the Diocese of Helena sent priests, sisters, and lay people to work in two parishes in that country. In addition to religious work, the diocese has been providing educational, medical, and social services since that time.

In the spring of 1975 Bishop Hunthausen was named Seattle's second archbishop. Under his leadership Archbishop Hunthausen and the church of Western Washington worked with other denominations and faiths, championed justice and peace efforts and further implemented the church reforms of the Second Vatican Council (1962–1965). The archbishop attracted international attention for his tax protest in opposition to the nuclear arms race and for a Vatican investigation of his ministry. The Vatican transferred some of the ministerial powers to Auxiliary Bishop Donald W. Wuerl in 1986 but restored them in 1987. Bishop Wuerl was transferred in 1987 and was named bishop of Pittsburgh a year later. Bishop Thomas J. Murphy of Great Falls-Billings, Montana, was named coadjutor archbishop of Seattle in 1987. Archbishop Hunthausen retired in 1991 and continues to provide retreats and evenings of reflection on ministry.

# Archbishop Denis E. Hurley, OMI

## Interviewer: John R. Page

**What was your capacity at the Council? Were you also a member of the Central Preparatory Commission?**

I attended the Second Vatican Council in my capacity as Archbishop of Durban, South Africa. I was appointed a member of the Central Preparatory Commission and attended all its meetings except the third in January, 1962. At the first session of the Council I was elected a member of the commission on seminaries, universities and Catholic schools. (The word "schools" was later changed to "education.")

**How many sessions of the Council did you attend?**

If by "sessions" it is meant the four periods of the Council, I attended them all. If the word refers to the general assemblies in St Peter's, I attended all of these.

**What was the most significant moment at the Council for you?**

The most significant moment for me was when, in September, 1964, it was announced that we had given a very impressive vote to chapters I, II and III of the *schema* on the church (*schema* being a position paper). Chapter I deals with the mystery of the church; chapter II with its membership, the people of God;

and chapter III with the hierarchy, and includes the very important section on episcopal collegiality.

## Of all the documents of the Council, which one is most significant for you and why?

The four constitutions—on the church (*Lumen gentium*), the liturgy (*Sacrosanctum concilium*), revelation (*Dei verbum*) and the church in the modern world (*Gaudium et spes*)—vie with each other in significance, but in the end, the most significant is the Constitution on the Church, for a number of reasons:

Firstly, in chapter V, [*Lumen gentium*] sets out the great overriding purpose of the church: the pursuit of holiness, a holiness that consists of the gift of divine life, the inestimable privilege of enjoying in our human life the presence of Christ and his Father and of the Holy Spirit, a presence inspiring the practice of and growth in love of God and love of creation, especially of its human dimension, the climax of known creation.

Secondly, in chapter VII, we read of the goal of humanity and of all creation in the glorious mystery of Christ in heaven.

Thirdly, in chapters II, III, IV and VI, we are given the varieties of membership of the church and also its organization, in regard to which the important issue of the collegiality of the bishops with and under the primacy of the pope is dealt with in chapter III. Finally, the role of the Blessed Virgin Mary as model of the church is beautifully described in chapter VIII.

A slightly disappointing feature of all this is that holiness—the great purpose of the church—and love, its most important manifestation, are not given all the emphasis they deserve. Without entering the detail on the Constitution on the Church in the Modern World, love should shine out as the greatest potential the church has when influencing the world, promoting peace and dealing with poverty.

## What's the most important teaching that came out of the Council?

The most important teaching to emerge from the Council is what has been said in the answer to the preceding question, and the involvement of the church in the world as explained in *Gaudium et spes*.

## Whom do you feel was the most significant figure at the Council?

In my opinion Cardinal Leo Joseph Suenens [1904–1966], Archbishop of Mechelen and Brussels, was the most significant figure in the Council. I say this for three reasons: firstly, because of the part he played in giving shape and balance to the agenda of the Council; secondly, because of his membership in a number of controlling organs of the Council; and thirdly, because of his magnificent contributions to discussions held in general assemblies of the Council. (Contributions to discussions came to be known as "interventions," a word adopted from languages of Latin origin.)

Prior to the Council, Leo Suenens had served as auxiliary bishop of Mechelen and Brussels; on December 15, 1961, he was named archbishop of that diocese and shortly afterward was appointed a member of the Central Preparatory Commission. I met him for the first time when he attended the fourth meeting of the commission held in February, 1962. He made no great contribution to that, being content to observe and reflect. It did not take him long to realize what several of us in the commission were concerned about: lack of clear purpose and a disorderly agenda. He came back to the next meeting a cardinal, having been created such on March 19, 1962.

He came back with a very clear plan for the agenda of the Council. It consisted of two parts rejoicing in the Latin names of *Ecclesia ad intra* and *Ecclesia ad extra* (*Ecclesia* meaning church, *ad intra* referring to its internal life, and *ad extra* to its relation to and activities in the world). I was very impressed, and after the meeting lost no time in congratulating the cardinal on what he had placed before us. It was a remedy for my anxieties and an answer to my prayers!

The Council was launched on October 11, 1962. During its first period, which concluded on December 7 that year, it dealt with three major topics: liturgy, revelation, and the church, along with two topics of less importance. The *schema* on the liturgy had been well prepared and was accepted as a Council document, subject to revision. But the *schemas* on revelation and the church proved unacceptable, and total revision was called for.

Before this first period of the Council came to an end, the Holy Father accepted what had been asked for in the Central Preparatory Commission and set up a coordinating commission of seven cardinals, one of whom was Cardinal Suenens. On December 4, His Eminence addressed the assembly and put forward his *Ecclesia ad intra*, *Ecclesia ad extra*, which was greeted with loud and prolonged applause.

"Moderators" were also appointed; basically their role was to preside over general assemblies but, as the Council progressed, they seemed to pick up other responsibilities. Again, Cardinal Suenens was one of the moderators. So the leadership to guide the Council through the rest of its history was in place, and Cardinal Suenens occupied a key position in it.

Within the coordinating commission, items on the agenda of the Council were assigned to various members for care and attention. Cardinal Suenens was allocated two major ones: an *ad intra* item, the church, and an *ad extra* item that ended up as The Church in the Modern World (*Gaudium et spes*). He was obviously carrying a very heavy load.

This did not prevent him from taking a prominent part in the discussion of various *schemas*. He had the advantage of a splendid backup of academic persons: theologians and other experts based at the University of Louvain. Among them, the most important was Monsignor Gerard Philips [1899–1972], who also became the principal writer of *Lumen gentium,* the Constitution on the Church.

A characteristic of the great debates in the Second Vatican Council was that the bishops of the western European bloc—France, Germany, Switzerland, Austria, Belgium and Holland—had the advantage of a magnificent pool of theologians, Scripture scholars, historians, liturgical experts and prominent promoters of lay apostolate, social concern and catechetics. It was this combination that brought the theological and other revivals forcefully into the consciousness of the Council, and neutralized and almost extinguished the traditional grip of the Roman Curia on the Catholic outlook. The struggle between these two tendencies was the drama of the Central Preparatory Commission and the first period of the Council. Clearly, Cardinal Suenens was a prominent, if not the most prominent, leader of the western European bloc. He was well served by his own particular Belgian brigade based in Louvain.

Along with all this, he was amply endowed with the gift of enthusiasm. This had become evident in his promotion of the lay apostolic movement known as the Legion of Mary. In the Council he strove to have the significance of the term Catholic Action broadened to include movements like the Legion. His enthusiasm for the Council was unbounded, and in the last period of his life, so was his enthusiasm for the charismatic movement.

Cardinal Suenens, during the treatment of the *schema* on the church, introduced the topics of the permanent diaconate and the recognition of a variety of charisms, that is, special aptitudes and activities originating from the Holy

Spirit and of great importance to the laity as well as clergy and religious. In the discussion on holiness, he pointed out how unbalanced was the list of canonizations, with 85 percent pertaining to members of religious institutes and 90 percent to three European countries.

On October 23, 1964, Bishop Emilio Guano [1900–1970] of Leghorn in Italy—*rapporteur* of the joint commission (doctrine and lay apostolate) responsible for the *schema* that became the Pastoral Constitution on the Church in the Modern World—announced that the question of artificial birth control would be removed from the competence of the Council since there already existed a special commission to deal with it.

Despite that, on October 29, Cardinal Suenens went ahead with his intention of speaking to the issue. He said it would be highly necessary that a commission of the Council work with the commission already established by the pope for the consideration of this question. (He was referring to the commission on Population, Family and Birth set up by Pope John XXIII.) He said that the issue of birth control should be considered from two points of view: firstly, in regard to church doctrine, that while the Gospel is unchangeable, doctrines relating to it will always be open to examination. It was possible, the cardinal thought, that in regard to marriage, too much emphasis had been laid on the Scriptural injunction "increase and multiply," but not enough on "they will be two in one flesh." The commission should investigate whether we had not urged the duty of procreation to the detriment of conjugal communion and put this in some jeopardy.

The commission, the cardinal said, should also face up to the population explosion, evident in many parts of the world; we should examine this problem in order to assist the church, "the light of the nations," to make known its mind. The commission should also give attention to what was emerging from scientific research, which was continually unveiling new dimensions of our humanity.

"I adjure you, brothers," exclaimed the cardinal, "let us avoid another trial of Galileo. One is enough for the church."

After a few more considerations, including the assurance that the final decision rested with the Holy Father, Cardinal Suenens moved into his peroration: "Venerable brothers, we have no right to be silent. Let us not fear studies about this issue. At stake is the salvation of souls and of our families, even of the world. Let us remember the word of the Lord: 'Truth'—both natural and supernatural—total and living truth—'will make you free.' I have spoken. Thank you." It must be remembered that the Latin word *dixi,* meaning, "I have spoken," was the usual way of terminating an intervention.

One can imagine what a meal the world [media] made of this speech. The news of it rumbled and roared around the globe to the extent that His Eminence found himself constrained to refer to it at the end of his contribution to the debate on missions on November 7. He maintained that he had been misrepresented. He had not said that the teaching on birth control should be changed; he had merely called for a thorough examination of the issue in the light of doctrine and science and had clearly indicated that the final decision rested with the Holy Father.

Pope Paul VI could not have been too pleased with this contribution of Cardinal Suenens to the debate on the family. Possibly it inaugurated the cooling-off of relations between pope and cardinal. Whatever the truth of this, the cardinal persevered in his vigorous participation in the Council and played a full part in the backroom struggle between the promoters of church reform and the guardians of the establishment, the Roman Curia. Despite an unending series of setbacks, the Curia never gave up in its resistance to change, relying on papal decisions to give it victory in a few skirmishes in the overall campaign.

Before the end of the Council, Cardinal Suenens had the enormous task of nursing what was first known as *Schema XVII* and later *Schema XIII* through a difficult first debate, through a midnight-oil-burning period of revising and correcting, to final acceptance and promulgation as the Constitution on the Church in the Modern World on December 7, 1965, the last working day of the Council.

Because all this left him with time to spare, he ran his own series of discussion groups on various Council topics.

## What was the most significant statement from the Council and why?

I would consider that the most significant statement from the Council is the conclusion to section 17 of the Constitution on the Church (*Lumen gentium*), which reads as follows:

Thus the church both prays and works so that the fullness of the whole world may move into the people of God, the body of the Lord and the temple of the Holy Spirit, and that in Christ, the head of all things, all honor and glory may be rendered to the Creator, the Father of the universe.

Being an ardent disciple of Teilhard de Chardin, I consider this the most significant statement from the Council, because it brings together the being of

God, Father, Son and Holy Spirit, and the being of the universe created by the Father and destined in Christ, its head, to give the Father full honor and glory through the church that is people of God, body of the Lord and temple of the Holy Spirit.

## What has happened that you never imagined would happen?

The outcome of the renewed vision on the relationship between the church and the world resulted in a far-reaching unsettlement of priests and religious, the abandonment by many of their chosen state of life and a drastic drop in vocations to the priesthood and religious life.

## What hasn't happened?

The collegiality of bishops. As things stand at present, it depends on the pope how collegiality is practiced and developed. Pope Paul VI took a small step in the direction of collegiality when he established the Synod of Bishops; but this is not really a collegial institution because, as the *motu proprio* describes its identity and operation, only the pope is authorized:

- to convoke the synod whenever this would seem appropriate
  and to indicate the place where it will be held;

- to approve the election of members in keeping with the
  prescriptions of sections V and VIII;

- to decide the agenda at least six months before the synod is held;

- to decide the program;

- to preside over the synod himself or through others.

The synod is a permanent body and all its meetings have conformed to these prescriptions.

It fell to me to represent the Southern African Catholic Bishops' Conference in some of the early synods. I deplored the absence of theologians. To a very large extent, theologians made the Second Vatican Council.

## Is there any issue you regret that the Council did not address?

There are two issues that I regret the Council did not address: priestly celibacy, and birth control in marriage.

## What has been the most significant liturgical achievement and what do we yet need to do to implement full, conscious and active participation?

The most significant liturgical achievement has been a better understanding of the liturgy and much better participation. Even better and fuller participation will depend upon the training of seminarians and young priests in the line of sensitivity to all dimensions of the liturgy.

## In your opinion, should there be a third Vatican Council, and what topic(s) would you bring to the table?

In my opinion there should not only be a third Vatican Council but an arrangement should be made for a council of the church every twenty-five years, so that every generation could experience a council and benefit from its impact. However, for Ecumenical Councils to achieve the best results, I think we should remember the Council of Jerusalem, and include others besides bishops as members: representatives of priests, deacons, men and women religious, and lay women and men. This might make it difficult for all bishops of the world to attend, but each episcopal conference could have representatives, as in the case of the present Synod of Bishops. Careful research will be necessary to work out how a huge and multilingual gathering of that nature should be organized. We have many examples to learn from in the great conferences that have been held in recent times on a great number of topics in various parts of the world.

This proposition concerning ongoing councils would be the main topic to be brought to the table of Vatican III.

## What Council teaching was most difficult to implement in the local churches?

I think that the most difficult teaching of the Council to be implemented in the local churches is the teaching on war—firstly, because the teaching itself is not devoid of complexities, and secondly, because it is not easy to have the clearer parts accepted by those who feel urged to embark on war.

## Is there any special historical or cultural significance that Vatican II occurred in the 1960s? Could it have happened earlier, later, in your opinion?

If Vatican II had not occurred in the 1960s, it might never have occurred up to the present time. Blessed John XXIII was unique in his conviction and courage about the necessity and value of the Council. The early sixties was a providential time, bringing together as it did the vision and courage of Pope John and the results achieved in an impressive array of revivals in the church: scriptural, theological, apostolic (especially in the matter of the lay apostolate), liturgical and catechetical.

Denis Eugene Hurley was born in Cape Town, South Africa, in 1915 of Irish parents. His father was a lighthouse keeper. After entering the Oblates of Mary Immaculate in South Africa, Hurley was sent to Ireland for novitiate, then to Rome (Gregorian University) for his philosophical and theological studies. He was ordained in Rome in July 1939, and was pursuing a doctorate in theology when the intensification of war in Europe forced his return to South Africa in 1940.

After returning to South Africa, he served as curate at the cathedral in Durban and then as rector of the OMI scholasticate at Pietermaritzburg. In December 1946, shortly after his 31st birthday, he was named a bishop and vicar apostolic of Natal; he was consecrated bishop on March 19, 1947. In 1951, when the hierarchy in South Africa was formally established, Hurley was named first archbishop of Durban and served in that post for 41 years. He was president of the Southern African Bishops' Conference from 1952–1960, and again from 1981–1987.

In 1959 Archbishop Hurley was named a member of the Central Preparatory Commission of the Second Vatican Council. (By 2003 the only survivors of the CPC were Hurley and Cardinal Franz König.) Toward the close of the Council, Hurley was named a member of the *Consilium* for the Implementation of the Constitution on the Sacred Liturgy (1964–1969).

Archbishop Hurley was a founder of the International Commission on English in the Liturgy (ICEL) and was present at its first meeting in Rome on October 17, 1963. He remained on the Episcopal Board of ICEL until 2001, and served as ICEL's chairman from 1975–1991.

The leading Roman Catholic opponent to apartheid, Hurley was convicted of treason by the South African government in 1984, but the case was dismissed on a technicality in the face of worldwide protest.

Archbishop Hurley has received numerous honors, most notably in 1999 when President Nelson Mandela awarded him South Africa's highest honor, the Order for Meritorious Service, Class I. From 1993 until 2000, Archbishop Hurley served in the prestigious honorary position of chancellor of the University of Natal. Archbishop Hurley died on February 13, 2004 as this book was going to press.

# Cardinal Franz König

## Interviewer: Christa Pongratz-Lippitt

**In what capacity did you attend the Council?**

I attended the Council in my capacity as the then Archbishop of Vienna. Every Roman Catholic bishop was invited to attend. I attended every session—and each one was fascinating.

**What was the most significant moment of the Council for you?**

For me, there were two most memorable highlights. First, Pope John XXIII's opening address in which he bade the bishops not to listen to the "prophets of doom" but to tackle present-day problems joyously and without fear. All the tension and uncertainty that had prevailed up to then was immediately wafted away. The address triggered a mood of great optimism and set in motion the church's opening up to the world.

And secondly, the ecumenical service in St. Peter's on December 7, 1965 marking the end of the Council, when Pope Paul VI announced that the Papal Bull of 1054, which had declared the Great Schism between the Western and Eastern Church, was now null and void.

## Of all the documents of the Council, which one is most significant for you and why?

*Nostra aetate,* the Declaration on the Relation of the Church to Non-Christian Religions and on the Jewish question, is in my eyes if not *the* most significant document, certainly one of the most significant. It underlines that the church "rejects nothing of what is true and holy" in other religions and stresses the importance of dialogue. The last three pages of *Nostra aetate* concern the church's relations to Judaism. This briefest of all the Council declarations was hotly disputed and took four years to pass. It was indeed almost a miracle that it was ever passed at all. *Nostra aetate* opened up a whole new dimension and pointed to a new way forward for the church's relations with the non-Christian religions and on the delicate Jewish question.

## What in your view is the most important teaching that came out of the Council?

I would mention at least two important teachings. The first is the Council's support for ecumenism. Pope John's decision to set up the Secretariat for Christian Unity and to invite non-Christian observers to the Council was path-breaking. By the end of the Council there must have been close to one hundred observers who joined in the discussions, rectified misunderstandings and brought in new aspects which found their way into the Council documents. This was already ecumenism at work.

And then there is the Council's emphasis on the importance of the lay apostolate. Vatican II stated clearly that the church is one communion. All the baptized are the pilgrim people of God and all share the responsibility for the church.

## Whom do you feel was the most significant figure at the Council?

First of all, the two popes—John XXIII and Paul VI. Pope John XXIII had the courage to take that initial, path-breaking step of calling and preparing a world Council; and Paul VI was brave enough to see it through. Both popes were central figures. I would also say that the bishops from Eastern Europe, which was at that time behind the Iron Curtain, played an important role, and also Cardinal [Leo Joseph] Suenens [1904–1996], who was in close contact with Paul VI and had a considerable influence on the decrees on the church. Oskar Cullman, a Lutheran observer, was also an outstanding figure.

## What was the most important statement from the Council, and why?

I think for me—but certainly not for everyone—the most important state-ment is the beginning of the Decree on Ecumenism, *Unitatis redintegratio*:

> The restoration of unity among all Christians is one of the principal con-cerns of the Second Vatican Council. Christ the Lord founded one Church and one Church only. However, many Christian communions present themselves to people as the true inheritance of Jesus Christ; all indeed pro-fess to be followers of the Lord but they differ in outlook and go their dif-ferent ways, as if Christ himself were divided. Certainly such division openly contradicts the will of Christ, scandalizes the world, and damages the sacred cause of preaching the Gospel to every creature.

## What has happened that you never imagined would happen?

I never imagined that, in his encyclical letter *Ut unum sint* (1995), Pope John Paul II would envisage a revised way of practicing the primacy and, without sacrificing the essentials of the papal mission, would acknowledge the need to make possible a new ecumenical orientation. I recall his invitation in *Ut unum sint*:

> Could not the real but imperfect communion existing between us per-suade church leaders and their theologians to engage with me in a patient and fraternal dialogue on this subject, in which, leaving useless contro-versies behind, we could listen to one another, keeping before us only the will of Christ for his church and allowing ourselves to be deeply moved by his plea 'that they may all be one... so that the world may believe that you have sent me' (John 17:21)?

## What has not happened?

According to the Second Vatican Council's Constitution on the Church, *Lumen gentium*, the bishops are called upon "to be solicitous for the entire Church" (LG 23). The expectation was that they would do this through regular synods of bishops held in Rome. But this has not happened.

In his encyclical letter *Sollicitudo omnium ecclesiarum*, (1969) Pope Paul VI took pains to remodel the advisory and controlling functions of the curial authorities, in order to bring them into line with the Council's intentions. But in the postconciliar period, the Vatican authorities have striven to take back autonomy and central leadership for themselves. The intentions of Paul VI's encyclical letter have not been realized, and today we have an inflated centralism.

## What has been the most significant liturgical achievement, and what do we yet need to do to implement full, conscious and active participation?

The most significant liturgical achievement has been the return to the vernacular. We must get back to the essential elements of the liturgy.

## Should there be a third Vatican Council?

I do not think that there should be a third Vatican Council. It would not be wise and would create confusion.

## What Council teaching was most difficult to implement in the local churches?

Ecumenism. People in the parishes were often of the opinion that it was the Vatican's job as it was too difficult to carry out at parish level. But discussion of theological differences is not enough. There are so many areas where we can work together ecumenically—in the fields of social and charitable work, for example— without running up against theological differences. Even if at the moment we cannot overcome some of the essential theological differences, we can change the climate of discussion by doing things together.

## Is there any special historical or cultural significance that Vatican II occurred in the 1960s? Could it have happened earlier or later, in your opinion?

It happened because John XXIII became pope and had the courage to call a Council. It would have been a good thing if it had happened fifty years earlier— but there was no Pope John XXIII then!

Cardinal Franz König is a cardinal in the Roman Catholic Church and Archbishop Emeritus of Vienna, Austria. He was born on August 3, 1905 in Rahestein, Austria. He attended the Pontifical Gregorian University, Rome; Pontifical Biblical Institute, Rome; Catholic University of Lille, Lille, France and earned his doctoral degree in 1930. He was ordained a priest in 1933, elected to the episcopacy in 1952 and became a leading expert on the Zoroastrian religion. He was named a cardinal by Pope John XXIII in 1958, and retired in 1985 on his 80th birthday. Cardinal König was part of the Preparatory Commission and attended all the sessions of the Second Vatican Council.

# Bishop Myles McKeon

## Interviewer: Russell Hardiman

In my time, they spoke of consecration of a bishop; only after Vatican II was it considered an ordination, so I was consecrated a bishop on September 12, 1962. On October 9, 1962, Redmond Prendiville [1899-1968], archbishop of Perth, Western Australia, and I, as his auxiliary bishop, flew out to Rome for the Second Vatican Council. All the priests of the diocese went out to the airport to see us off.

Halfway between Perth and Singapore, one of the flight officers asked, "Would you by any chance be Bishop McKeon?" I said, "I am." He shook hands with me and said, "Well, I'm your cousin. This is my first trip to Australia as one of the pilots. Before I left Liverpool, my father told to be on the lookout. 'You never know, you might meet a cousin of yours who became a bishop in Australia only recently and his name is McKeon.'" I said, "Well, I'm the man, and what is your name?" He said, "Paddy O'Toole."

We arrived in Rome on schedule and went to stay at the Casa Palotti near the Ponte Sisto, just downstream from the Vatican, a *pensione* run by the German Pallottine order.

## What was the most significant moment for you at the Council?

The beginning of the Second Vatican Council. We were all excited, of course. The special buses for the bishops picked us up from the various places where we were staying. It was very colorful, as we were all in our purple *soutanes* [cassocks]. There were hundreds of thousands of people in Rome for the occasion, and we were cheered all along the way up to St. Peter's. We had to wear an alb and a cope with our ordinary purple cassocks, so it didn't take long to get dressed. I was dressed about ten past seven and then we had to sit around and wait until eight a.m. for the procession to St. Peter's. The Council was to start at ten in the morning.

I had just got my outfit on when this tall, stately bishop came along; he shook hands with me and said, "I'm Lawrence T. Picachy SJ [1916–1992]." (He afterwards became a cardinal in Calcutta.) I said, "I'm Myles McKeon." He said, "You're from Perth, Western Australia? I got a letter from friends of mine just before I left home, telling me you would be here and that I might meet you." He didn't expect to meet me on the first morning out of nearly 3,000 bishops, archbishops and cardinals.

All the bishops from all over the world were present that morning—2,993 members, only seven short of 3000. Everybody who could walk at all was there— and some of them had to be practically carried. At eight in the morning we moved from the halls where we had vested, down the corridors and out into the open square. As far as the eye could see, we saw nothing but people everywhere. The procession started at eight sharp; it took a solid two hours for the last one to come in. That last one was Pope John XXIII.

Pope John was carried in, as was usual in processions, on the official chair, the *sedia gestatoria*, so that he would be elevated while he was giving his blessings to the thousands of people all over the place.

There was no particular order of seating at that first session. When the Holy Father arrived, of course, there was a great clap for him from all the Council fathers as soon as he came in, and then there was a bit of a holdup. Pope John tapped the side of the seat and told them to lower the chair because he was going to walk up. This was out of keeping with the ordinary procedure, and the men who carried him wanted him to remain as he was. However, being the pope, he won the argument; he said, "Do you want me to disgrace myself in front of all my bishops, to have them think I couldn't walk up St. Peter's?" Actually, to see him walk up, he was short and very heavy and he practically ran up; he went up at a trot!

Then he gave his formal address to the Council fathers as to what the Council was all about and what were the expectations. The main thing he had to say was that he expected and prayed for a renewal in the church, with a true emphasis on what renewal meant. That it was renewal: *renovaris* is the Latin, to make new or to bring it to a complete—you might say refreshing—renewal of the church. The Italian word he used was *aggiornamento*; he explained that very minutely, saying that he wanted to have an evolution of doctrine and of the teachings of the church. He emphasized that the evolution was not meant to be revolution, but the unfortunate thing is that as the teachings of the Vatican Council became known or studied, a lot of people who should have known better did go for revolution rather than evolution; and that is why we have had so much trouble.

The pope spoke of opening the windows, letting in the fresh air into the church. But he didn't mean that everything should be opened so that a storm could blow through the church and do damage rather than good. In spite of all the teachings and statements to the contrary, the more the documents were studied and people really got down to the very kernel of the teachings, the more they realized the teachings were something to be regarded as sacred and beautiful.

The extraordinary thing about that opening day was to see Pope John XXIII, who wasn't young, walking up St. Peter's main aisle to start the Vatican Council. That first session did not finish until a quarter past two in the afternoon, and that man was as fresh at the end as he was at the beginning. It was in itself a tremendous experience to just be part of that and see Christ represented through an elderly man speaking to the whole church throughout the world and speaking with tremendous vigor with no sign of being tired. He had no concept of time at all.

## Whom do you feel was the most significant figure at the Council?

Pope John XXIII was an extraordinary genius. He met all the bishops of the whole church in turn in national groupings. It went on night after night after night.

He received as a group all the bishops from Oceania, from Australia, the islands in the Pacific, and from Papua New Guinea, New Zealand and so on. We were scheduled to meet him at six p.m.; we were all there in good time. We waited and waited, and we saw him about half past seven. He was busy receiving other bishops; it was just a case of seeing them all. Time was not of the essence of any of his programs.

Cardinal [Norman] Gilroy [1896–1977] did the introductions; he knew the whole group by name. He came to Bishop [Edward Michael] Joyce [1904–1964] from Christchurch, New Zealand, who is a tall man about 6'4" or 6'5" and about 18 or 19 stone in weight [260–275 pounds]—huge! John XXIII just looked up at him and then looked down, and sized him up from top to bottom, then gave him a poke in the stomach and said, "Bravo, you're a fine, robust man just like myself." That was his style.

When he sat, a cushion was put under his feet because he couldn't touch the ground with his feet; his chair was too high. He beckoned to us to sit down and make ourselves comfortable. As he started talking, he just took a kick at the cushion and then the feet were in and out after that as he pleased. He spoke to us for about an hour, just a nice chat in the form of a welcome; he hoped that we would not be disappointed by all the comings and goings at the Vatican Council, and that we would all be able to make our contribution to the sessions.

We now call him Blessed John XXIII. He called the Council against opposition in Rome itself. When John announced it to some of the Curia, they replied, "Have it in three years' time? That's impossible. It's impossible to prepare for it in three years' time." John said, "All right, prepare for it in two years' time."

Pope John XXIII was always regarded as "the grand old man." When the chips were down and there was something to be done, there was no messing around. It had to be done when he wanted it done, and he looked on the calling of the Council as very urgent. Why? He had been Papal Nuncio and delegate in different parts of Europe and in Constantinople, which is not an easy area. He knew the church. In his career, he was in constant contact here, there and everywhere. He knew that in the church there was a shocking cry going out for change in so many areas to update the church, and to have an evolution, as he said in the first session of the Council. He knew that was a matter of urgency. As somebody put it, "The pot was boiling madly in different parts of the world and unless there was something to control it, when the pot boiled over it would blow the lid off and then we'd be in trouble and there would be nobody and nothing to control it." So the pope said, "Let us have a Council. Let us listen to the church all over the world."

## What were the sessions like?

We started every session of the Council at nine each morning with Mass. All the different orders or rites in the church had their own rituals. Morning after morning we had these special rites, the singing of Byzantines, Copts and Ukrainians, and many others besides the Roman Rite. The custom was that bishops of the various churches in different regions celebrated daily Mass. Then each day the Word of God was enthroned, as a connection with the practices of the earliest Councils in the church when this ritual was a prominent daily feature.

I'll just give you an idea of each day of the Council.

St. Peter's had been refurbished so that all sat in a kind of choir format facing one another across the central aisle, with blocks of seats and desks for us all. The desk was a kind of board that could be let down, with something supporting it. The seats, in blocks of sixty, were very comfortable and just ordinary. When you first came in, you received your numbered seat, and that was your seat for the rest of the Council.

After Mass, Archbishop [Pericle] Felici made announcements that had to be made in the name of the Holy Father. Felici was a great character and had a great sense of humor. He introduced each day and you got a clear picture of what was being dealt with. Then he announced the name of the president of the Council, the person who was in charge of all that day's proceedings. Of the presidents, Cardinal Gilroy of Sydney had his fifteen minutes of fame when he was the first to ring the bell on a cardinal who had exceeded the time limit. When Gilroy rang the bell and said, "*Satis* [enough]," there was huge applause, which gave impetus and support to the president's right and power to control proceedings. There were twelve presidents who took charge of the proceedings in rotation each day. After Mass and the announcements, the day's working papers were distributed.

The daily sessions of the Council went from about quarter to ten in the morning until quarter past twelve in the afternoon. In the afternoon, various committee meetings and groups analyzed what had been said at the morning session.

Every single document that has been produced by the Second Vatican Council has been studied paragraph by paragraph by all the Council fathers, and voted on paragraph by paragraph. It was long, tedious work, but at the same time you felt that it wasn't dealt with in a haphazard or slapdash way. You had the best ecclesiastical scholars of the world involved with the bishops of the world in the production of the documents.

It wasn't easy. Every document was in Latin. All the Council proceedings would be in the Latin language.

## Everything was in Latin?

I had found it a lot of drudgery in the seminary to do all the moral theology, canon law and so on, the whole thing in Latin. But it became part of your life and when you got questioned in class, you stood up and away you went in Latin. Sometimes you would use an English word, and the professor would say, "*Sufficit* (that's enough). Sit down, please." Speaking English wasn't tolerated. For me, and for bishops who studied in Rome, of course, and those who studied in England, Ireland and most European seminaries, the fact that the Council was conducted in Latin was no great problem. But others, especially in areas of the U.S.A., did not use the Latin language in their studies; they found it difficult to get through it. And there was no letup.

The interest in Latin also concerned the oriental rites or Eastern churches united with Rome, then commonly called Uniate Churches. These were the churches of the Eastern Mediterranean areas, in a lot of the places where St. Paul did his preaching. In modern times, areas such as Syria and Lebanon came under French influence, and French was often the European language of these countries. Similarly, Noumea [New Caledonia] was French-speaking. Indeed, French is the first language in parts of Canada; groups from different parts of Canada spoke French and nothing else. But at the Council, they all had to speak in Latin. We were all waiting to see what they would do. There was no apology from Patriarch Maximos IV Saigh [1878-1967] (of the Melkite Church in Syria and elsewhere); he just spoke in French. I shouldn't say this but they were a very proud sort of people, who looked upon themselves as something special.

The first session of the Second Vatican Council was very important. We really got badly bogged down for the first month, as we were dealing with the very difficult subject called "The Sources of Revelation." Draft texts were issued to us, drawn up by a committee that was regarded as a committee from the Holy Office; they were conservative, afraid of change, and a lot of them were determined that change wouldn't occur.

When a document was presented, the first thing you had to do was study it—whatever it dealt with, liturgy or anything, you name it—and then discuss it at the Council sessions. The key issue was whether the document would be accepted as the basis for discussion and eventual voting, or whether it should be returned for further preparation.

The document, "The Sources of Revelation," provoked huge discussion. In a matter of four weeks, 654 bishops spoke on that document. (When you spoke at the Council you got ten minutes a time to say what you had to say and then sit down. If you didn't sit down, you were *told* to sit down by the presiding President of the Council for the day.) Everyone was getting tired of it, as we didn't seem to be getting anywhere. It was a very difficult subject, on which ecumenism would depend on a lot in the future.

The whole assembly was divided. Some bishops were for the draft document as it was, and other bishops were against it. The "younger" crowd was considered against it, which was true, as a lot of the older men didn't know what was at stake. I myself didn't know what was at stake at all until my friend, who was a professor of Scripture, explained it to me.

After four weeks, it came to a vote as to whether we should accept that document for further study or not. Although they didn't like the words "conservative" and "progressive," the element of difference was there, whether they liked it or not, and it is a useful way to describe it. When the final vote was taken, the conservatives won the day by 411 votes; there was a great cheering by them and terrible depression on the part of the other group.

I've never felt so downhearted in my life as I did that day. I was staying with a group of conservatives; one was an archconservative, Bishop Bernard Stewart [1900–1988] of Bendigo, Australia (Lord, have mercy on him), and my own archbishop was a bit that way, too. There were five of us staying at the one place and sitting at the one table, having the same discussions. I thought, "This is one day when I must shut up and say nothing." Bishop [William] Brennan [1904–1975; bishop of Toowoomba, Australia] (Lord, have mercy on him) used to take pity on me and take sides with me often, although he was conservative himself. However, after that vote, we came home, sat down, said grace, and Bishop Bernie Stewart couldn't hold it in. He turned to my archbishop and said, "Well, Redmond, thanks be to God, the Holy Spirit is with the church still. All those young whippersnappers, they don't know what they are voting for or talking about. They were put in their place well and truly today. I hope they have learned their lesson." My archbishop didn't say yes or no to him, and when he tried to start the conversation a few times, nobody was joining in.

Word got out that evening that the pope was going to veto the vote. That night twenty-two of the top men from Rome—cardinals, bishops and archbishops—approached John XXIII and tried to get him to change his mind. He just let every single one of them know he was in charge, and he saw this—and he was so right—as a tremendously important moment for Scripture in the life of the church.

Next day in the Council, Archbishop Felici told us that the Holy Father had followed carefully the discussions of the Council fathers on "The Sources of Revelation." He had noted the vote and now, as Vicar of Christ on Earth, Supreme Head of the Church, he was casting his vote in favor of the minority. The place went wild, and it was nearly ten minutes before the President of the Council could get a bit of silence.

The Council never looked back after that. That was the turning point. I came home that day delighted, and I said to Bishop Brennan, "Well, Bill, thank God the Holy Spirit has come back to Rome after a twenty-four hour absence." My archbishop could have cut my throat.

When the document on revelation came back to us, it was a new document altogether. Nobody was game any longer to take any conservative view, or your own private view. You had to know why you voted for a new document, which was a great thing.

The trouble was that Catholic scholars were so far behind in the study of Scripture at the time of the Council. When our men got the green light by that vote of John XXIII, it was tremendous. At the Biblicum, a Jesuit house in Rome, I met two famous scholars, who in the years preceding the Vatican Council had been practically silenced by the church in the field of Scripture. But after Pope John's vote, that all changed. They did a tremendous job. And they were the most humble men you could ever meet; they would sit down and talk to you in very plain language about the Scriptures. They did a magnificent job once the door was opened to them.

While we waited for the new document on revelation to come back, we went on to the liturgy draft document. Of course, there were fire and brimstone during that discussion. Everyone was having a go; it was liturgy, liturgy and liturgy. The next day this old bishop got up and gave us a great talk on St. Joseph, and the absence of any mention of St. Joseph in the Mass, and how there should be. The President tried to stop him several times but he wouldn't be stopped. He caused a great laugh, of course.

The next morning, Archbishop Felici got up and announced that Holy Father had listened to the talk given by bishop so-and-so, and from that time on St. Joseph would be included in the canon of the Mass, in the first eucharistic prayer. This is the type of thing that happened.

During the first session's discussions on the liturgy, bishops from different parts of the world were saying that it was now coming to the stage where the church must face up to reality and forget about saying Mass in Latin in China, and saying Mass in Latin in Africa, and saying Mass in Latin all over the world. There must be concentration on the liturgy to the extent that bishops and priests in their own territory would be able to deal with all documents of the church in English. They would be able to say Mass in English and so on, and relate the sacraments to the people, so that people would know what was happening instead of just being present and hearing a whole lot of garbled prayers. Even at a baptism, how did anyone know what was going on? The priest was saying and doing the whole thing in Latin.

At the first session of the Council, I was fortunate to meet a priest who was a professor of Scripture at Notre Dame in the United States, an Irishman who afterwards became professor of Scripture at Maynooth College in Ireland. He had just been over to Jerusalem studying Scripture and examining the modern insights in Scripture. He was one of the scholars with the American bishops. I said to him, "Look, John, you are just the man I need to give me a complete and clear insight into the whole thing from a modern standpoint." He was invaluable because I got to understand what we were all talking about and what we should be talking about. There were a lot of things I was out of date with. He told me the books I should read; I got them and studied them, which made the whole thing clearer to me.

He was one of the *periti,* the experts. Many bishops brought their own advisers, theologians or Scripture scholars to help them. We used to have regular meetings dealing with different subjects.

Along with many others I used to attend the American press conference conducted every afternoon in English. It was good to listen to the various theologians from all over the world, and I got to know quite a few of them.

Among the hierarchy a tremendous friendship developed. We were all in it together, so to speak. It was a great experience to meet the bishops from other countries and to realize that, everywhere you looked, they had their own problems, their own specific problems.

## Of all the documents of the Council, which one is the most significant for you, and why?

One of the great documents of the Council is the Decree on the Church's Missionary Activity (*Ad gentes divinitus*), devoted to the missionary nature of the church shared by all the baptized. Pope Paul VI emphasized its importance by coming and introducing it himself.

During the conciliar debate, it was most interesting to listen to the bishops of the Third World and to realize what their lives must have been like, and to hear the comments of missionary bishops about the implications in their cultures of the universal celibacy demanded of priests. Later, it was not possible to discuss issue of celibacy.

From my background as Director of Propagation of the Faith, I was very conscious of the support for the missions and of affirmation for the missionaries from so many countries—men, and women too, answering the call of God to go out into the various mission fields. Out of my class of thirty-five at St. Jarlath's College, Tuam, in Ireland, seven were a very close-knit group; six became priests, five in the Third World; some are still alive in Japan.

To give you an idea of the spirit of the Council, one night the superior of the Columbans in Rome invited me to dinner at their generalate. He said, "The Columban bishops who are at the Council will be there." I asked, "How many?" He said, "Twelve." When I sat down in the middle of the group that night at dinner, suddenly I realized that every single one of them had done long years in prison for God in China and in Korea. Right beside me was a bishop who was in the headlines as giving an example of ecumenism (before the word became popular during and after the Vatican Council); he is still remembered in Korea today. He was one of few who survived the "hundred days' death march," as it was called in Korea. There were about three-hundred people on that death march, all Christians and Catholics. Most of them died along the way. Any who got ill were just abandoned by the roadside, and those who carried on had to listen to the guns of the communists as they shot dead those who had failed. When the small group arrived at the end of the hundred days' death march, among them was a Catholic bishop, supported on his right by a Methodist minister and on his left by a Salvation Army captain. As they struggled over the finishing line, all three fell to the ground. They couldn't go another step further. They were thrown into prison until the end of the Korean War.

Today the church has spread like wildfire in South Korea. Many Catholics in North Korea still exist under the communist regime. There are so many South Korean priests now that the foreign missionaries who worked there—the Columbans, the Maryknoll Fathers and the Maryknoll Sisters from the U.S.A.—have gone on to other missions to bring the Gospel to those places where it has not been preached.

## What was Paul VI like?

Pope John XXIII had died in June, 1963, and was succeeded by Cardinal [Giovanni Battista] Montini as Paul VI. Paul VI thought he was always in the shadow of John XXIII until the famous occasion when, during the Council session, he visited the United States to address the United Nations. He left one morning from Rome and after a flight of six or seven hours, he addressed the

U.N. General Assembly at eight that evening. Everything stopped in Rome to watch him on the TV. He made the dramatic appeal that war must cease. "There must be no war, never, never, never again. Otherwise we run the risk of destroying the whole world." These words were the headlines. Next morning, we sat down to resume Council business at 9:30 a.m., and in walked Paul VI. On that morning he came into his own; now he spoke as Paul VI, Vicar of Christ on earth. The ovation was deafening.

Paul VI was regarded as one of the greatest popes who ever lived. He had everything that was best in a pope. He knew what was happening; he had been Archbishop of Milan. Academically, he was way out in front; spiritually, it was lovely to see him when he celebrated Mass and when he came to meetings. He was friendly—the warmest individual you could ever meet.

In 1970, I made an *ad limina* visit [a bishop's five-year report to the pope] just after Paul VI had announced that he would visit Australia. He just sat me down beside himself and put his arm around me and asked me what I thought about his visit to Australia. I said he would get a great welcome. He said, "Do you think I am too old?" I said, "Not at all, not at all." I showed him the area of my diocese on the map. "*Mamma mia!*" he said, "It is as big as Italy!" He made you feel completely at home and he commanded the respect of all the Council fathers.

### How did the Council end?

The final day of the Council, December 8, 1965, was in itself a tremendous experience. All the proceedings were held outdoors in St. Peter's Square. Apart from all the Council fathers, there were visitors from all over the world. Messages to the world prepared by the Council were addressed to various groups, for instance, a special address for the youth.

There was a special address given for young women. To me, it was a very good statement; unfortunately, I noticed it has been left out of some of the editions of all the Council documents. Get a book with the documents of the Council, go right to the end where they give the various concluding addresses that were sponsored by the Council, and if there isn't one on women, look around further and see if you can get one. It would be a pity to miss it.

When the Council came to an end, it was a sad sort of day because we all had met so many other bishops from various parts of the world and had come to know and indeed love them; we felt that the Council united us as one.

The years have taken their toll of the Council fathers. At the final session in 1965, forty-four bishops represented Australia; and forty years later, forty-two have gone to God. Bishop Jobst, Bishop of Broome in Western Australia for some thirty-two years, is retired and lives in his hometown in Germany. And then there is just myself, apart from Bishop Dogget of Wewak in Papua New Guinea, who in his nineties lives in retirement in Sydney. The Council was one of the greatest experiences of our lives. It gave an insight into the church that I don't think any bishop or anybody could possibly have who hadn't experienced the Council.

## What happened after the Council?

When I came back from the Council, there was the big—in many ways difficult—work of bringing the message of the Council to the people, and then dealing with huge changes in the liturgy. Australia was one of the first countries in the English-speaking world to introduce English into the Mass. In other countries there were long delays and many obstacles because people were rejecting the whole idea; bishops had a hard time. But here in Australia, people accepted it.

We had the books printed long before any other bishops. A friend, a bishop in Canada, asked me if we had done much about the liturgy or introducing English into the Mass. I said, "Yes, we had." The people had accepted our books very readily, and even before the Council was ended, they were ready to introduce English into the Mass. He asked me, "Would you by any chance have one of those books?" I had one with me; the poor man was absolutely thrilled to get it and amazed to see that before Council was ended, we had the English books ready.

After the Council, I called on a friend in England, the archbishop in Birmingham [Francis Grimshaw, 1901–1965]; he was asking me if we had a lot of trouble with the introduction of the English Mass. I said, "No, we got a smooth sort of a passage." "Well!" he said, "I came home from Rome a week ago and I came in here to my office in the morning after I arrived back; I saw stacks of letters all over my desk and I just put down my head on my desk and said, 'God help me.' I noticed my secretary had opened the letters; as I took one of the piles of letters on the desk, he came in and said, 'Your Grace, don't bother your head about them. They are all the same—stacks of abuse for the idea of introducing English into the Mass.'" The bishop added, "I know I have to go around parish to parish and get nothing but abuse. I try to get them to see the point." I don't think he finished his rounds; he died shortly afterwards.

In Perth, the archbishop was ill, in hospital, so I had to hold forth in front of 175 priests, presenting them with the proposition of saying Mass in English within the month. It was a frightening experience, but it gave me an insight into priests—how much humanity they had. Before long, I knew that they felt sorry for me rather than anything else. After the presentation of the Mass in English, I threw it open for questions. The questions went on and on; some of them were getting tired.

Father Joe McCormack (Lord, have mercy on him) stood up and said, "I think I'm the oldest man here in this group of priests. Anyone older than 85?" There was nobody, but they gave Joe a great clap. "Well," he said, "now I've been saying Mass—imagine saying Mass for over sixty years in Latin and in a month's time I must start saying Mass in English, and I'll be delighted. I think it's going to be hard on me; it's going to be very hard. Now I'm the same as you here, we've had enough and the poor bishop is tired, listening to you." He held up the book and said, "Now we all must study this and we all must present this. We must all do what our assembly expects us to do and what the church expects us to do in a month's time. Well, I'm going to study it, whatever you do." That was the end of the questions.

The day after the official introduction, I went down to Claremont to see how Father Joe got on. He answered, "Well! I was still up at half past one in the morning, trying to make sure of it, and I went into seven o'clock Mass a bit sleepy." (At that time, of course, we did not yet have Mass facing the people— that came later.) "So," Father Joe said, "it went fine. I was quite pleased with myself, but I suppose I was getting proud, and the next thing I went completely blank. I didn't know where I was in the Mass. It was a great test also for my assembly. I turned around and said, 'I'm lost. Tell me, did I do the consecration yet?' Only one woman knew. She stood up and said, 'No, you didn't do it yet, Father.' So I said, 'Well, I'll do it now and we'll continue from there.' So that was my experience." So beautifully human, but it was a great example.

The attitude of these priests facing a new situation epitomized for me the new collegial spirit and hope engendered by the Council. This had been obvious in the unity of the Council fathers; now it had crossed over into the spirit in the diocese, and everybody was committed to do their best.

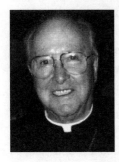

Myles McKeon, bishop emeritus of Bunbury in Western Australia, was auxiliary bishop in the metropolitan see of Perth, Western Australia, from 1962–1969. He was appointed Ordinary of Bunbury in Western Australia in 1969, and retired in poor health in 1982. He was born near Westport, County Mayo, Ireland, in 1919, and was ordained a priest for Perth from All Hallows College, Dublin and went to minister in Western Australia. He was Director of Migration, Welfare and the Propagation of the Faith, as well as being curate in several parishes in Perth. At the time of Vatican II, he was the third most junior bishop, having been consecrated only four weeks previously. He has recorded over fifteen hours of oral history of his ministry in Australia.

# Bishop William Power

## Interviewer: Bernadette Gasslein

*This interview took place the day after the installation of Raymond J. Lahey as the eighth bishop of Antigonish [July 12, 2003]. The diocese of Antigonish is home to St. Francis Xavier University and the Antigonish Movement, a people's movement for economic and social justice that began in Nova Scotia during the 1920s, and Coady International Institute at St. Francis Xavier that sprang from it.*

**What do you think was the most important teaching to come out of the Council?**

It seems to me that it was the notion of freedom. The Council created an atmosphere whereby the freedom of the sons and daughters of God was more recognized. The accent had been on the church as a society, and when that's the case, the emphasis is on rules and regulations. When you look at the church as a community, as in a family, there are tolerances, a certain freedom; you're able to recognize that God can call people to different kinds of missions and work. This freedom was recognized in a way that had consequences.

## Do you think that we've kept up that sense of freedom today?

Well, I think it's something you can't stop once it's released. You see, you can't control with rules and regulations. We're talking about a community. The variety of people in any community makes for differences, but it is the sense of community or love that holds everybody together. Canada is a very good example, with ten different kinds of provinces, and ten different kinds of mentalities, yet we all hang together somehow or other. You can say to someone from Newfoundland or from here or from British Columbia, "I'm a Canadian." It's the same way in the church. Once you own that sense of freedom, once the document on the church says that we are a people, a community, that's a different thing. To me, that's what makes sense of the Council. I don't think an individual bishop could have brought about that sense of freedom in his diocese. He might have been able to do it in a certain sense, but he'd have run into regulations.

## So the change that the Council effected in terms of the vision of and theology of a people brought about this underlying change in the sense of freedom.

In that sense, the principal Council document was that on the church, *Lumen gentium*. It set the tone for the whole thing.

## And in that particular document, was there anything that you thought was the key to the whole?

Chapter I, The Mystery of the Church. When you conceive it as a society, you feel you can sociologically get hold of it—and you can't. The church has its human dimension, just as the incarnation has its human dimension, but it's basically a mystery. We're all united in Christ, and taken to God the Father. You don't get to that by a survey. It's a reality and it's a mystery. In the document itself, the other thing that struck me is the chapters: first, the mystery of the church; second, the people of God. The third is the hierarchy. The fourth is the laity. The fifth is the call to holiness. The sixth is religious. If you implement that, you get to the real role of the laity.

## How do you see the real role of the laity?

For that we need to look at the document on The Church in the Modern World (*Gaudium et spes*). The thing that I found so interesting, and which was most appealing to me, is that this document was born in the Council. There was no preparatory document for it; in the third session, it was surfaced, and between the third and fourth sessions, the document was prepared for the fourth session. It's about the role of the laity in the church. When you say "the role of the laity" to people of my time and immediately after me, too—I'm sixty-three years ordained—they respond, "He or she would make a fine eucharistic minister, or a fine lector or a fine manager of the parish...." It's all inside the church. But what about unions, public life, family life? The laity has to take responsibility in these areas. The priest can't raise a Christian family, or run in politics.

This document was never anticipated. Cardinal [Leo Joseph] Suenens [1904–1996] of Belgium voiced it first. I don't know whether he thought of it first, but he was the first one to voice it. Up until then we had been talking about the church, looking at her belly button so to speak, looking inside, the church *ad intra*. Isn't it about time that we began looking at the church *ad extra*, at how does the church accomplish her mission in the world? The Lord sent the apostles to all nations, so everything has to be sanctified and redeemed. The Council said that the primary role of the laity is the sanctification and redemption of the temporal order. Because we haven't found a way of realizing that sufficiently, we have brought the laity into one of their callings, which is religious education, liturgy, service to the sick, all these particular things that traditionally were done by religious but were seen as the mission of the church.

France, Belgium and Germany created what we used to call the lay apostolate, with which I was involved in the forties and fifties. Called "Catholic Action," it was an attempt at various levels of society to create a movement whose primary purpose was to prepare people for their apostolate in the world. Now, the definition of Catholic Action—with which I could never fully agree—was the participation of the laity in the apostolate of the hierarchy. But it's the participation in the apostolate of the church. And that was a bone of contention in the Council. It came out the right way, thank God.

**So you think we still have a too-narrow concept of church, despite what we heard at Vatican II?**

It's the implementation of Vatican II. This is why I can't agree with the idea of having Vatican III now; it's too soon. You don't change the mentality, the outlook, the way of living and doing of an outfit that has 150 nations in it in the space of 25, 30 or 50 years. It gradually comes. Bishop Lahey's installation ceremony yesterday would have been impossible when I was installed in 1960. A woman reading the papal bull! A woman as the chancellor of the diocese! When I came here, there were forty-five priests associated with St. Francis Xavier

University: five in the Extension Department, five in Xavier Junior College in Sydney, and thirty-five here in Antigonish in administration and teaching. Now there is one priest involved in the university, as chaplain.

The Council contributed to the possibility of change. An individual bishop would never have been able to get away with the kind of celebration we had yesterday—the ambiance, the atmosphere! When St. Elizabeth Ann Seton, [1774–1821] the founder of the Sisters of Charity of Halifax, was canonized on the square of St. Peter's [September 14, 1975], only late Saturday night did the mother general find out that she was going to be allowed to read the next morning. And secondly, she was to wear a veil. Now, she was out of the habit, she had a suit, but she had to have a veil. Remember that, in the old days, you had to wear certain regalia when you were in the presence of the pope.

**Whom did you think was the most significant figure at the Council?**

The two popes. And probably Cardinal Suenens. In my opinion, he was a very intelligent man. I don't think he was an original thinker, but he had a mind that could take two or three things and put them together quickly. He was very influential from that point of view. Cardinal [Paul-Emile] Léger [1904–1991, archbishop of Montreal, Canada] was very influential in his own way. But it was mostly the European cardinals. I used to admire so much the cardinal of Cologne, Cardinal [Joseph] Frings [1887–1978]. He was blind. He always used to walk with his arm through another priest's arm, and when he made an intervention at the Council, he had to memorize it.

**Were there any people in the background of the Council whom you thought were particularly influential? I think of people like Congar, Chenu, Rahner, Haring and Ratzinger.**

Well, obviously, they had their big influence on the commissions, as they weren't allowed to address the Council. But the mystery of the death and resurrection was portrayed perfectly by them. I was involved with the young Christian workers at the time when *Humani generis* [1950] came out from Pope Pius XII, which was against new kinds of things. There were protests, they tell me. I couldn't document this, but the provincials of some Dominican provinces in France were removed. [Yves] Congar was exiled to Cambridge for two years; [Marie-Dominique] Chenu and [Henri] de Lubac weren't allowed to teach. [Bernard] Haring hadn't come into his own by then; this was in the fifties. But these same fellows who were put through that third degree, that death, became the stars of the Council.

These people were the fruits, in my opinion, of the Catholic Action movement. Once you take the methodology started by Canon [Joseph] Cardign [1882–1967] in Belgium—observe, judge and act, which is the virtue of prudence—and you start applying it socially, or environmentally, then you stimulate a lot of thinking that brings forth a lot of questions. If they're theological questions, you go to theologians for answers or to Scripture scholars for answers. This was remote preparation for the Council.

## What about John XXIII?

Because he was basically conservative, John XXIII, who had a degree in history, had a sense of the times and a sense of immediate dependency on the Holy Spirit. He told the cardinals, "The Holy Spirit gave me the inspiration to have a Council." He was so close to God, it was just unbelievable. You felt it when you saw him. He had a great sense of humor, which is always a good sign. "How many people work at the Vatican?" he was asked. "Oh, about half," he replied.

## He also was a pastor.

Oh, yes. Interestingly, he spent most of his time in the diplomatic service, but he had a pastor's heart. I still remember the full-page picture in *Life* magazine of him as nuncio at a New Year's reception he gave for the president and all the ambassadors. The full-page picture was of him in the black cassock with the red buttons, zucchetto, cross, and he's got a cigarette in this hand and a glass of champagne in other. I'm sure he did it just to make people feel at home. A full-page picture. That's in the fifties. He went from there to Venice, from Venice in 1958 to being the pope.

I don't agree with the ways of the present man, John Paul II, but I trust him. He's a real mystic in the full theological sense of the word. I would trust him even though I don't agree with the way he's doing things. Somehow, he's done a hundred visits—his last one in the former Yugoslavia. People growl, "Why doesn't he stay at home and do his homework and get things done?" but his travels have caused the unity. When we see advertisements for news, his picture is always in them. He's made the church present through himself.

# How did you change during the Council?

When I went to the Council, I didn't know what I was going to. I had the advantage of my involvement in the YCW (Young Christian Workers). On a Saturday night, I'd sit around with four or five fellows eighteen to twenty-three years old, and have a beer, and settle all the problems of the world. Cultural, social—everything was fair game. You could question anything. I used to joke and say, "Hey, good thing that door's shut—I don't want to be suspended." I get to the Council, and hear a cardinal saying the same thing we used to say in those closed rooms. So I had this remote preparation, but I never expected to hear bishops at the Council saying the things they said. I can still remember the bishop of Bruges in Belgium [Emiel-Jozef De Smedt, 1909–1995], saying, "We must get rid of triumphalism, clericalism and legalism in the church." Two thousand eight hundred bishops sitting there listening to all that.

But then you'd go in the coffee shop—there used to be one on each side in St. Peter's and you'd get to know a few people after a while, and you'd run into some of the English-speaking bishops who hadn't been exposed to what I had been exposed to previously, and they'd say, "Did you hear what that fellow said out there? Good God, what's the church coming to?" They were getting an education in the process.

# What hasn't happened since the Council that you thought would happen?

I'm prejudiced, but the role of the laity in the church—we haven't figured out how to train lay people so they understand and realize their call. To be fully Christian in the sense that we're speaking of, the laity are going to take an awful beating. First of all, you have to have some kind of community, and you have to have some kind of deeper training in religion, the spiritual life and spirituality, because otherwise you're going to say, "Forget it! I'm not going to get myself into this, lose my job because of this." It requires a formation or training.

Those movements that had existed in Canada and in some other countries which were doing, or attempting to do, such formation have all disappeared. In my opinion, nothing is preparing the laity for that particular role. That's all part of the providence of God, too, you know. Maybe we're going to experience being the weak things of this world that confound the strong, just like the old church in many places. You take the church in Mexico, and what it went through. It's beginning to come out of it, beginning to get a few crocuses at least, but I think this is what's going to happen in North America.

The YCW taught you how to say Christian things without using traditional words, words that would scare the people out of the room. Movements that would prepare people for that—they change people inside, so that they will begin to speak in their own language the things that are in the Gospel. John XXIII said at the opening of the Council, "We must preach the Gospel, but because the world has changed we must find new ways to express the Gospel so it will be understood today." The current pope says quite distinctly that we must find new ways of developing the laity for them to fulfill their position, their job in the church. That's what I'm talking about.

My experience of the YCW did that for me—other movements have done it for others—and at the same time gave me back a fuller perception of my priesthood. If priests don't have a similar experience, they can't stand this kind of life. I used to stay with a priest in Montreal who was alone in a three-story stone rectory. Unless you're motivated by something or distracted by something—he was a great baseball fan—these guys go up the wall. I wouldn't be surprised to hear about priests committing suicide because if you have no hope, it's terrible.

### You get that hope from being in relationships with people.

Exactly. And struggling with the same questions together, struggling with the same issues. Yes. It's a spirituality of death and resurrection.

### That was one of the central points of the Council?

That's why the liturgy was transformed: because of the paschal mystery. All I came out of the seminary with was the resurrection as proof of the divinity of Christ. For so many centuries we were so concerned about fighting the Protestants and proving that we were right; we had the resurrection as one of the proofs that Jesus was really the Son of God. Never did we talk about the consequences of the cross.

### What was the most significant liturgical achievement of the Council?

Two things. First, the vernacular; second, the revival of the Word of God. Up until then, the Liturgy of the Word, as we call it now, was something you had to get through to get at the essence. We used to have Mass once a week [at the Council] in the Oriental Rite. We had one from Egypt, the Chaldean rite, I think: the deacons came processing down the aisle waving two big fans, like those the pope used to have. The music was totally unfamiliar; many of us associated it with a certain form of dance! And then the whole thing was in their language, and long.

I had gotten to know a couple of the English-speaking bishops whom I met in the coffee shop. One bishop said, "I didn't understand a word out there today. I don't even know when the consecration took place. I couldn't tell." And I said, "It must be something similar to what our people experience when we have Mass in Latin." "I guess so," he responded. The discovery process was going on, and it was so powerful because it was the liturgy that did it to him. There were all these kinds of experiences of minds opening to see things that had been right in front of them before.

Only a few years earlier, when the United States Liturgical Conference held its meeting in London, Ontario, the Vernacular Society which wanted the vernacular to be implemented more quickly, was told, "Hold your meeting a day ahead of time, but not with us." They didn't want the bishops objecting to the presence of the Vernacular Society. That was only in the fifties, and yet you get a bishop saying this in the sixties.

When liturgy is properly done and properly explained, it's a very powerful tool for formation. That's why old Pope John pushed it as the first document for discussion. Because it was the liturgy, right away you'd have a commonality among the bishops.

### The bishops had new experiences?

They had the same experiences, but they viewed them differently. They felt comfortable because they were surrounded by bishops; they felt comfortable saying it. You know, if a bishop was surrounded by lay people, he wouldn't say a thing like I just quoted for fear he'd disturb them, unless he felt very much at home with this group of laity. But when we went back to the second session, we were seated according to the date of our consecration, so we were sitting with much the same people whom we'd sat with at the first session. It was a lot like a class reunion. That generated a sense of trust for each other; we felt comfortable with one another. We weren't supposed to applaud, but when one of the bishops made an intervention that pleased everyone, everybody applauded.

### So there was a sense of fraternity, a sense of camaraderie, a sense of comfort.

And then you'd get a greater sense of church.

**You were actually learning this experience of being the people at the same time as you were experiencing this freedom you talked about as well.**

That's right. And that's very difficult to do in a diocese.

## How did you bring that home?

Fortunately, this diocese has such an experience with the social aspect of being church—there were always small groups, "kitchen meetings" they used to call them, about the credit union, and co-ops, because Father Moses Coady's basic notion was adult education through economic cooperation. It wasn't primarily the material; it was primarily the education of people.

Secondly, we had the tradition of the Scots with their clans. Remnants of that are here still. For instance, if the bishop consults the priests (and the people, to a degree), and they advise such a thing, and the bishop decides exactly the opposite, that's fine—but we had a say in it. That fitted in with the notion of the church that we brought to life, but the working that out in church life was very difficult.

The senate of priests—as it was first called, and then the council of priests—was always very difficult. What topics do you bring to them? What topics do you raise there? We said, "The council of priests is to assist the bishop in the governing of the diocese," but what does that mean in the concrete? That's what we had to work through when you say, "apply these to the diocese."

I couldn't go in and start saying that they should be interested in the social, because most of the priests were members of the board of directors of the credit union or the co-op. This was characteristic of the diocese, to be interested in social questions.

## And it still is?

Yes. About 4,000 people have come from about 125 nations to little Antigonish to the Coady Institute. You know how difficult access is [130 miles from the nearest airport in Halifax]. But that's part of the mystery of God, in my opinion. God picks the weak things of this world to confound the strong, and that's where I think the church is heading, into a dying kind of period.

In this diocese, there has always been a plenary assembly of the clergy every year. Eighteen years ago, one of the questions priests were raising was their concern that the youth weren't going to Mass. Well, those youth are now in their 30s.

We used to always say, "Oh, he'll meet some good girl, and that will straighten him out." Now it's the guys who are straightening out the girls! The balance that used to be doesn't exist anymore. Change is universal.

## It's not just a church change; it's a whole social change.

God help us if we hadn't had the Council, because the world was changing, and has changed at a very rapid rate—and we'd be stuck. We'd be a museum piece by now because to do something with the church conceived of as a society with rules, regulations, you'd almost have to defy authority in the church.

## Some people would like us to go back to that fortress.

Of course! They're looking for security.

## Or a way of establishing that kind of Catholic identity in the world.

Yes! But that's passé.

## I tend to agree with you; I don't think we're going to be able to rely on an institutional identity. It's a personal identity, a personal Christian mission.

But you've got to have a group. That's why the future's going to be small groups to leaven the larger group. It doesn't mean that everybody has to be in small groups in a parish, but there has to be a leavening of some kind. The problem is that most people think in terms of the leavening—we'll get them, they'll get involved and that will be great. Various movements are good, but they must get beyond the internal ministries of the church to living Christian life in the world.

## Otherwise, we're almost back to a clerical model of the laity?

Exactly. I remember that Bishop Alexander Carter [1909–2002 Sault Ste. Marie, Ontario, Canada] made an intervention on the laity. He began, "This document has been conceived in sin." After a dramatic pause, he continued, "The sin of clericalism." It was more seen as the laity helping the priest.

## But isn't there also room for lay people to work within the church?

You can't just change one portion of it. What we're talking about, unconsciously, is the training of priests. I've heard priests who don't understand the role of the laity, as I perceive it, say, fifteen years ago, "Well, so-and-so would make an excellent person, with a little direction." Priests would be lost—some of them are feeling lost now. We haven't got the control, the power we used to have—which means, basically, that we need a new spirituality.

## Say more about that spirituality.

[It's] a spirituality that has to be a much more profound appreciation of the resurrection of the Lord, which expresses itself in the cultivation of virtues that facilitate our recognizing that God calls each of us to a mission. To quote the prayer of Cardinal [John Henry] Newman [1801–1890], "Each and every person is given a mission. They may not necessarily recognize it, but they have it."

When priests recognize that lay people are capable of doing certain tasks or ministries, they may ask, "What am I going to do if I let him take care of the books?" because that's where they devote a good portion of their activity. Priests are suddenly going to have to let go of this kind of thing, and devote themselves to prayer and spiritual reading, to much greater preparation of the Word of God. That's a real, full change.

I'm talking about those who are already priests. The younger fellows are going to conquer the world, which is only normal. No matter what you take up, that's what you're doing—you're going to be the best. Well, what is the best when it comes to being a priest? The best is the person who dies the best in order to bring Christ to life. So you're into something that is not just "thirty days' prayer and you'll get what you're asking for," as my poor mother used to say.

Secondly, we have to present Christianity or the church or the mission of each person as a challenge. I think one of the reasons for the lack of vocations is that we don't present it to youth as a challenge. All youth have to have a challenge of some kind, whether it's to be the best ballplayer or climb the highest mountain or do the most stupid thing in the world, whatever it is. The proof of that is World Youth Day, when the kids come from all around the world, and are almost happy to be caught in the rain, because that's part of the experience. It's a challenge.

What's required is a basic orientation. The modern vocation to religious life is to be found in L'Arche and in the work of Catherine [de Hueck] Doherty

[1896–1985], because it fits. You don't commit yourself for life, but for a year or two years, and only after these kinds of commitments, after five or ten years, do you do anything of a definite nature. Youth don't want to commit themselves, because they've grown up in change, and they say, "If I commit myself, maybe next year things will be different." They've known nothing but change.

Many people hesitate to do anything of a permanent nature. And now, with the employment situation—part-time employment, temporary employment, everything—you work here one day, the next day you work at another company, and all the kids growing up with McDonald's, working a couple of hours, and so forth, so everything is in flux. There's nothing to get hold of.

And the priest stands here with the standard of the cross—permanent. He knows it's permanent. Nobody's around. That's why the priests have been crucified, though they don't realize it. That's the terrible thing. They're entering into the death and resurrection of the Lord by this loneliness. Instead of doing something by coming together, it's very difficult for them to come together and share together because they came out of an individualist background. They're scared stiff that someone may say, "Don't tell me you believe that!" And that's where the humility comes in. See, all these fundamental virtues have to be developed. We have to become a people of faith, hope and love. How you do that in this kind of a climate, that's the trick.

**You said, "The best is the person who dies the best." It strikes me that when we start taking the values of Christ, of peace and justice according to the Gospel, when we start taking them into the world, most of us are going to end up dying in some way or another.**

Yes! The difficulty then is that it is equally true that everyone has the responsibility of developing talents that God has given them. So it's very positive; it's not death. I'm sure people in the diocese thought I was a pessimist when I first came, because I'd be talking problems and they talked positively. That's the beauty. The new bishop seems to have grasped that. Perhaps it's his theology or spirituality, and he caught the sense that's here. Even when I retired and I was living on campus, if I'd say something negative, they'd come out with something positive. They don't do away with sin, but sin isn't magnified as if it's a terrible thing, and we're not ever going to get to heaven because we're sinful. No. Sin is a reality, but the death and resurrection of the Lord is a reality. They may not put it in those words, but that's what they mean.

**And grace is as much a reality as sin—and more so.**

Yes, more so, because it conquered. The Lord conquered death and evil. But it's finding the formula. The Spirit raises up people necessary for every age. You see, in the days of St. Francis of Assisi, Franciscan spirituality put the accent on poverty because of the affluence of the particular society he came out of. Then you get the Dominicans, with the search for truth, and Ignatius with the poor originally, believe it or not, and discipline and obedience, and so forth. Then John Eudes and the Sulpicians—they were in a very difficult time again. When you say, "What would be characteristic of a spirituality for today?" the answer doesn't just come jumping out. It's going to have to evolve. A hundred years from now, they're going to look back and say, "Why didn't they see that? It's as obvious as the nose on your face."

**You said no to Vatican III—not yet. What do you think needs to still grow and happen before Vatican III can happen?**

We need to implement more of Vatican II.

**If you were making today a list of things that you wanted to see implemented, where would you start? After you get the laity understanding their vocation, what other things would you do?**

What I know is if the laity with their abilities and intelligence and so forth could come to the point where I would like to see them, then we would see creativity taking place. We would see things beginning to happen. Otherwise, if it's hierarchical—and by hierarchy the Council means bishop, priest and deacon—if the solutions come from the hierarchy, they will be a clerical kind of solution. If somebody, were to ask me what would be the spirituality of a bishop for our times, I would tell how I jokingly say, when I go to help somebody, "The Vatican Council said the bishop is supposed to be of service. I'd do this."

**But there's a profound truth in that joke.**

Well, of course. That's why I'd say it. Then they'd say—or more likely, think it—"Hey, he really means it." And that's a witness.

**That you're not to be served, but are the servant.**

Yes. The pope's most illustrious title is *servus servorum Dei*, servant of the servants of God. I could hold forth on the renewal of the episcopacy, but to hold forth on the renewal of what the laity should do? It should be the laity in conjunction with the bishop, who is the father of the community. It's fun to be—I call it fun, because it really was—fun to be a bishop in the time when society rejects authority. You have to use a whole bunch of different terminologies. You can't say, "I demand that you do this in obedience," but "The community needs this particular service and I think that you're the one who seems to have the qualifications to be able to do it. Would you be willing to go along with this?" You're asking obedience, but in a language that's so different.

**Recently I heard a bishop define the promise of obedience that a deacon makes at his ordination as "Ask nothing and refuse nothing."**

But you've got to be in a canonical state to accept that.

**Some of us who were sitting in the church thought, "I don't think any of us would ever be obedient under those conditions." Because that's not even human.**

That's what I mean.

**What legacy from Vatican II would you want to give to a new bishop today?**

Be yourself, first. Respect people, in the fullness of the term. The first and primary teaching of the Roman Catholic Church is the dignity of the human person. Jesus Christ died, was crucified and is risen, and by his blood, through the power of the Holy Spirit, we become the children of God. We are the sons and daughters of God. That's the foundation of everything. So, be yourself. Respect yourself as a son of God—a chosen son of God, if you're a bishop. Because that's a fact of life that you have no control over, you have no say in. You can refuse it, that's about all you can do. If you connive for it, God help you, because then you're never sure whether the Lord wanted you to be a bishop or not. Be kind to priests. They're having a hard enough time without you accentuating the difficulty.

**What from Vatican II would you want to hand on to twenty-year-olds—from a Council during which they weren't even born?**

I would say, following Father Joseph Cardign, who had extraordinary dynamism in him, "One young worker is worth more than all the gold in the world." That's what I'd say to them today: "One young person is worth more than all the gold in the world." Their value, each and every single one of them. Their value, because they are made to the image and likeness of God, and if they happen to be Christian, God has chosen them to be part of his family, sons and daughters of God. Therefore you have to live as a family. You must respect people. You must help people.

## What would you say to people who are discouraged because they think that Vatican II has been forgotten?

I guess the only thing I could say is the fundamental theological virtues of faith, hope and charity… we have to live in faith, hope and charity. That we don't see it doesn't mean it's not happening. The grain of wheat falls in the ground. You don't see it die; you see the fruit later on. If the church is going to change and become what I believe God intends it to become, it has to die. The old has to die before the new fully comes up. A whole lot of the new has to come forward in so many ways.

I'm thinking of my installation. It was in the afternoon with no Mass; Benediction of the Blessed Sacrament, that's all. It was 1960. The administrator presented the crucifix to Archbishop [Joseph] Berry [1902–1967], the metropolitan [of Halifax, Nova Scotia], and myself; we processed down; then they sang the antiphon to Saint Ninian [the cathedral patron]. I chanted the prayer for the Apostle of the Picts and Scots, and then Archbishop Berry escorted me by the hand over to the throne that used to be on the side, and presented me with the crosier, the symbol of office, as was done yesterday. Then the laity spoke and presented a gift; then the religious, then the priests—every priest came up, genuflected, kissed the ring and so forth. And then we had Benediction. That was it.

Yet we had that glorious celebration yesterday, and a new way of doing it—summoning Bishop Lahey to come in by himself. Yesterday was a celebration of the whole people—all the faithful. So when people say that not much has happened, we had evidence yesterday of what has happened.

William E. Power was born in Montreal in 1915, where he was educated and ordained a priest for the Archdiocese of Montreal in 1941. He served as a parish assistant, as vice-chancellor and diocesan chaplain to the Young Catholic Workers (YCW) and the Christian Family Movement. He also served as a national chaplain of the YCW. Named bishop of Antigonish, Nova Scotia, in 1960, Bishop Power was present at four sessions of Vatican Council II, and attended the synod of bishops in 1974. He also served on the executive committee of the Canadian Conference of Catholic Bishops and was the vice-president and president of the conference. He was chancellor and chairman of the board of governors of St. Francis Xavier University, in Antigonish, Nova Scotia, 1960–1987. He became bishop emeritus of the diocese of Antigonish in 1987. Bishop Power died on November 29, 2003 as this book was being edited.

# Bishop Remi De Roo

## Interviewer: John B. Foley, SJ

**Were you present at the Second Vatican Council. What was your capacity?**

Well, I was just another bishop among some 2,500 others. When I was appointed as bishop of Victoria, British Columbia, on October 31, 1962, the Council was already in session. I was immediately called to the Council and provided with my Council passport.

I spent a block of time during the first session, but I was not given any official assignments. The commissions were already set up. My main occupation was to work as a team with several Canadian bishops. I was privileged to consult and to work with a number of outstanding theologians. I was basically involved in many things, without being given any particular functions.

**Who were some of the theologians?**

The outstanding theologians that I remember—and this is not in order of importance but just as they flash across my mind—certainly [Dominican Father] Yves Congar, one of the great theologians of the Council. I believe he merited as few others did the title, "Father of the Council." Consider only his massive book on the laity published in 1952. His *Jalons pour une theologie du laicat* was a pioneering work which helped to lay the foundations for what Vatican II would teach about the laity. The title was mistranslated by an editor who probably hadn't read the book. It was called *The Laity in the Church* [Christian Classics]; but one of Congar's points is precisely that the laity are the church, not simply members in the church. Pius XII had recognized this in an address to the cardinals in 1946.

I also worked with [Dominican] Dominique Chenu, a close associate of Congar's. He was renowned for his theology on creation and on human labor. In fact, one of my interventions [oral presentation to the Council] was made at his suggestion.

I worked at length with Father Jean-Marie Tillard, whom we lost to cancer so long ago, a very great loss. Although French-born, from the islands of St. Pierre et Miquelon in the Atlantic, he did extensive teaching and writing in Canada. He was a stalwart in the field of ecumenism, working with the World Council of Churches, and a specialist in the sacraments. His book, *The Bishop of Rome* [Health Policy Advisory Center], is a definitive work on the papacy. He also contributed substantially to a number of insights on the sacraments. He and I together prepared an intervention on the question of marital life, proposing that the Council recognize the sacramental nature of conjugal intimacy. I remember him well and am very grateful to him.

In those early years I was associated to a lesser extent with Gregory Baum, a very fine Canadian theologian who is still very active. He received an honorary doctorate from the University of the Assumption in Windsor, Ontario, and I was honored to make the presentation. Every Sunday morning the Canadian bishops called in the better known avant-garde or leading theologians to hear the latest research. [Jesuit Father] John Courtney Murray was one of the guests whom I was asked to invite. I got to know a bit more about [Jesuit Father] Karl Rahner, and spent considerable time talking with [Dominican Father] Edward Schillebeeckx. Though born in Belgium, he was active mostly in Holland. I consider him a theologian's theologian.

Of course, I had incidental contacts with quite a number of bishops, particularly those who served as representatives of their conferences. The key man in our Canadian team, Maurice Baudoux [1902–1998], Archbishop of St. Boniface, Manitoba, was also my archbishop. He was really an extremely well-informed man, one of the most catholic or universal bishops I have ever known. He was constantly up to date on ecumenism and relationships with the Eastern churches. Another young scholar, Antoine Hacault, was his theologian at Vatican II, and became his auxiliary in 1964. Antoine had been my classmate through the years. He became the archbishop but also died of cancer a few years ago.

We were doing a lot of work with the other conferences. They [the various groups of bishops] were in the process at that time of reclaiming their own authority, to counteract the organized opposition of the Curia. So we in turn organized—some of us were known as the "Group of twenty-two." We were from many countries, exchanging views with other bishops' conferences which had already been formed. As the work of Vatican II became more intense and the focus sharpened around some key issues, we met more frequently. Our intent was to provide the more forward-looking perspective, as against the bishops who sought to retain the perspective of the past. Later, when bishops who spoke for groups were given priority over those who presented individual submissions, it was important to have these consultations and to get multiple signatures on our interventions. Often we found ourselves working against the clock.

## What would you name as "basic issues"?

Well, there are so many. The basic issue taken up by *Dei verbum* (the Dogmatic Constitution on Divine Revelation) was, of course, the old question about the two sources of revelation. Just recall the antagonism that split Catholics and Protestants before Vatican II—Protestants waving the Bible as the sole authority, and Catholics responding, "Yes, but don't forget that the church existed before the Bible. We've got the magisterium to tell us what is authentic or orthodox and what is not." It was a dialogue of the deaf.

## Did you say "dialogue of the deaf"?

Yes, where people did not hear or understand one another. That standoff was resolved, thankfully, by the Second Vatican Council declaring that it was not a question of the Bible versus tradition or the magisterium. However meritorious and worthy, those were means and not an end in themselves; they were instruments. Revelation is really a person: the person of Jesus Christ. I suggest this may be possibly the farthest-reaching point of Vatican II, really, in terms of its implications. Revelation is a person, not a written document. Jesus Christ is not only the messenger but also the message; in other words, the one announcing is also the one announced.

# A little bit of Marshall McLuhan, another Canadian.

Yes. And the proclaimer Jesus is also the one proclaimed: the Messiah, the Christ. We have yet to develop all the implications of that, particularly in the sphere of liturgy. It is extremely important, foundational background to the liturgy, because then the liturgy becomes not just the question of a head-trip, but also a question of relationship with Jesus. We celebrate his actual living presence through the paschal mystery, Pentecost and the remainder of the church year or liturgical season.

You know, at the very heart of the work of redemption is another insight of Vatican II that we rediscovered: the biblical understanding of work. Remember the time when Jesus was really jumped on by the Pharisees and Sadducees— "you've got six days to perform your miracles but not on the Sabbath and particularly not in the temple." Jesus' comeback was, "My Father is always working, and I too am working" (John 5:17). Here we rediscover the real meaning of work. With John's Gospel one understands the ultimate, the deeper meaning of the liturgy. The Vatican Council II teachings are clear: liturgy is the work of bringing about the divine reign, through our relationships with God, worship, adoration, celebration, relationship with Scripture, with our environment, ultimately with the Holy Trinity.

Yes, these are the famous four relationships that your wonderful confrere [Jesuit Father] Walter Burghardt, brought out in his lectures. He reminded us that biblical justice is really four relationships being put in proper order: Relationship to myself as image of God. Relationship to my neighbor as the other, also the image of God. Relationship to all of creation. Finally, relationship to God. There you have basically what the Bible teaches about justice. Liturgy means bringing about the work of justice—in other words, restoring the universe into its proper relationships by worshiping God through liturgy in all its forms.

# Wonderful. Is this making its way into the church?

Slowly.

There were two articles in *America* [February 24, 2003] and they represent two different sides to the issue. [Jesuit Cardinal Avery] Dulles takes the very conservative side, and John W. O'Malley [a Jesuit professor of church history at Weston School of Theology, Cambridge, Massachusetts] took the more forward-looking stance.

**Dulles has written another article, about "what Vatican II really said was this."**

Beware the man who says, "This is what Vatican II really said," because Vatican II reflected four or five different schools of theology. It takes a brave soul to say, "I alone know exactly what Vatican II said."

**Exactly. Different schools of liturgy and liturgical music.**

Which is quite appropriate. After all, when Jesus walked in our midst he did not compose a book, but brought to their perfection the Law and the Prophets. His oral teaching eventually led to the formulation of various traditions which in turn spawned a variety of churches. Read Raymond Brown's book, *The Churches the Apostles Left Behind* [Paulist Press]. Read the commentaries on the Gospel of John, and you realize that there is quite a different church around the beloved disciple than the one that focused around Peter.

**And Paul.**

Precisely.

**Of all the documents of the Council, which one is most significant for you and why?**

Well, it's hard to say that one constitution is more important than another constitution, because we're talking about what constitutes the church. There are obviously many salient points in Vatican II. For instance, the recognition of revelation as a person—Jesus as not only the messenger but also the message. In other words, the incarnation. That touches every dimension of creation and of human life.

**This connects with Schillebeeckx—with Christ as a sacrament of God, church as a sacrament of Christ.**

Yes. Right. But then go on from there, to rediscover that the reign of God as not necessarily identified solely with the institutionally structured church. We've moved well beyond *Mystici corporis* [1943] and certainly well beyond Leo XIII, for whom the perfect society could tell the civic world—governments and emperors—what to do. Boniface VII, to go even further back. But even Pius XII still identifies with what you might say is the structured body aspect, the mystical body side of the church. Since Vatican II there has been more insistence on the people side, on relationships, on the community of the *laos*.

It is interesting to remember that lesson from history that the early church was people. Structures were secondary; mind you, we needed them, but they came gradually. The church spent several centuries seeking to understand itself, through all the councils—Nicea (325), Constantinople IV (869–870)—you know, the seven founding Ecumenical Councils, the only ones accepted by the Eastern Orthodox as well as by the West. When we recite the Nicene Creed, we remember how it took centuries of struggle to clarify several doctrines. The structures also became more and more all-embracing. Not that they weren't important from the beginning. I am not anti-structure, not an iconoclast. But the structures grew. Gradually, around the tenth or eleventh century, the focus became so strong that we lost sight of the church as people. An expression attributed to the late Cardinal Yves Congar says that first the Eucharist made the church; then the church made the Eucharist.

We witnessed more splitting of hairs around points of doctrine with the Scholastic method, the Greek and Roman and Aristotelian philosophies coming in, and—as the Eastern bishops used to tease us—we got fully engrossed in trying to put mysteries into boxes. It took Vatican II—this is a major shift—to reawaken the church to the fact that that other dimension, the people of God, was just as important as the structured mystical body aspect. So here you have two of the major tensions: the shift away from, you might say, the apex reached in Pius XII, of the church as structured body, as fortress, and back to the church as the pilgrim people of God.

## How do you differentiate the people of God from the mystical body?

Well, they are all part of the same mystery, the body of Christ in history. But you can see that the focus on the mystical body is on the structural dimension—legal, juridical, theological, call it whatever you like. Whereas when you focus on the people of God, you are talking now of the spiritual, relational, theological dimension. They fit together, two sides of one coin. Much depends on which side you are looking at.

## It's important to keep looking at all the sides.

Absolutely, it's a mystery. The field has opened. We learn from Vatican II that there are no longer two classes or levels in the church. In the Mystical Body concept, you definitely have two classes, superiors and subordinates: the hierarchy and the laity. Lay people may be invited by mandate (which means clerical control) to participate in a limited way, in the "apostolate of the hierarchy," as Pius XI and XII said. Well, since Vatican II it's not only participating in the apostolate of the hierarchy. It's being called from birth, by faith and baptism, by the gifts of the Spirit, called to be equally responsible for the totality of the church. Even the so-called "temporal and the spiritual," as split aspects, fade into insignificance now in the light of our rediscovery of pneumatology, the theology of the Holy Spirit, and the realization that the incarnation embraces everything. No longer this perceived chasm between the temporal and the spiritual orders, different realities, although Vatican II didn't really get much beyond that type of language.

But let us move along from there. Consider the pilgrim people of God, called to be a messianic people. All the people of God, equal in dignity and in capacity to serve—not only dignity, also capacity to serve. This opens the whole field of ministries. All the people of God are called to the fullness of sanctity. There is an entire chapter on holiness in the document on the church and that holiness implies also the call to mysticism. This is different from the spiritual stages of life, which we learned from Tanqueray, read in our seminaries. There the mystics were seen as somewhat queer people—admirable, but suspect, beyond the reach of ordinary believers.

## Out on a mountaintop somewhere.

Yeah. Now we join Rahner's insight—you know, the Christian of tomorrow will be a mystic or won't be a Christian at all. Although gifts vary, everyone now is called to the fullness of perfection, in their own way.

So you can move along from there. The church, then, basically, is people, a people gifted with the Holy Spirit. Who decides whose charism is more important? The whole concept of the hierarchy shifts, then, from dominance and the magisterium—the teaching church, as it were—to a partnership.

## A partnership of service.

Service, absolutely. It runs like a refrain through Vatican II: the ministry of service. Not domination by one group with authority over the other. So the stage is now set. But then, since we must not focus only on the church, as we were often reminded during the Council sessions, a new document, *Gaudium et spes* (The Church and the Modern World), spontaneously arose out of the very impetus of the Council itself. And now who is to say which document is the most important? From a practical pastoral point of view, in terms of post-Vatican II applications, it's *Gaudium et spes*. Unless you want to remain focused on the mystical dimension, and say it's the one on the liturgy. It's a question of point of view. The documents are all important, all intertwined.

## Liturgy was one of the first, if not the first.

*Sacrosanctum concilium* (Constitution on the Sacred Liturgy) and *Inter mirifica* (Decree on the Media of Social Communication) were promulgated in 1963. The others followed.

## Who were important in the insights into liturgy as to what it is and how it works?

Well, liturgy was really prepared by about fifty years of labor, toil, struggle, misunderstanding, and ostracism of a whole raft of people. Religious in their monasteries beginning to experiment with new expressions of worship and prayer. Laity who were calling for the return of the chalice, the right to receive Eucharist under both species, and for the vernacular—the Scriptures read in local languages. All of that in a sense coalesced over time. The Council reached a point where the bishops, realizing they were going to have difficulty getting any agreement, decided, "Let's start with liturgy. Maybe that's the place we can get a consensus."

## What an insight. Do you find that today there might be tendencies to go back on any of this new liturgy?

Not just today. From the word "go," there was determined opposition. It came from a totally different mindset. I don't blame the "ultraconservatives." Let's say those who are more the ones looking to the past. They who saw the deposit of faith as an object to defend. Something that is complete but can be protected by the magisterium. Any attempt to play around with that, to change the formulations, was seen as abhorrent. It is symbolic that Cardinal [Alfredo] Ottaviani, the most prominent, visible leader of the opposition, had as his motto "*Semper idem*," nothing is to change. (He headed up the Vatican Commission on Doctrine, which saw itself as the most important and ultimately decisive commission.)

However, the "progressives" saw differently. For them, revelation is a person and reflects the growing presence of Jesus in history. While we have the fullness of revelation in Jesus, its living out in history will obviously develop. That's another major shift of Vatican II. Before Vatican II, to talk about the development of the doctrine was anathema. Since Vatican II, John Paul II himself is now using the expression "development of doctrine." Thus Cardinal [John Henry] Newman [1801–1890] was vindicated at Vatican II. In that sense, Cardinal Newman is one of the great fathers of the church. Cardinal Congar is reported to have said that Vatican II is Newman's Council. While he is no longer alive, many of his ideas came forward to greater fruition. Incidentally, [Pierre] Teilhard de Chardin was also vindicated in part by Vatican II. In *Gaudium et spes*—I forget now which article, but one finds the text there: The future belongs to those who give reasons for hope to the rising generation. That's almost a direct quote, though not acknowledged as such. Several bishops spoke about Teilhard at Vatican II. No question but that we owe a lot to his genius.

**That's not a known factor. If you asked people, "Did Teilhard influence Vatican II?" they'd say, "I don't think so."**

No, they haven't read the documents.

**Or Teilhard?**

You have to have both.

**Is there any issue that the Council did not address?**

Oh, yes. The Holy Father himself saw fit to reserve unto himself issues of morality around conjugal life, particularly the question of birth control. The ordination of married men, that too was deliberately reserved. Then there were other matters that simply were left untouched for the simple reason that you can't do everything in four relatively short sessions. We must confess, there was still much preoccupation with the completion of Vatican I [1869–1870]. That produced a strong focus on the bishops and their relationship with the pope. It is remarkable what a long section in the documents deals with the relationships of the bishops and the pope.

Another unresolved issue of Vatican II: How can you have, on the one hand, the college of apostles—granted, always with Peter at the head, and never without the head—having full and complete authority and infallibility, and at the same time the pope—even acting on his own, obviously in communion with the college—also having full and complete authority? That remains a significant problem today.

105

## You're not saying that authority is unimportant and should not be a part of the church, are you?

No, on the contrary, Jesus gave all authority to his church. Authority is extremely important. But how will it be exercised in the most fruitful manner for all concerned? Jesus made it clear that ministry is meant to give life, not to lord it over people.

Among other issues left to be resolved: How to explain that, on the one hand, through faith and baptism all members of the church are equal in dignity and capacity to serve, and then insist on an "essential" difference between the priesthood of the ordained and that of the laity? Unresolved issues—I wouldn't try to tackle this one here. Issues like that one may long remain unsettled. That's understandable.

The debate around war and peace was another one without a final solution. This was partly due to the Communist specter of Russia still hanging over Europe. As a result, some European bishops were very cautious. Paul VI on October 5, 1965, addressed the United Nations in New York. A momentous, historical occasion. I feel it was definitely the mind of the church when he spoke for all the bishops: "No more war. War never again." Pope John Paul II has said almost the identical thing, declaring that war today is a defeat for humanity. That's the mind of the church, but not in the Council documents. They waffle on this point, leaving open the question of the so-called "just war."

## Is that not one purpose of the documents: To open a question which is then to be resolved later?

Well, there are both. The documents can also resolve questions, settle issues. Just recall other Ecumenical Councils, especially the first seven. But yes, documents can also bring to the level of the conscience of the church universal some unopened issues that need further maturing. In that sense there is no question that Vatican II itself caused a lot of thinking to mature and move forward.

For example, in 1943, Pope Pius XII, a brilliant scholar—Vatican II owes a lot to him, for many things in Vatican II don't go beyond his insights—in his encyclical promoting biblical studies, *Divino afflante spiritu*, welcomes the contribution of modern scholarship in the field of Scripture. He was roundly vilified, excoriated by Cardinal Ernesto Ruffini [1888–1967; archbishop of Palermo]. I understand he wrote in *Osservatore Romano* that the pope really had lost it. The Curia subsequently did not accept *Divino afflante spiritu*. It took Vatican II to bring this matter forward.

Another example: Pope Pius XII in 1946 was talking to the cardinals—I imagine most of them must have been about 80 or so, half-asleep—but anyway (I say that deliberately because of what is going to follow), he said that the laity must be aware of not only belonging to the church but—and I can still see before my eyes the printed text—they are the church. He repeated himself: They—are—the—church. Then he continued with the language about the "soldiers of Christ" in the front trenches and their important contributions. In 1950, Pius XII called for open speech in the church. It took Vatican II to bring that forward, to say that there must be more freedom. Thus it produced what, in a sense, may prove to be the most telling of the documents of Vatican II, the last one, on religious freedom (*Dignitatis humanae*). Finally the Council picked up on something that came from Cardinal Newman, which was presented to Vatican II repeatedly by the most brilliant English theologian in Vatican II, Christopher Butler [1902–1989], then Abbot and later Bishop Butler, who became auxiliary bishop of Westminster.

In October 2002, I was invited as the closing speaker at a special symposium at Heathrop College. It marked the fortieth anniversary of the opening of Vatican II and what would have been, had he lived, the 100th birthday of Bishop Butler. I'll never forget two things about Bishop Butler. The first one was his defense of the vilified scholars—you know, theologians, Scripture scholars, et cetera—then his reminding the Council fathers that we were all dependent on the brilliant gifts of these people. For the good of the church, they must have complete freedom of research. We had no reason to suspect that they were less than true believers, honest members of the church. You know, he himself had experienced persecution and knew what it was all about. He was himself a triple Oxford, a brilliant mind. His younger brother, an Anglican canon in Victoria (as you know, Christopher Butler was a convert), referred to him as "a walking intelligence."

However, the other point he then made was to say, "Look,"—and I'll never forget the Latin expression—*"ne timeamus quod veritas veritatem noceat* (why should we fear that truth should in some way endanger truth)?" Admire the logic! Regretfully, that is not the atmosphere in our church today, or in many other centers of authority. This is maybe one of the major challenges unresolved since Vatican II—when will we finally trust the presence of the Holy Spirit in all the faithful baptized? We profess it in our official documents, but in practice do we follow it? Church leaders too often still doubt the orthodoxy of the common people.

## Whom do you feel was the most significant figure at the Council?

Pope John XXIII inspired as he was by the Holy Spirit to convene the Catholic bishops of the world with many outstanding scholars, representatives from other churches, and a host of other participants in "his" Council. Compared to him, the other members were minor players, no matter how rich or significant their individual contributions.

## What was the most significant statement from the Council, and why?

*Dei verbum*, the constitution on revelation. It takes us to the very heart of revelation and the purpose of the church. Revelation is more than a book or a teaching authority, no matter how inspired and meaningful. Revelation is a person, Jesus Christ. He is not only a divine messenger sent from the Godhead with inspired teachings subsequently entrusted to the apostles and disciples. The person of Jesus Christ is, in his very self, also the message: his total being, his actions, his attitudes, as well as the words he spoke make God visible in the flesh. In Christ, God personally enters our history forever to dwell with and in us. Jesus is not only the bearer of Good News, not simply the announcer, but equally the One Announced, the One Proclaimed as well as the Proclaimer. We need no further revelations. Our aim now is to become Christ-like and to facilitate the transformation of the entire creation in his image. All earlier Council documents are fruitfully read again in this light. Thus we see how the Council itself matured and developed.

## What has happened that you never imagined would happen?

A major shift or development in ecclesiology, reclaiming the early tradition when the church was, in effect, the people. It was still not primarily considered as the structured institution. This later development resulted in people having the impression that there were two degrees of membership in the church. First-class members were the "hierarchy." In second class came the "laity." This mis-reading of church history conveniently ignored the fact that at the beginning there was only a community of disciples, the *laos*, or pilgrim people. Leadership emerged, under the direction of the twelve apostles, but there was no dominant class. Authority was linked to service, a theme frequently recalled by Vatican II. The establishment of the diaconate illustrates how the apostles saw their mission primarily as prayer and proclamation of the Gospel, not administration. Everyone was called to worship and evangelize, not just the "leaders" in or with whose "hierarchical apostolate" the laity would more recently be invited or called to "collaborate" or "participate." Recall Pius XI and XII concerning "Catholic Action": The laity were "mandated" by the "hierarchy" to share in the "hierarchical apostolate." Even today we still notice how many bishops continue to speak as if they truly constitute the church. This "teaching church" continues to instruct the members as from above them or apart from them. History and the gifts of the Holy Spirit prove, rather, that all members of the church need to be constantly taught.

### Is there any issue you regret that the Council did not address?

Certainly, the universal priesthood of the *laos* could have been further clarified. But equally important for me would have been a clear proclamation by Vatican II concerning the mission of the "poor" (in the biblical sense) as subjects or agents of salvation history. Contrast this to the attitude of many people who feel they are somehow "benefactors" when they help the poor. Church leaders still encourage us to extend as charity that which is due in justice. We have yet to catch up with what Pope Paul VI tells us in his encyclical on the Development of Peoples (*Populorum progressio*) [1967]. When will we effectively apply the "preferential option for the poor" to normal church life?

*Gaudium et spes* could have further matured the question of the "universal priesthood" as applied to daily life and to our mission toward the whole of creation. It could have stressed the universal call to evangelization and to mysticism (note Paul's Letter to the Romans). The shift from an "extrinsicist" divinity to an "immanent" God still needs to be situated at center stage in church life and in the relationships of the pilgrim people to the whole of creation. "Secular" need not be opposed to "spiritual." The Spirit of God is at work throughout creation and history. There is but one benevolent plan of creation and redemption, centered on the call of everyone to "love in action," whereby society and the universe are being more effectively "humanized" under the leadership of Christ.

### What has been the most significant liturgical development and what do we yet need to do to implement full, conscious and active participation?

The laity as a whole are gradually reclaiming their rightful place as subjects, adults, responsible agents of their own spiritual destiny. Yes, always in partnership and collaboration with the ordained leadership, but no longer in a relationship of dependency, of perceived immaturity on the part of the "followers." I admire the women scholars who are providing the most creative leadership today in this domain. I also hope for an ongoing conversion on the part of the ordained. When will they fully and effectively recognize their ministry as service, not privilege or domination? How many ordained priests truly believe their priesthood is meant to insure that all the baptized believers exercise their own triple priesthood as "prophets, priests, and sovereigns"? And for those who do so in theory, how is their ministry carried out in practice? Do they make manifest that laity and clergy are equally responsible for the good of society and of their church? How many are aware of and responding to the call for public opinion in our church, as implied in several documents (*Lumen gentium* 37; *Gaudium et spes* 43, as well as several indications in *Apostolicam actuositatem*)? How many lay people remain fixated in the mode of "helping Father with his parish"? How many parishes see themselves as places of outreach, offering their resources to facilitate the reign of God throughout society, their arms outstretched to the world?

## A third Vatican Council?

Not yet! Too many calls for a third Vatican Council sound to me like a cop-out. How about first effectively applying the gains made at Vatican II? Further to this, is it possible today for the Western/Latin Patriarchate of Rome to effectively convene a Council that would be perceived, "received" as a truly ecumenical, universal? Are we prepared to include the three major monotheistic religions, all the sons and daughters of Abraham, Sarah and Hagar, in proclaiming globally our shared faith in the One God? Would anything less make an effective impact on today's global village? Is our vision prepared to look beyond "housekeeping" in our territory, toward worldwide evangelization? Are we still in a posture of maintenance, or are we ready to hear the call of the Holy Spirit beckoning us into ongoing and universal mission that is truly catholic in the full sense of the term?

## Was there any special historical or cultural significance in Vatican II occurring during the 1960s?

I believe the Holy Spirit inspired Pope John XXIII, and his successor Paul VI, who effectively brought the Council to its conclusion, to preside over a providential period of preparation for the Third Millennium. I applaud the repeated calls of Pope John Paul II to recognize that the best way to enter the new millennium is to use Vatican II as a "sure compass," a reliable instrument to guide our church into the future. Vatican II could hardly have happened earlier. It was apparently given consideration by Pius XII (possibly also Pius XI) and set aside. I believe that under the previous popes, a council would only have deepened the alienation between the church and society. Possibly one of the best illustrations of this are the efforts being made by well-meaning people today to turn back the clock, as if looking backwards to a supposedly ideal yesterday is the best way to promote the Gospel! History is moving forward rapidly, and the Spirit of the Risen Lord of history beckons us to hasten forward toward new horizons. Did not Jesus promise that he would be with us through his Holy Spirit, bestowed upon us? Who else are we waiting for?

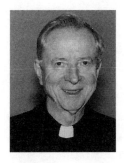

Remi De Roo was a priest of the archdiocese of St. Boniface, Manitoba, before becoming bishop of Victoria, British Columbia, Canada (1962–1999). He received his B.A. in Latin philosophy in 1948 at the Collège de Saint-Boniface, and his doctorate in sacred theology (S.T.D.) in 1952 from the Angelicum University in Rome. A member of the Canadian Conference of Catholic Bishops (CCCB), he was a founding member of the World Conference on Religion and Peace (Kyoto, 1970) and former vice president of WRCP Canada. He was the first chairperson of the Human Rights Commission, Province of British Columbia, (1974–1977) and a member of the CCCB Theology Commission (1987–1991). He retired in 1999, but continues to lecture as one of the bishops who took part in the Second Vatican Council.

# Archbishop Leobard D'Souza

## Interviewer: Nihal Abeyasingha

**What was your capacity at the Council?**

During the Eucharistic Congress in Bombay, at the age of 34, I was consecrated a bishop on December 3, 1964, by Pope Paul VI with five others representing the continents of the world. I was present for the last session of the Council in 1965.

I was young, with little pastoral experience. For me to be participating in the Council was a unique thrill and a proud moment. The timetable for the daily sessions was well settled; I followed it, savoring every moment and admiring the clockwork procedures and meticulous help we received. My signature was appended, I think, to most of the Council documents that were passed during the last session of the Council. With the little Latin I had, I followed some of the interventions made on the floor, but their contexts and contentions did not grab my mind, as I had been absent from the previous sessions. Since I had subscribed to these documents, there arose in me a strong desire to study them later. During the monsoons I held classes for the sisters of Jabalpur on the Council documents.

## Of all the documents of the Council, which one is most significant for you and why?

Undoubtedly the premier document was *Lumen gentium* (Constitution on the Church). The rediscovery of the nature and role of the church offered to the faithful a dynamic picture of the significance of the people of God. Under this rubric, the functions and roles of the various people in the church got clearer meaning and deeper understanding. Underscoring the common priesthood based on baptismal consecration was a doctrinal step forward after Trent, and governed other documents that followed.

## What's the most important teaching that came out of the Council?

I feel that the most significant teaching of the Council, for a historian, was *Dignitatis humanae*, the Decree on Religious Liberty. It laid to rest the ghost that had haunted the thinking of the church since the days of the Enlightenment. Now the church could come into the open and speak the language understood in the world. Our present-day concern for human freedom and rights has force and validity precisely for the stand taken in this document.

## Whom do you feel was the most significant figure at the Council?

No one figure emerges from the Council except John XXIII, with his uncanny wisdom and sense of history. If one would hazard a view, I believe that precious confluence of some fearless fathers and the experts who framed the drafts in back-room committee meetings was indeed a moment of special grace and light of the Holy Spirit. Otherwise one cannot explain the depth and length to which some teaching went.

## What was the most significant statement from the Council and why?

As a young bishop, I felt the call of Paul VI to the Council fathers to become the church of the poor was very significant.

## What has happened that you never imagined would happen?

That the Council took place at all was itself unimaginable. We studied under the shadow of the towering intellect of Pius XII, whose allocutions covered and attempted to answer every major issue faced in the modern world. There was nothing further to be added. In fact, the preparatory commission envisaged a brief Council endorsing his teachings. But it was not to be. The Council became indeed the work of the fathers who were called to prepare the pastorals for the modern world. Pius XII was brought on board not slavishly, and the documents were given a thrust that put the church in the front line to meet the challenges and opportunities of the modern world. The import of the documents, which the fathers signed, came home to them when the people read, studied and took their statements seriously.

## What hasn't happened?

Many things that were ardently anticipated never happened because of the preemptive actions of the overzealous and their unilateral interpretations in the post-conciliar era, particularly with regard to liturgical renewal. For the so-called mission world, liturgical inculturation went for a cropper [was a disastrous failure]. Another important issue was collegiality, which did not really come to its fullest understanding and acceptance. Episcopal co-responsibility for the universal church was watered down to periodic discussions and consultations.

## Is there any issue you regret that the Council did not address?

I regret that the issue of family planning and its methods was off the agenda; it made the solution much more difficult to accept. I think if the fathers had debated the issue, they would have trotted out a clear and unequivocal statement on abortion, which would have had greater credibility in the world today.

## What has been the most significant liturgical achievement, and what do we yet need to do to implement full, conscious and active participation?

Obviously, vernacularization of the liturgy was the most significant liturgical achievement for the people. This made the faithful in the pews of churches everywhere in the world fully conscious and active in their participation and made inculturation possible and desirable.

## In your opinion, should there be a third Vatican Council, and what topic or topics would you bring to the table?

I'd definitely like to endorse Vatican III, but not immediately; I think the geopolitical events of the present times will dictate its timing. The pressure will come from outside the church. Multi-religious issues engaging the world will scream for common resolve, comprehension and the widest acceptance. If we cannot live together, we will destroy ourselves together—for the very best reasons, despairingly.

## What Council teaching was most difficult to implement in the local churches?

I feel the most difficult teaching to implement meaningfully is the role of the laity in the church.

## Is there any special historical or cultural significance that Vatican II occurred in the 1960s? Could it have happened earlier, later, in your opinion?

Looking backwards, it's too easy to say when the Council should have taken place. It's pure speculation. History cannot justify itself. History only records, interprets and celebrates. The march of events and decisions cannot be explained except as the work of the Holy Spirit, who uses the intelligence, will and imagination of people to give expression to their faith and love. They become the *dramatis personae* of such a great event as the Second Vatican Council.

## Two documents, the Constitution on the Church and the Constitution on the Church in the Modern World, contained shocking new concepts of the church—about the church as sacrament, and the admission that the church did not sometimes have all the answers to problems. How did you react to these statements as a newly ordained bishop who was trained in scholastic theology?

As a newly ordained bishop, my acquaintance with *Lumen gentium* was a wonderful revelation, the answer to a search. As a member of the Sodality of Our Lady in St. Xavier's, Calcutta, in the 1950s, I belonged to a group of students who were enthusiastic and dynamic for the apostolate. Among the studies we undertook was the mystical body of Christ, arising from the encyclical of Pius XII; we grappled with the theology but never came to a proper understanding. The search continued into the seminary and deepened when I did ecclesiology in Rome. It was *Lumen gentium* that put it all together and gave depth and breadth to my understanding of church.

Scholastic theology was a good, clear and certain guide—I would say excellent for tenderfoots. But like Fr. Bernard Cooke's bag, it always had bits and pieces sticking out. The gnawing questions and thoughts never were fully answered. In our Roman days we were warned by our professors of the trans-alpine theologians whom they considered dangerous. Come the Council, these theologians became the experts. John XXIII had the wisdom not to prevent these experts from coming into the Council; they took some documents to greater lengths than was acceptable. The Council was God-sent. Scholastic theology received a lesson that other philosophies had contributed to human thinking and must be taken aboard if only to make doctrine understandable to modern thinkers.

### How would you reassess the restatement of the universal priesthood of the faithful? Do you remember your reaction to this?

The doctrine of the common priesthood of the faithful was invoked to make the role of the laity theologically clear. Because it was reversing Trent, it was not trumpeted. It revolutionized the pastoral [*Lumen gentium*]. It has been one of the more difficult teachings to implement in the postconciliar era. Rubrics was our bugbear before the Council; thank God, a sensible attitude to the liturgy put an end to the wooden, stylized rubrics of old. However, I do miss the dignity, beauty and majesty of a well-conducted liturgical ceremony.

### What do you think of including in seminary studies such negative events in church history as the Inquisition and the Crusades?

I think you did well to put church history in the syllabus of the university, but it cannot be handled by just anyone. If Islam has to be dealt with by an Islamic scholar, and Buddhism by a Buddhist scholar, a Christian scholar must teach church history. The Crusades and the Inquisition cannot be swept under the carpet. They are facts—facts that have a lesson to teach the world and us. Religion cannot be used as a weapon to suppress freedom and truth. The Holy Father made bold to ask for forgiveness and we must continue to ask for forgiveness for the harm we have done and not repeat it ever.

### Are we seeing a deepening of the spirit of Vatican II or a return to the pre-Vatican II mentality?

I feel that there has been a back-pedaling to the thrust of the Second Vatican Council. Some fears, not unprovoked, arose because of the preemptive and over-enthusiastic actions and thinking of some immediately after the Council. Paranoia caused some harsh measures, which sapped the élan after the Council and dried up the magnificent flow of theological literature and its wide readership in the late sixties and seventies. I think the repressive methods used to deal with the extremists, who by and large had the church at heart, could have been handled more calmly and firmly if peers were give an opportunity to battle out their findings in their respective fora. We would have benefited from the debate and would have come out with a more acceptable theology.

Born January 18, 1930, Leobard D'Souza was ordained a priest December 22, 1956, in Rome. He was consecrated bishop by Paul VI on December 3, 1964, and became bishop of Jabalpur, India, in December 1965, archbishop of Nagpur in September 1975, and archbishop emeritus in February 1998. He served as chairman of the Catholic Bishops' Conference of India (CBCI) for Labor 1970–1974, chairman of the National Biblical, Catechetical and Liturgical Center (NBCLC) from 1974–1983, chairman of the Christian Life Commission 1975–1983, and chairman of Caritas, India, 1983–1991. He is presently teaching church history at St. Charles Seminary, Nagpur, conducts pastoral workshops, and is a spiritual director.

# Archbishop Augusto Trujillo Arango

## Interviewer: Pedro Rubalcava

I was auxiliary bishop of Manizales in Colombia when Pope John XXIII announced the celebration of the Council. I remember that there was great jubilation in Colombia and the local church prepared with great anticipation and joy to participate in this great event. All of our bishops attended; at that time there were almost fifty of us in Colombia. I participated officially as bishop of the diocese of Jericó, according to the public document by Cardinal [Amleto] Cicognani [1883–1973], dated October 10, 1962.

I recall the historic opening celebration presided over by Pope John XXIII— to be in Rome in the presence and company of all the bishops of the world had a great impact on me and to this day has made an incredible impression. I attended all of the sessions of the Council and I sat in seats 844, 748, 774, 690 and 725, respectively, in the Council chambers during this time.

There were so many important people with key roles at the Council; among them I believe that the popes, of course, were significant as they presided over the events. Certainly, Cardinal [Leo Joseph] Suenens [1904–1996] of Belgium was a strong figure, as were all the cardinals who served on the board of directors.

The four constitutions—*Lumen gentium, Dei verbum, Sacrosanctum concilium* and *Gaudium et spes*—and their prophetic and inspired teaching born of the Council were of great importance to the church and continue to be for us in the twenty-first century. Certainly, as church, we should not doubt the importance that not only the constitutions had, but the nine decrees, the three declarations, John XXIII's apostolic constitution *Humanae salutis* [1961], the message of the Council fathers, and during the Council, Paul VI's *Ecclesiam suam* [1964]. The Council made three declarations: on religious freedom, on Christian formation of youth, and on the relationship of the church with other non-Christian faiths. It is my opinion that these were of great significance and, because of their content and import, continue to serve us to an unequivocal extent to this day, though perhaps they are not fully realized.

In retrospect, I think that all that occurred following the Council was what was expected and even desired, and we are still experiencing some of the fruits and struggling with the impact these forty years past. Slowly, we have been seeing the realization of some of the conciliar reforms, and I can honestly say that nothing put in motion as a result of the Council was contrary to its original intent.

I consider that the themes that were dealt with in the Council were an inspired response to the needs of the church at that time, and they continue to be our guide since then.

The beginning of the renewal of the liturgy and all that revolves around the way in which we celebrate the holy Eucharist, the purification of the popular piety, and the liturgical documents that were born out of this new liturgical transformation—all continue to have an impact to this day. To achieve full, conscious and active participation of the people, we have to implement an understanding of the liturgy and allow the need for this understanding to keep progressing and evolving in the participation of the community. We have indeed come a long way, but there is growth needed and surely more growth to come. Indeed, it seems that the liturgical teachings and changes were and have been the most difficult to implement. It was necessary, at the time, to implement these progressively, step by step, while at the same time allowing the priests and people to begin to understand the essence and need for these changes. Needless to say, this was and is one of the great challenges of the Council.

Personally, and in gathering the thoughts and wishes of those with whom I have shared the needs of the church, I believe it would be of the utmost importance to celebrate a third Vatican Council. Perhaps this is a direction toward which the pope would lead us. Our world has changed incredibly, even in a mere forty years, and it needs to hear the teachings of hope and answers the church has to offer, given the reality and problems presented by the new millennium. There would be much to study and examine: new social problems; the urgent need for world peace; the ever-increasing need for respect for human life, given the permanent criminality of many countries at present; ecumenism, the search for unity in the church; the question of a celibate priesthood; further clarity in the role of women in the church without the issue of ordination of women; the inculturation of the Gospel message; the political responsibility and ethics of Catholics in public life; the relationship of faith and politics; the New Age—how we deal with all its ambiguities and rarities; Christian morality; and finally the search for an authentic Christian spirituality.

In my opinion—and as you can see—there are many issues that need to be addressed, were there to be a new council. Perhaps it was changes that were occurring at the time that led the church to respond with the Second Vatican Council. There have been many historical events that have occurred after the Council and that have shaped the church's response to, for instance, the problems of war and peace in the world, and its permanent and unceasing calls for peace, and its World Day for Peace each New Year. I believe the world has respected and admired greatly the popes since the Council—John XXIII, Paul VI and John Paul II—and let us not forget the figure and teachings of Pius XII.

Archbishop emeritus Augusto Trujillo Arango of the archdiocese of Tunja in Colombia was born in Santa Rosa de Cabal in Colombia on August 5, 1922. His early education was under the tutelage of the Marists and he received his bachelor's degree with the Vincentian fathers. He attended the major seminary of the archdiocese of Manizales in Colombia and did further studies at the Sulpician House of Studies in Washington, D.C., as well as at Catholic University, where he obtained a theology degree in 1947. He has served as a parish priest and as seminary professor at the major seminary in Manizales, where he later became prefect. Archbishop Trujillo also served as vice-rector of Colegio de Nuestra Señora (College of Our Lady) in Manizales, and later as rector of the minor seminary in Manizales. He was named titular bishop of Nisyros and auxiliary bishop of Manizales on April 25, 1957, by Pope Pius XII and ordained bishop on June 9, 1957. In 1960 Pope John XXIII named him bishop of the diocese of Jericó. In 1970 he was named archbishop of Tunja by Pope Paul VI. He retired in 1998, having served as bishop under four popes. He remains active in the Instituto Ravasco (institute for higher learning) and resides at the Monasterio de la Visitación (Monastery of the Visitation) in Manizales.

# Archbishop Gennaro Verolino

## Interviewer: Daniel McCarthy, OSB

### You were ordained a bishop in 1951?

Yes. I was ordained a titular bishop of Corinth.

### You have been a member of the Roman Curia from the beginning?

Well, yes; I was a diplomatic person of the Holy See. I began young, and I was sent into diverse nunciatures. My first position was in Colombia at the end of 1931, then afterwards Italy, Portugal and other places as a diplomatic person. After a certain time, they called me to Rome, where I remained until I went into retirement.

During the Council, I was in Rome at the office of the Secretary of State. I participated in the Council as it developed. When the sessions were open to all, I was always present; every day it was in session I went to the Council. I followed all the sessions; I was present, but I never gave an address. I always voted.

### Did you go in a particular capacity?

I went to the Council simply as a bishop—all the bishops were invited—but I did not have any specific task, no special charge.

### Was there a more memorable moment of the Council, as you see it? Was there energy in the city?

But what need I say? It all was interesting. It seems to me that the city went about its business. The people did nothing special. The Romans were tranquil in their homes.

## Did the Council sessions take place in Latin?

Well, yes, Latin was spoken in the Council. But there were some who wished to speak in another language (French or English), perhaps because they did not know Latin well. There were also those who could translate. In general, though, everyone was speaking in Latin.

## When did you celebrate Mass in Italian for the first time?

Well, I still say it in Latin. I have permission. When the occasion arises in a public church and the people expect the Italian, I recite it in Italian.

I have only said Mass in public a few times because generally I say it here in the house, where I have a small chapel. Here I say the Mass in Latin. Certainly, Latin has its advantages. It is the language of the church. It is suitable for solemnity. It is adapted better to philosophical and theological concepts.

## At Saint Anselm's [San Anselmo], we say Mass in Latin in the cloister, but away from the cloister, in Italian.

Yes, the people expect the national language. Without doubt, with the national language, one is better able to understand and this was the decisive reason for which it was changed.

## What did the Second Vatican Council change in the church? In your life, in your diplomatic career, not much has changed.

No, I remain as before. I never had an assignment in direct contact with the people, with the faithful. I was in the office of the Secretary of State or in the nunciatures; I was a person, let us say, of the office, an administrator. The Holy See continued to have its nuncios and its ambassadors, and then around the nuncio there is an entire office including desk workers, auditors, et cetera, all as before; nothing has changed in that regard.

## Were there any effects of the Council on the diplomatic corps because of ecumenism?

Before the Council there were always good relationships, and this continued to be so following the Council.

**And the relationships with the other ecclesial communions, the dialogue we have developed, for example, with the Protestants, with the Anglicans and, above all, with the churches of the East?**

These contacts derive from the commissions. However, today there are so many encounters for discussing issues, but I do not participate. I read about it in the newspapers.

**Is there a desire in the church to change anything more?**

I am not in contact with the people, so I don't know if the people want it. But in general the people don't want and don't like to change. In general, the people prefer to maintain the traditional prayers. Everyone, even their parents, their grandparents, pray in the traditional manner. They prefer to continue in the same manner. Tradition is a great force.

**Can I ask you how old you are? Are you 96 years of age?**

Oh, yes, exactly. I was born in 1906.

**You have seen in life many changes in society, technology, even going to the moon. And two world wars.**

Two. Yes, many things have happened. Now we are moving toward disarmament, thanks be to God, making peaceful the years that endure. Peace is the essential thing. For the Christian life and the life of the world, it is essential that human beings love one another rather than fight one another.

**The bishop who ordained me was with you at the Council. You didn't know one another, but he was there together with you.**

We were more than, two thousand. It was an important time. So many wanted to speak, to have an active role. I never requested to speak. I was present only to listen. There were diverse opinions, but substantially there was no controversy.

Archbishop Gennaro Verolino was born in Naples, Italy on November 3, 1906. Ordained a priest on December 23, 1928, he received his first diplomatic appointment three years later as the secretary of the Papal Nuncio to Colombia in 1931. Since then he followed a diplomatic career serving in other countries including Portugal. He was ordained a bishop of the Roman Curia on October 7, 1951. He was later called to Rome and worked for many years in the office of the Secretary of State. He was in Rome during the Second Vatican Council, attended almost every session, and voted in every balloting. He has since retired.

# PART 2

# *Peritis* and Staff

# Gregory Baum

## Interviewer: Christina Ronzio

**What was your capacity at the Council?**

I was appointed by Pope John XXIII as *peritus* (theological expert) at the Secretariat for Promoting Christian Unity, which was one of the commissions created to serve Vatican Council II. The reason for my appointment was the fact that I had written a doctoral dissertation at the University of Fribourg [Switzerland] that touched upon ecumenism. When the pope created the Unity Secretariat, he made Cardinal [Augustin] Bea [1881–1968] its president; the cardinal in turn appointed Monsignor [Johannes] Willebrands [b. 1909; later archbishop of Utrecht, The Netherlands] as acting secretary, who then looked for theologians who had studied Catholic-Protestant and Catholic-Orthodox relations. Monsignor Willebrands wanted the *periti* to come from all parts of the Catholic world. At that time, I was the only theologian in Canada who had worked in the field of ecumenism and had published a book—my dissertation—on the topic; that is why I was appointed. Prior to the Council, I attended three different meetings of the Secretariat, and during the Council I was present at the four sessions, and several times between sessions. The Unity Secretariat was responsible for three of the more controversial conciliar documents: the Declaration on Religious Liberty (*Dignitatis humanae*), the Decree on Ecumenism (*Unitatis redintegratio*) and the document that began as a statement on Jewish-Christian relations and later became the Declaration on the Relation of the Church to Non-Christian Religions (*Nostra aetate*).

## What was the most significant moment at the Council for you?

That is a difficult question. During the Council I lived in the Roman monastery of the Irish Augustinian fathers—I was an Augustinian priest at the time—and spent my entire love and energy on the Council. I would get up early in the morning for Mass and meditation, then spend the morning at the Council and the afternoon at the Unity Secretariat, and finally enjoy the company of theologians and bishops in the evening, often eating in Roman restaurants, discussing the issues debated at the Council and kindling our hope. I was young at the time and never got tired. Many of us at the Secretariat lived on an emotional high throughout the Council. The issues debated touched upon faith, hope and love; the spiritual climate was open to new interpretations; and a lively debate involved Catholics from all parts of the world. The experience of dedication, dialogue, friendship and solidarity created for many of us an unforgettable sense of what it meant to be Catholic.

I still remember my excitement at the opening speech of Pope John XXIII—a text that we should continue to read—in which he proclaimed that the church, while almost two-thousand years old, was ever new, ever young, ever capable in the Holy Spirit of being reborn and renewed. He disagreed with the prophets of doom who recommended cautious policies for the church, inspired by fear. At the meeting of the Protestant and Orthodox observers, for which we at the Unity Secretariat were responsible, I praised the pope's speech in such enthusiastic terms that Monsignor Willebrands asked me to calm down. I did shut up at the time, but I did not calm down during the entire Council.

## Was there a sense that you were living in an important historical moment?

The Council represented a truly historical moment. The Catholic Church changed its mind on several important issues. For instance, it defended religious liberty. During the nineteenth century and into the twentieth, the papacy had severely condemned "the rights of man" first formulated by the American and the French revolutions, including the freedom of religion. The popes argued that error has no rights. In the 1950s, Jesuit Father John Courtney Murray still got into trouble with Rome because of his defense of religious liberty. During the Council, there were still powerful circles opposed to changing the church's official teaching. What helped the progressive bishops was that in his encyclical *Pacem in terris* [1963], Pope John XXIII had praised the Universal Declaration of Human Rights [1948] of the United Nations, including religious freedom. The

Vatican Council's proclamation in 1965 of the Declaration on Religious Liberty (*Dignitatis humanae*) was a historical event that changed the church's relationship to society and other religious communities and offered a new interpretation of the freedom brought by Jesus Christ. For us who labored at the Council, it was a great event to experience that the Catholic Church is able to change its official teaching. Catholics should never forget this.

## Of all the documents of the Council, which one is most significant for you and why?

Again, this is a difficult question. Many documents were highly significant. The Constitution on the Church in the Modern World (*Gaudium et spes*) redefined the church's mission in history as a ministry of justice and peace and an effort to have the Gospel influence the culture in which she lives. *Gaudium et spes* remains a relevant text for our day, especially since we have not yet fully translated its vision into reality. I have taught many courses on *Gaudium et spes* and always found that students were touched, thrilled and empowered by this document.

Also of great importance was the Declaration on the Church's Relation to the Non-Christian Religions (*Nostra aetate*), which not only redefined the church's position on Judaism and the Jewish people but also appreciated the divine truths, echoes of God's Word, found in the other world religions. For the first time in its history, the Christian church here expresses a positive view of religious pluralism. What were the theological grounds for this new approach? It was the faith proclaimed by early church fathers that the eternal Word of God, incarnate in Jesus, addresses the hearts and minds of people everywhere, often through the wisdom or the religious truths they have inherited. Karl Rahner believed that people in the future would remember the Vatican Council because it introduced a new openness to the world religions.

Pope John Paul II has emphasized interreligious dialogue and cooperation. This is especially important because of a new theory, adopted by American right-wing social scientists, that a clash of civilizations is almost inevitable. They argue that civilizations are grounded in a particular religion and these religions have incompatible values; we are thus threatened by a clash between the Christian West and the Muslim world. John Paul II has rejected this theory. He promotes the dialogue of civilizations. The pope strongly opposed the war against Iraq [in 2003] because he feared that the American policy would lead to a further estrangement of the Muslim world. Since the Vatican Council, Catholic solidarity crossed boundaries.

## Whom do you feel was the most significant figure at the Council?

Again, this question has no single answer. Pope John XXIII was the wonderful catalyst who made the Council possible. He was seconded in the *aggiornamento* by several European cardinals from France, Belgium, Holland and Germany; without them the Council would not have achieved a great deal. Then there were the great theologians, such as [Jesuit Father] Karl Rahner, [Dominican Father] Yves Congar and many others, who were influential in the writing of the texts. It is worth acknowledging that for several decades beginning in the 1930s, the Catholic Church found itself blessed with a whole group of outstanding theologians, a historical phenomenon which, in my opinion, had no parallel since the time of the high Middle Ages. During the Reformation, the Catholic Church had no major theological thinker. The presence of great thinkers is something that cannot be planned: it happens; it surprises us; it is experienced as a special gift of God. Today we are no longer quite as blessed. The Vatican Council was convoked at a time when great thinkers had prepared the ground for the conciliar renewal and were available as authors and advisers of the conciliar documents.

## What has happened that you never imagined would happen?

Some Catholics claim that the Council has been poorly applied in the life of the church. Hans Küng has said repeatedly that Pope John Paul II betrayed the Council by reversing the conciliar orientation toward collegiality and decentralization. The Council did emphasize that the local or regional church was not simply a province of the universal church, and the local bishop not simply a papal representative. Each regional or local church fully incarnates the ecclesial mystery and hence exhibits its own vitality and creativity. This theology of the church as a community of communities calls for a certain decentralization of the ecclesiastical institution. After the Council, a beginning was made with the creation of the national bishops' conferences and the World Synod of Bishops; yet under John Paul II the power of the national bishops' conferences was severely limited and the World Synod of Bishops became completely controlled by the Roman Curia.

Let me also mention the conciliar doctrine of collegiality. According to Vatican II, the pope is not a monarchical ruler: As member and head of the episcopal college, he always teaches and rules in communication with the bishops, sometimes at an Ecumenical Council in the presence of the bishops and, more often, alone after consultation with the bishops. According to Vatican II, the local bishop is not simply the responsible leader of his diocese; he also exercises co-responsibility for the governance of the universal church. Furthermore, the idea of collegiality suggested that in each diocese the bishop should recognize the co-responsibility of the priests and the people. The Vatican Council envisaged a participatory church. In my opinion, it is not unjust to say Pope John Paul II has reversed the orientation toward participation and restored the monarchical regime in the Catholic Church.

At the same time, the present pope has promoted other conciliar teachings with great energy. He has become a champion of human rights and a promoter of interreligious dialogue. He has supported the ecumenical movement and redefined the church's relationship to the Jewish people. He also expressed his respect for the religion of Islam and advocated cooperation and solidarity between Catholics and Muslims. On matters of economic justice, John Paul II is boldly progressive. These are aspects of his thought rarely reported in the media. He wrote a radical encyclical on labor (*Laborem exercens*, 1981), in which he rejected both Marxism and liberal capitalism and advocated something very close to democratic socialism. He has repeatedly warned against the neo-liberal globalization of the economy that is presently taking place. After September 11 [2001], he pleaded for an international campaign against terrorism that would not inflict harm on innocent people. He criticized the bombing of Afghanistan [2002] and condemned the preemptive strike against Iraq [2003].

Because of his promotion of solidarity, justice and peace in the world, John Paul II deserves great admiration. We may criticize him for his monarchical style, but we should praise him for his understanding of the church's ministry in society and the boldness of his public stands.

## What hasn't happened?

As I said above, what hasn't happened is the decentralization of the church. John Paul II is daringly progressive *ad extra* (in matters dealing with the world) and highly conservative *ad intra* (in matters internal to the church.) The distinction between the church *ad extra* and *ad intra* was already made at the Vatican Council when the bishops decided to produce a document on the church (eventually published as *Lumen gentium*) dealing with matters *ad intra*, and a document on the Church in the Modern World (eventually published as *Gaudium et spes*) dealing with matters *ad extra*. Yet this distinction was based on the illusion that one can separate these two aspects of the church.

If the church recommends dialogue with outsiders and participation as the ideal for society, then inevitably Catholics will also want to have dialogue and participation within the church. The pope's bold teaching on social democracy and religious pluralism prompts Catholics to expect participation and pluralism within the church. The malaise of many Catholics today is that the official church is in contradiction with itself, affirming one ideal for humanity and another for the Catholic community. Here is a startling example: In his encyclicals, John Paul presents men and women as "subjects," i.e., as historical agents co-responsible for the institutions to which they belong. Governments, the pope argues, must respect their citizens as "subjects." Even when they introduce policies serving the common good, governments sin against the subject character of their people if they have failed to consult them and allow them to participate in the public debate. But if this is true, Catholics want to be responsible subjects in the church; yet here they are simply ruled from above. The church fails to apply its social teaching to its own institutional existence.

At the same time, the emphasis of Vatican II on human conscience has encouraged Catholics to do their own thinking and decide what the Gospel means to them as Catholics. They feel free to differ from certain official teachings, such as birth control, and freely publish their theological reflections. Priests as part of the ecclesiastical apparatus must be careful, but lay Catholics have produced a vast theological literature in total freedom. For this creativity, there is reason to be grateful.

## Is there any issue you regret the Council did not address?

The Council did not address the issue of women in the church nor did it deal with birth control and matters of sexuality in general. The bishops wanted to talk about birth control on the Council floor; some of the cardinals had already started, when word came from Paul VI that this topic was not to be discussed. I remember listening to this announcement; it was a shock to many of us that the pope did not trust his own bishops. Later, Paul VI created a study commission on birth control, yet when he read their report in favor of changing the church's official teaching, he decided not to follow their recommendation, and published an encyclical (*Humanae vitae*, 1968) condemning artificial birth control. Why does the Catholic Church retain the traditional views on women and sexuality while the Anglican and Protestant churches have modified their teaching? One factor is surely that the men who make the doctrinal decisions in the Catholic Church are not married, do not experience sexual love and have no children to educate and to learn from.

According to the polls on Catholic practice in North America, it would seem that Catholics prefer the sexual ethics taught in the Anglican and Protestant churches.

## What has been the most significant liturgical achievement and what do we need to do yet to implement full, conscious and active participation by our assemblies?

I am not a specialist in liturgy at all. I find the new liturgy introduced after Vatican II quite admirable. It is in the vernacular, it is flexible, it allows the presiding minister to move freely from ambo to altar and back, and it permits a creative pastor to have wonderful worship with his assembly. Even though the liturgical texts are everywhere the same, I am always amazed at the difference between the liturgical celebrations from parish to parish. There is no substitute for artistic creativity.

## In your opinion, should there be a third Vatican Council?

A third Vatican Council at this time would tear the church apart.

What is lacking in the church at this time is open conversation among the Catholic people and their leaders at home and across the nations and continents. Bishops don't reveal what they think because Rome demands conformity. Only after a couple of glasses of beer will bishops reveal their frustrations at the lack of honest dialogue in the church. Even in relatively small matters, such as the translation of liturgical books, the bishops are supervised by Rome and often find their pastoral judgments rejected by a Roman congregation. Since a good number of theologians have been censured by Rome in recent years, many priest theologians and priest ethicists are afraid to publish their theological studies. Only the laity are perfectly free to dialogue and explore the contemporary meaning of God's self-revelation in Jesus Christ, yet their conversation tends to remain outside the wall erected by clericalism.

What we need is an authoritative theology of pluralism internal to the church, i.e., a public recognition of different theologies and spiritual cultures within the same Catholic faith. In Canada, the traditional practices of Native Peoples are now being honored in the church, while in the past they were condemned as pagan superstitions. The Native Peoples have created their own spiritual culture in the church, demonstrating that theological unanimity among Catholics is a fiction. A useful starting point for renewal would be a World Synod of Bishops, uncontrolled by Rome, on the topic of pluralism within the church and the positive role played by responsible dissent.

135

## What Council teaching was most difficult to implement in the local churches?

Catholics in the U.S.A. and Canada adopted very quickly the more open attitude toward outsiders, Protestants, Jews and members of other religions. Thanks to the Council and other historical developments, the position of Catholics in North American society has significantly changed. It is my impression that Catholics who resisted the liturgical changes were in parishes where the priest was unable to offer theological explanations of the new rite; yet, in my opinion, the changes introduced by the Council and implemented in subsequent years have on the whole been well received by churchgoing Catholics.

The Council has brought forth a new Catholic mentality. It is a curious fact that confessions have gone down and almost disappeared among North American Catholics, even though no one had promoted this development. What happened, I think, is a change of mentality. Among the factors that have produced this change is the new emphasis of the Council on the primacy of conscience, the disagreement of Catholics with the official teaching on sexual ethics, and an expanded sense of sin that included the unjust structures in which we in North America live and from which we derive many benefits. Prompted by the church's recent social teaching on international justice, we have become aware of the moral ambiguity of our existence: We profit from our location in the wealthy corner of the globe, while others are excluded from the resources that sustain their lives. The cup of coffee in the morning relates us to the coffee picker overseas who may receive a starving wage. The malaise created by the sinful world in which we live cannot be articulated in the confessional. What we desire is a public liturgy of repentance and forgiveness made up of biblical texts that lament our involvement in a sinful world, that promise God's forgiveness of our compromises and adjustments, and that urge us on to continue doing good, helping other people and yearning for an alternative world.

## Is there any special historical or cultural significance that Vatican II occurred in the 1960s? Could it have happened earlier, later, in your opinion?

In the 1960s, western society experienced great optimism. After World War II, most countries adopted a guided capitalism, following the economics of John Maynard Keynes, which produced enormous wealth that improved even the lives of workers and the lower middle class. Keynes had argued that capitalism is an unstable system that will do well only if government helps it in times of crises.

When industries slow down, government should invest in production, create new jobs and spend money to enliven the economy. Keynesian capitalism was accompanied by the welfare state, especially in Europe, Australia and Canada. The economic upswing and the new security produced a culture of optimism in the West. People looked upon the planning for social change as a good thing. The idea of planning change also haunted John XXIII, the progressive cardinals and bishops, and theologians gathered at the Council. Some of this cultural optimism was reflected in *Gaudium et spes*, where we read that the economic system that has overcome poverty in Europe should be exported to the Third World to rescue the people there from their misery. It is interesting to contrast this with the documents of the Latin American bishops' conference at Medellín [1968], which offered a totally different picture of the world. Looking at the economic system from the margin, the Latin American bishops recognized that the economic process that has made Europe and North America wealthy has made their own continent much poorer. The World Synod of Bishops held in Rome in 1971 dropped the optimistic stance of the Vatican Council and fully accepted the Latin American perspective. When the United Nations in the 1970s asked for the creation of a new economic order, they were supported by the Catholic Church.

### So the Council couldn't have happened later or earlier?

Essential for the Council was the work of the great theologians to whom I referred earlier: Karl Rahner, Henri de Lubac, Yves Congar, Urs von Balthasar, Marie-Dominique Chenu, Hans Küng, Edward Schillebeeckx and several others. Their work flourished by the decade prior to the Council. An earlier Council would not have been able to draw upon their achievements.

### Which phrase or paragraph from any of the Council documents, for you, conveys the spirit of Vatican II?

For me, it is the first sentence of *Gaudium et spes*, which says that the joys and the sorrows of the people of this world, especially those who are poor and afflicted, are also the joys and the sorrow of the followers of Christ. Solidarity with people everywhere, especially those in trouble, is something entirely new in the Catholic tradition. No Catholic author prior to the second half of the twentieth century could have written such a sentence. In the past, we were not concerned about the well-being of heretics, schismatics, Jews and other outsiders. Now this has changed. Faith in Jesus Christ summons us to share in joys and sorrows of the whole of humanity and to wrestle with them in the service of love, justice and peace. Every time I read the first sentence of *Gaudium et spes*, I still get goose pimples. It represents an extraordinary leap in spiritual awareness.

## Do you think it was significant that the first document to come from the Council was the Constitution on the Sacred Liturgy?

I think that the conciliar document on the liturgy was the first document to be promulgated because the liturgical movement had existed for a long time and produced a great deal of research. Liturgical centers in different countries, including the United States, had influenced the thinking of vast numbers of Catholics. The Catholic community was ready for the liturgical renewal. It is possible to argue that if the document on the liturgy had been produced at a later session, it would have included the new insights brought out in some of the other documents. For instance, the concern for the world expressed in *Gaudium et spes* was not integrated into the Constitution on the Liturgy. In the present liturgy we simply pray for the Catholic Church, its leaders and its members; we do not offer prayers for the world, except on Good Friday when we list humanity outside the church according to their spiritual defects. At present, we correct this lack by the Prayer of the Faithful, which allows worshipers to express their concern for the sorrows and the injustices experienced in their day. If the conciliar document on the liturgy had been published at a later point, the new solidarity with the human family would have found expression in it.

## What relationships did you form at Vatican II, either with other consultors or bishops, that have had a lasting impact on your life and work?

This is a big question. Vatican II influenced my entire life as a Catholic theologian and activist. Immediately after the Council, a group of theologians created the international theological review called *Concilium*. It was published in five languages, sometimes in seven languages. I had the honor of serving on its board of directors for twenty years from 1970 to 1990. The board of directors met once a year to discuss theological developments in the church and then to prepare the several issues for the coming year. At these occasions I met Rahner, Küng, Congar, Schillebeeckx and other theologians whom I greatly admired. The aim of our review was to explore the letter and the spirit of the Second Vatican Council. Since most of us had participated in the Council and experienced that the church's magisterium is capable of changing its mind (on religious liberty, the ecumenical movement, the right of conscientious objection, the divine covenant with the Jewish people, God's salvific presence outside the church, etc.), we were keenly aware, more than other theologians, of the extent to which the magisterium reflects the spiritual culture in which the church is situated.

When the Vatican insists at this time that its official teaching is carved into stone and can no longer be debated, Catholics who remember Vatican II are likely to smile. The contextuality of the magisterium was in fact recognized in a brief note written by Cardinal [Joseph] Ratzinger [b. 1927]when, a few years ago, the Congregation for the Doctrine of the Faith rehabilitated the thought of the Italian Catholic philosopher Antonio Rosmini, whose writings had been formally condemned in the nineteenth century. Fidelity to God's self-revelation in the history of Israel and the life and teaching of Jesus Christ demands on ongoing dialogue with all believers and with the culture in which the believers live. In the terms used by John XXIII and the Vatican Council, we must pay attention to "the signs of the times" as we formulate the meaning and power of the Christian Gospel in our day.

## Did that annual meeting sustain a sense of the spirit and energy of the Council?

Yes, I think so. After a few years *Concilium* recognized that the church was alive on all continents, that European and North American theologians should not monopolize the conversation, and that theological representatives of other Catholic communities should be asked to join the board of directors. To avoid men monopolizing the conversation, women theologians were also appointed to the board. For two decades or so after the Council, *Concilium* played a unique role in the worldwide theological community. Eventually, theological reviews everywhere became open to new ideas and allowed the voices of women and representatives of Catholic communities in the less developed world to be heard. To correct *Concilium*'s preoccupation with contemporary theological issues, the review *Communio* was founded. This was a good idea, for the renewal of the church demands a rereading of the Christian authors of antiquity and the Middle Ages. When we read them in a new light, they have much to say to the contemporary church.

## One of the things you said earlier was that priests weren't really well prepared to help the assembly know what the spirit of Vatican II was. What might have been done to help the clergy understand the spirit of the documents?

After the Council, many of us were involved, year after year, in summer institutes where hundreds of priests, sisters, brothers and lay people eagerly studied the new approaches of Vatican II. In those years the great European theologians were invited to North America; their public lectures were attended by thousands of Catholics. Vast numbers of Catholics were thrilled by the theological renewal. Yet priests who did not study the conciliar documents and the new literature and stayed away from educational opportunities were unable to explain the new liturgy and the new attitude to their parishioners. Such parishioners often remained troubled; unless they subscribed to Catholic reviews or good diocesan newspapers, they were left in a state of confusion. Should the bishops have forced the priests to attend courses in theology? Obligatory study is of doubtful value. Studying theology is exciting only with an open heart. We must be ready to be addressed, and this cannot be commanded.

### Is there anything in our culture today, or our experience in Canada, either within the church or within society, that prevents us from hearing the message of Vatican II?

Many social critics argue that individualism has become the dominant dimension of present-day North American culture. I am thinking, for instance, of the work of the American sociologist Robert Bellah. This new individualism is nourished by the economic system in which we live. I mentioned earlier that after World War II, the capitalist economy relied on the intervention of the state, provided full employment and raised the income even of workers and the lower middle class. This created a culture in which social solidarity had an important place.

Yet after 1975 or so, there took place a turn to an unregulated market system, following the so-called monetarist theorists who trusted that competition alone, without government interference, would improve the economy and produce greater wealth. In fact, the new economy (called neo-conservative or neo-liberal) widened the gap between rich and poor countries and between rich and poor in each country.

When competition becomes the dominant cultural orientation, unaccompanied by solidarity, it generates individualism, preoccupying people with their own well-being. Because of this cultural turn, even Catholics find it more difficult to appreciate the divine summons to solidarity, emphasized by the Council and Catholic social teaching. Even the new interest in spirituality, often interpreted as a postmodern phenomenon, is strongly marked by the individualism of the age. Religion here become a personal journey and loses its world-transforming dimension.

At the same time, there are Catholic movements inspired by the social outreach fostered by Vatican II and Catholic social teaching. These movements are promoted by Catholic faith and justice centers, by religious orders, male and female, by Catholic papers, reviews and books, and more especially by the bold social teaching of the bishops and John Paul II. These Catholic movements also promote peace in our time. In fact, they were opposed to the bombing of Afghanistan [2002] and the preemptive war against Iraq [2003]. When I lived in Toronto, I was involved in these movements there. Now I live in Montreal, in the French-speaking province of Quebec, where the Catholic left is still an active community. I am on the editorial board of the Jesuit monthly *Relations* and participate in progressive Catholic networks such as *les Journées sociales* and *l'Entraide missionnaire*.

The reason why the social outreach emphasized by the Council and Catholic social teaching is not well received in most parishes is not only the impact of contemporary individualism on the Catholic conscience. Often, good people troubled by personal difficulties want Sunday morning worship to be a period of quiet repose in God and not be disturbed by a homily on the social sins in which we live. This touches a spiritual problem. How can we rejoice in God and at the same time be deeply troubled by the cruelly unjust world? Of all the mystics, St. Augustine has lived this spiritual paradox most intensely. This is the area where many of us struggle today. The God who comforts us is also the God who makes us grieve over the suffering of others. God's gift is a blessed restlessness.

## A hundred or two hundred years from now, what do you think Church history will say about Vatican II?

I already mentioned that Karl Rahner predicted that future generations would remember Vatican II as the Council that reconciled the church with religious pluralism. At this time, the big cities of North America and Western Europe are the home of significant Muslim, Hindu and Buddhist communities of recent origin. Can we live together in peace? Are we as Catholics willing to honor their religious traditions? Can we rejoice in religious pluralism or must we regard it as a sign of unfulfillment? These are important topics with implications for society's domestic and international policies. I have just attended a three-day colloquium in Montreal on religious diversity in the city, at which I was asked to discuss the topic from a Christian point of view. In my opinion, the Catholic Church has greater theological resources for dealing positively with religious pluralism than the other Christian churches. We all learn together.

**What advice or encouragement would you give to someone like me, who was born after the Council and perceives herself to be living out of the vision of the Council, in the current ecclesial climate where you have people on one side of the aisle screaming at the other people, "You're liberal!" "You're conservative!"?**

Is this really true? This is certainly not my experience in Canada. Canadians tend to be compromisers. The different trends in the church do not seem to create hostile divisions, except for tiny groups committed to extreme positions, usually made up of people who never had the chance to be educated. Even after I resigned from the priesthood in 1976, I continued teaching Catholic theology at St. Michael's College [Toronto] and working with the social justice committee of the Canadian Bishops Conference and later the Quebec Bishops Conference. Maybe Catholic life in the U.S.A. is more polarized. I think it is important not to be alone, and to belong to a network of Catholics engaged in dialogue and cooperation. Conflicts in the church are nothing new. *The Catholic Worker*, with its pacifist stand, and *Commonweal*, with its opposition to Franco, created divisions in the church. Once we take a good look at church history, we find that tensions and conflicts existed in many periods.

**What do you think is the best way to communicate the spirit of Vatican II to people who have never heard what the church says? So often in my work I have people say to me, "Since when do we do this?"**

"Since when do we do this?" is a good question. Since when do we celebrate the liturgy in the vernacular? Since when do we receive the Eucharist in the hand? Since when do we preach the Gospel as world-transforming power? Since when do we accompany our Protestant friends when they go to their church? Since when do we respect the spirituality of the Native Peoples, formerly repudiated as pagan? These seem to me good questions that deserve a careful answer. Some Catholics who have been away from the church for decades are greatly surprised when they try to come back. Some of them wish the church had remained the way it was when they left it. But upon reflection, they do admire the new solidarity, the spirit of *Gaudium et spes*, the love of the Other, the gift of universality.

**Is there anything else, any memories of the Council?**

I will tell you honestly that I have not kept any of my papers from the days of the Council. Foolishly or wisely, I decided in the monastery not to keep letters, papers or photographs, a practice which I never abandoned. When several years ago the National Archives in Ottawa telephoned me, asking me to give them my papers, I had to tell them that I had none.

Still, I remember forever the wonderful years of the Council. They shaped my life as a Catholic and a theologian. I have experienced that pentecostal events are possible in the church. The sociologist Emile Durkheim speaks of "times of effervescence" in the life of societies that allow them to renew themselves. Pentecostal events happen; they cannot be manipulated; institutions may initiate them, but they cannot foretell whether the Spirit will summon forth effervescence. Today many exciting things are happening in different corners of the church: new forms of discipleship, the emergence of a social spirituality, innovative models of holiness and new theological developments. We want to be close to these corners, yet whether a Pentecostal event is around the corner, nobody knows.

Born in Germany in 1923, Gregory Baum came to Canada from England in 1942. He earned a B.A. in mathematics and physics from McMaster University (1946), and continued his studies in mathematics for an M.A. from Ohio State University (1947). His studies in theology resulted in a doctorate of theology (D.Th.) from Fribourg University in Switzerland (1956). He took up the study of sociology at the New School for Social Research in New York City (1969–1971). From 1959–1986 Dr. Baum was professor of theology and religious studies at St. Michael's College at the University of Toronto. He was professor of Religious Studies at McGill University from 1986–1995, and has been professor emeritus since 1995.

# Primo Carlo Braga

## Interviewer: Aurelio Porfiri

Transcribed and translated by Marina Madeddu

### Could you explain to us your role during the Council?

I was not a Council father; I was not, and am not, a bishop. I was on the staff of the Secretary for the Commission of Sacred Liturgy before, during and after the Council. In addition to this collaboration and direct presence in the deliberations, I took part in the other discussion points, because it was easy to be in the *aula* (conciliar hall) and because of the contacts with the bishops who were members of the liturgical commission and others who were easy to meet. But I will talk in particular of the liturgical aspect of the conciliar deliberations.

### In your opinion, which was the most important moment of the Council?

Everybody knows that the liturgical *schema* opened the conciliar deliberations. The fathers found it the most organic and complicated, because it had been prepared by sixty years of studies and pastoral experiences in all the nations, starting from the principles and reforms proposed by Pius X. Nevertheless, the discussion on liturgy was also for some bishops a discovery of important doctrinal and practical elements.

## Which was the most important teaching of the Council?

First of all, the rediscovery and assimilation of the liturgy's real concept, familiar to the Fathers of the Church and to the first Christian generations, but in part hidden by less vital and more philosophical concepts that followed, such as the idea of liturgy as rite, liturgy as worship act that goes from man to God, and the loss of participation by God's people. The real worship, as the constitution on the liturgy teaches, is the offering to the Father of the salvific work made by Christ, made present and applied to the church and to her members through the liturgical action.

## So what is the Council's definition of liturgy?

Liturgy is the action of Christ, the continuation of his priesthood, and the sacramental action of all the church, celebrant priest and believers, united by the communion in the mystical body. All the church celebrates and takes part in the mystery, according to everyone's condition. An important statement of the Council concerns believers' "right" to take part in the liturgical celebration because of their baptism. The previous teaching, the liturgical movement and the liturgical pastoral, had insisted on believers' "duty." The Council starts from their "right," which implies also rites corresponding to the believers' capacities.

## Can we talk about the church's "sociological" view of believers?

Of course, but it's above every purely human conception. The church, which celebrates and effectuates the mystery of Christ, is above a purely social vision. She is the body of Christ, his bride. She is a mystery born from his cross, which comes back to life, and renews herself continuously in eucharistic celebration, which shows the world, and realizes in it, the salvation made by Christ. When the Council fathers began the discussion on the church *schema*—which was built on a theology old by that time—they requested explanation of the concept of church-as-mystery, which they had just passed in the liturgy *schema*; they also requested a new writing of the Preparatory Commission's text.

## What principles resulted?

First of all, the need for proper education of the bishops, priests and believers who form the church under the sign of the liturgical assembly, which allows their conscious, active and full participation. Second, the need for a reform of all church liturgy—to purify it from additions made during the centuries, and have it correspond more to the mentality and spirituality of our time—so that the liturgy can answer not only to the Western world's culture but also to the culture of the other peoples who approach the church. That is the problem of the reform, but more than that, of inculturation. The reform had already been started by Pius X, Pius XII and John XXIII, but there was a need to go deeper to open the liturgy's treasures to all cultures. The introduction of living languages into the celebrations is a sign of that reform, which has gradually reached, with the necessary papal approval, beyond the Council's document.

## Which are the practical applications?

I can talk only about some of them: the use of living languages; the extension of the Gospel reading during the Mass and the sacraments, and the homily to explain it, at least during the feasts; concelebration and Communion under both species; the sacraments' relationship with Eucharist and so their celebration during Mass; a simplified Liturgy of the Hours, but at the same time a richer one for the spiritual life of presbyters and God's people; recommendations to bring back art and music to more authentic service of the liturgy.

## What is the relationship between *Sacrosanctum concilium* and the other Council documents?

The value of the Constitution for the Sacred Liturgy (*Sacrosanctum concilium*) is perfectly clear only together with two other important Council documents: the Dogmatic Constitution on the Church (*Lumen gentium*) and the Pastoral Constitution on the Church in the Modern World (*Gaudium et spes*). The church, born from the cross of Christ, revives and renews herself in the Eucharist as a memorial to the cross. The church, bride of Christ, prays and realizes with him the world's salvation in the liturgy's celebration. The church, cause of renewal in the world, finds in the liturgy the peak and the source of her pastoral activity, of catechesis, of charity, of renewal offered to the world. These three documents, read together, give a rich doctrinal, spiritual and practical complex, which is the support of the conciliar doctrine's structure.

## In your opinion, who was the most important figure of the Council?

I could say those who worked on the formulation of the Constitution for the Sacred Liturgy. It is impossible to talk only about one person. We must remember many great experts and pastors who, even unaware, prepared the ground for the

Council. There were bishops who gave fundamental contributions during the Council—for example, Cardinals [Giacomo] Lercaro [1891–1976], [Giovanni Battista] Montini [1897–1978], [Joseph] Frings [1887–1978], [Bernardus Johannes] Alfrink [1900–1987], [Julius] Döpfner [1913–1976] and other European ones, together with good groups of theologians and liturgists, and some South American bishops. But there were also bishops, often not so famous, who in their pastoral and spiritual sensibility suggested small changes and interventions that gave more sense to the document's text. I cannot forget who "coordinated" the work: Monsignor Annibale Bugnini [1912–1982], Secretary of the Preparatory Commission, and Father (later Cardinal) Ferdinando Antonelli [1896–1993], Secretary of the Council Commission. Their direction was essential to reach the Constitution's goals.

The Council fathers' successors must have the same spirit to realize the inspiration, not only literally, of the Council. The opposed fringes must be understood and drawn into the mainstream of the church; they must be helped to discuss their positions without rigidity and to leave their doctrinal and pastoral isolation.

## What can be done to improve the conscious, active and full participation of the believers?

We have to work very much to realize completely the Council's dictates: to develop more illuminated and sensible education of pastors, who must form and guide God's people; to rekindle the forms of celebration, which risk becoming sclerotic and insignificant like some before the Council; and to renew a creative and generative spirit of liberty in the church.

## What happened that you would have never imagined, and what did not happen that you expected?

It is not easy to answer, because everyone had his hopes and fears. I found positive the vote for reception of the liturgy *schema* (only four votes opposed) and the collaboration in the conciliar assembly to bring the *schema* back to the Preparatory Commission's dictates. At the same time, some parts and some implementations (like the use of living languages, the extension of concelebration and Communion under both species) were changed.

The reform's implementation could have been negative: There was too much caution and fear. This is not strange; other deliberations were effectuated later in the everyday and practical church life.

# In your opinion do we need a third Vatican Council, and what would be the problems to discuss?

The dictates for an authentic renewal of the liturgy in the Second Vatican Council's spirit are in the new liturgical books, but their implementation cannot be left to amateurs or nostalgic people, or be obstructed by fear. We need hope and courage to complete this renewal. The result will depend on the sensibility and the courage of all the church, guided by her pastors.

Today, a new Council would be useful to spread what was said in the Second Vatican Council, especially from a doctrinal point of view. Maybe it could ask more audacity and perseverance in implementation of the Second Vatican Council.

Primo Carlo Braga was born in the diocese of Piacenza, Italy, on January 1, 1927. A member of the Congregation of the Mission, he was ordained priest in Rome on June 24, 1950, and studied theology in Rome at the Pontifical University of Saint Thomas (formerly called the Angelicum). In February 1956 he was offered a position in the Historical Section of the Congregation of Rites. He was a member of the commission for liturgical reform of popes Pius XII and John XXIII before becoming assistant in the secretariat of the pontifical commissions for the sacred liturgy of Vatican II: antepreparatory, preparatory and conciliar. After the Council, he worked in the secretariat of the *Consilium* for liturgical reform and in the Congregation for the Divine Worship until 1970. In 1970 he served in the Institute of Pastoral Liturgy of CELAM in Medellín, Colombia, for six years, working in many Latin American countries. He was Professor of Liturgy at the Collegio Alberoni, Piacenza, for nine years. Currently, he pursues his liturgical studies and is responsible for the Centro Liturgico Vincenziano, which publishes the journal *Ephemerides liturgicae* and the corresponding series "Bibliotheca EL"; he contributes to various symposia and Italian journals.

# Pierre-Marie Gy, OP

## Interviewer: Michael S. Driscoll

I was in service to the French Episcopal Commission for the Liturgy and as such was named as a *peritus* [expert] to the pre-conciliar preparatory commission and, after the Council, named again as a *peritus* for the *Consilium* for the implementation of the conciliar liturgical reforms. I worked with Johannes Wagner and Aimé-Georges Martimort in drafting the Constitution on the Liturgy. After the Council, on the *Consilium* for the implementation of the reforms, I worked with bishop members and other *periti*. My particular value to the French bishops was at the time of the debate on the liturgy. Because I had been working in the field of liturgy internationally and knew many people, I could help the French bishops make contacts with English-speaking bishops. Shortly after beginning this job, I was put in contact with some American bishops regarding the use of the vernacular in the liturgy. Some of them came up with some weak arguments against the vernacular, and they seemed unaware of where the Council was heading in these liturgical matters. The Council made the liturgy and the liturgical movement known to the United States.

As an aside, let me say that in the American culture there is both a quality and a risk—the quality is the ability to discover new things and to begin anew from scratch, whereas Europe is an old culture and moves much more slowly. The danger is that sometimes assimilation into a culture is a matter of time and possibly there is a risk of going too quickly.

# How many sessions of the Council did you attend?

I can't remember. I do recall being present at the session that discussed the Constitution on the Liturgy; but after this had been voted on, I asked to return to France in order to resume my work there. I also remember introducing Cardinal [Joseph-Marie Eugène] Martin [1891–1976] of Rouen, who was the head of the French liturgical commission, to Cardinal [Augustin] Bea [1881–1968]. This was at the time when the Preparatory Commission was forming. There was fear of appointing either a French or German, and as a result Cardinal Martin was assigned to the Ecumenical Commission.

I remember another occasion in 1956 when Pope Pius XII was implementing the reform of Holy Week. Cardinal [Francis] Spellman [1889–1967] of New York, who was a good friend with the pope, was intending to ask for an indult to be excused from the reforms of the Easter Vigil. This was reported to Cardinal Bea, who retorted, "Spellman knows Pius XII, but Pius XII also knows Spellman." As a result, Cardinal Spellman was given an additional year to prepare for the implementation but nevertheless had to implement the reforms. Pius XII was reported to have said to Spellman, "I will appease you but lead you."

# What was the most significant moment at the Council for you?

I've never asked myself this question. Possibly two moments: the way the pope [John XXIII] announced the Council, and from the beginning, the appointment of commission members. It was interesting that those presumed to be appointed in fact were not. I suppose that being together during the Council changed the way bishops saw things. The encounters the bishops had among themselves and with the *periti* changed them greatly.

# Of all the documents of the Council, which one is most significant for you and why?

Evoking a text of Giuseppe Dosetti [1913–1996, an Italian university professor who later became a priest], all the documents shed light on the others. The later documents completed and complemented the earlier ones. The articulation between *Lumen gentium* (constitution on the church) and the decree on priests (*Presbyterorum ordinis*) showed that the latter document completed the former. Rather than classifying these in nice tidy compartments, it is better to take them all together. I think that one has to be cautious of the idea that new things replace or imperil old ones. For example, the priesthood of the faithful doesn't diminish the ordained priesthood. The Council did not authorize us to minimize the sacrament of penance and reconciliation or the ordained ministry.

### What about the discussion of *Sacrosanctum concilium* (Constitution on the Sacred Liturgy) before *Lumen gentium* (Dogmatic Constitution on the Church)? Did this have any bearing on the future of the Council?

One day I was walking toward the Vatican and I met a famous theologian whom I knew who told me that the Constitution on the Liturgy was going to be voted in, but the Constitution on the Church was going to be returned to the Preparatory Commission to be reworked. And that's what happened! It wasn't that liturgy was judged more important, but the text for the Constitution on the Liturgy was in good shape and could be approved. This might not have a lot of shock value and may displease some Americans who would like something more dramatic, but that is what happened.

Recently I gave the Marquette Lecture in which I recounted what Cardinal [Yves] Congar once told me. Apparently John XXIII on several occasions during the Council went to his summer residence at Castelgandolfo in order to study and work on the most difficult dossiers. He did this in order to make sure that the majority had paid enough attention to the requests of the minority. In the cases where a minority was very far away from the majority, he made a special effort that the majority not leave the minority behind. This was his method for maintaining communion within the Council. He was concerned to bring every-one along in the decision-making—the minority as well as the majority. According to a Roman rule there must be a two-thirds majority to elect a pope. If there is one third strongly against a person, he will never be elected pope. This is for ecclesiological reasons—in the spirit of communion.

Once the Abbot Prou of Solemnes, who was the leader of the minority position, came to see me. [The Benedictine monastery of Solemnes was well known for its conservatism. This monastery had worked for the reform of Gregorian chant and had produced the major liturgical books prior to the Council.] After the vote was taken—a vote that he did not support—the abbot announced, "The vocation of Solemnes is to follow the pope, so we will follow." Curiously, this abbot became the most effective opponent to Archbishop Lefebvre [the well-known archconservative who, after the Second Vatican Council, repudiated its decisions]. When Abbot Prou came to see me, he was opposed to other Benedictine monasteries that wouldn't celebrate the liturgy according to Vatican II.

## What's the most important teaching that came out of the Council?

I may be wrong, but there seems to be the misunderstanding that the Council was replacing ordained ministry by lay ministry. I think that the true articulation was to affirm both. Nevertheless, the Council makes the distinction between ordained and lay ministry, recognizing the superiority of ordained ministry. Once again I think that the most important teaching of the Council was the ecclesiology of communion.

## Who do you feel was the most significant figure at the Council?

There are two significant figures for me—John XXIII and Paul VI. John XXIII had the charism to call for the Council and Paul VI the vision to see the Council through to the end. Recently some people have protested against the beatification of John XXIII and Pius IX together—as though one canceled out the other. I think that this was extremely unfair toward John XXIII. He would have responded, "You don't understand my theology and spirit of communion." Even to his family he declared, "I am Giuseppe, your brother," demonstrating his familial, inclusive spirit.

## What was the most significant statement from the Council and why?

I think that the most important statement was the connection of the church to the world and the Gospel to the world. *Gaudium et spes* expressed clearly, on the one hand, not the social organization of yesterday but the evangelical announcement of hope to the world—even if the world of our day is already different from the world when *Gaudium et spes* was promulgated, the message of the Gospel must retain its purity and intensity. Forty years have elapsed since *Gaudium et spes*. We no longer find ourselves in the same situation. To the extent that I understand the world today, there is greater insistence upon the freedom of the individual—but didn't St. Paul call this a form of slavery?

## What has happened that you never imagined would happen?

Some people regard the Council as a rupture with the past. I don't agree. For other people, the Council created a sense of rupture within themselves. But in liturgical matters, still others saw the introduction of the vernacular as an opening, not a rupture. [A curious phenomenon is that many rubricists were pushed to an antirubrical position.] For example, there were bishops at the Council who were not very strong in Latin yet fought against the use of the vernacular. When

John XXIII came to the preconciliar Commission on the Liturgy, some members were already addressing the question about liturgical language, but they were looking more specifically at the breviary. They noted that many priests were saying the Office without understanding it, and they judged that this was a great shame. So the Commission broached the question about the vernacular for the breviary. This doesn't mean that they did not regard Latin as a real treasure of the church. Rather than posing Latin against the vernacular languages, it is better to affirm both. It is not either/or, but both/and.

## What hasn't happened?

Let me say that it takes time for assimilation of the Council. We need a certain amount of time, even more than forty years. If someone thinks that it is time to correct the reform or, as some say, "to reform the reform," it makes me think that they did not understand the reform in the first place. The work of the reform is still before us. For example, pastors still have much to do to enter more prayerfully into the eucharistic prayer.

## Could we say that the work of the revision of the rites and liturgical books is over, but the work of the liturgical reform is still before us?

I wouldn't say it that way. But I would say that the key is the assimilation of the treasures of the liturgy. I think that there is the tendency, particularly for priests, to look at the practices and devotions of their childhood and the time when they were in seminary with great nostalgia. They tend to want to enshrine this memory. But the reform of the liturgy must complete and correct these memories.

## Is there any issue you regret that the Council did not address?

I have never asked myself this question. Rather, I would say that it would have been an error if the Council tried to deal with everything. It is like the end of the New Testament, recognizing that there remain many more things that could be added.

## What has been the most significant liturgical achievement and what do we yet need to do to implement full, conscious and active participation?

Very simply, I see two great achievements. First, the dialogical nature of liturgical prayer, and second, the ability to hear the Word and understand it. In the first case, when the faithful respond to the priest in all the dialogues like "The Lord be with you," "And also with you," this is a wonderful development that has been achieved everywhere in the world. Second, except in the case of the hearing-impaired, the fact that the readings are proclaimed and people can hear and understand them, this is also a great achievement to the extent that the Word moves through people's ears to their hearts.

Two other things that are developing but are not yet fully realized are the assimilation of the eucharistic prayer, which I've already addressed, and Communion under two kinds. If you permit a Dominican to evoke the memory of St. Catherine of Siena—she wrote many beautiful texts about the Precious Blood, even after the practice of offering the chalice to the laity had disappeared—this seems very evident to me. If St. Catherine of Siena were among us today, she would convince Catholics to receive Communion from the chalice. I rejoice that American Catholics have fared better in this regard than the Old World of Europe. This can help us understand better the importance of the cup.

Regarding the common cup, the bishops reflected with care on this matter. In consultation with the American bishops and the National Institutes of Health, they found that there was no problem from the standpoint of public health. Even during the Council some bishops were concerned about the transmission of germs. Consequently, some Swedish Lutherans undertook this study; they discovered that if great care was taken, no more germs were transmitted than what one finds on public transportation. Probably greater care has to occur in evangelizing people today about the importance of the cup. We need to help people get over their unfounded fears about receiving from the cup. Maybe we have to help people unlearn what they have learned from their mothers about not drinking from someone else's glass.

### In your opinion, should there be a third Vatican Council, and what topic or topics would you bring to the table?

This question reveals an error regarding the place of the Council in the life of faith and devotion. Instead of asking whether there should be another council, we should ask what else can we do to favor the assimilation of Vatican II. Maybe we have forgotten the ecclesiology of communion of which I have spoken earlier.

## What Council teaching was most difficult to implement in the local churches?

I don't know, for two reasons. First, in France, to receive the Council means something different than for the United States. Maybe we haven't received it deeply enough. Secondly, there is a difference in countries that must be factored into the question.

## Is there any special historical or cultural significance that Vatican II occurred in the 1960s? Could it have happened earlier or later, in your opinion?

The questions that we ask today were not in the minds of people at the time of the Council. Our questions reflect forty years of experience since the Council. In the sixties there were great changes in western civilization, so that if the Council didn't happen, these changes would have had an ill effect upon the church. What we need to see is how we can be witnesses to the Gospel for a transformed world.

Normally we are unconscious of change until after the fact. For example, regarding conservatives, Père Congar used to say that you have to speak to them as much as those estranged from the Catholic Church. In France we call them the *intégristes*, and I think that their greatest problem is their ignorance of history. If they had lived at the time of St. Pius V and his missal, they would see that Pius himself would have said, "Do your best to understand [the reforms of Trent]. Don't be stupid about this matter." Even Paul VI wanted a more measured application.

Père Pierre-Marie Gy, OP, born in Paris in 1922, is one of the most influential liturgical scholars of our time. His area of study at the famous École Nationale des Chartes in Paris was in medieval studies. His doctoral dissertation was on the history and theology of the ritual of the sacraments. From 1949–2001 he was a member of the Center for Pastoral Liturgy, which in 1964 became the official liturgical center for the French episcopate. Together with Johannes Wagner and Aimé-Georges Martimort, Père Gy was one of the principal architects of *Sancrosanctum concilium* and of the postconciliar liturgical reform. Throughout his scholarly career Père Gy's primary concern has been to help re-establish the unity between sacramental theology and the church's liturgy, both as historically understood and as celebrated.

# Pierre Jounel

*Note: At the time of compiling* Voices from the Council, *Pierre Jounel had suffered several heart attacks and was no longer able to give interviews. This chapter is taken from a 1994 interview. Interviewers: Olivier Cagny and Pierre Faure, 1994. First published in* Célébrer, *no. 254, October-November, 1995. Used with permission of Éditions du Cerf and the National Center for Pastoral Liturgy (CNPL). All rights reserved. Abridged, edited and translated for this publication by Paul Inwood, 2003.*

Pierre Jounel was ordained priest for the diocese of Nantes, France, in 1940. From 1942 to 1952 he taught philosophy and theology in Sulpician seminaries at Orléans and Rodez, and then fulfilled a childhood dream, going to Rome to do research in the Vatican Library on the cult of the saints. From 1953 he worked at the Centre de Pastorale Liturgique (CPL) in Neuilly, Paris, which later moved to the center of Paris and become the national center (CNPL). In those days, professors of liturgy learned their trade essentially on the hoof, but Jounel had had access to a remarkable liturgical library while he was at Rodez. This, coupled with ten years of pastoral experience in a Parisian parish, formed Jounel into a liturgist who tried to balance research, teaching and pastoral practice. In Paris he was first of all given the task of editing the two journals, *La Maison-Dieu* and *Notes de pastorale liturgique*, and found himself working alongside [Aimé-Georges] Martimort, [A.M.] Roguet, [Pierre-Marie] Gy, [Henri] Dalmais, [Jean] Daniélou, [Louis] Bouyer, [F.] Boulard, [A.] Chavasse, [Joseph] Gelineau and others.

After the promulgation of the revised rites for the Easter Vigil, Jounel was sent all over France in 1955–1956 to help implement them. In many parts of France the Easter celebrations took on a new life (though they never became as popular as Christmas Midnight Mass), but in other countries this did not always happen. Jounel states that the Italian clergy, in particular, made little differentiation between the Easter Vigil and a Saturday evening anticipated Mass, getting through the whole rite in forty-five minutes. This was what provoked the 1988 instruction on the celebration of Easter, which, says Jounel, was not necessarily aimed at abuses in other countries and certainly not in France.

The Holy Week reforms of the 1950s were not the result of work by the CPL or its sister liturgy institute at Trier, but both of them had sensitized their respective bishops' conferences in advance so that when the reforms came about there was support for them in the upper echelons. In fact, these reforms were the work of a small commission set up by Pius XII in 1947; it worked in secret, a fact justified by the hostility of the Roman Curia to liturgical reform in general and to these reforms in particular when they finally appeared. Pius XII had been well aware of this hostility.

In 1956, Jounel went to the international pastoral liturgy congress in Assisi and met for the first time the future Cardinal [Ferdinando] Antonelli [1896–1993] and Fr. [Annibale] Bugnini [1912–1982], at that time president and secretary respectively of the commission for liturgical reform. Jounel was invited to join their work in 1958. Initially, this was a simplification of the Rite of Dedication of a Church and mapping the outlines of what became John XXIII's revised Code of Rubrics.

1956 was a key year for another reason: the Institut Supérieur de Liturgie was founded at the Institut Catholique in Paris. The new body had been founded to compensate for the inadequacy of liturgical teaching in French seminaries, but in fact there were far more overseas students than French ones. Jounel taught courses there for 26 years alongside [Bernard] Botte, [Pierre-Marie] Gy and [Irénée] Dalmais; the kernel of his teaching was incorporated into the four volumes of "L'Église en prière."

Jounel loved to teach. For him, a guiding principle was the active participation of the faithful in the paschal mystery, as asked for by Pius X at the beginning of the twentieth century and as extensively promoted by the great Benedictine liturgist Odo Casel until his death in 1948.

Of this preconciliar period, Jounel states:

It is important to note that, up to the Council, the CPL never asked for a reform of the rites. Its directors, especially Canon Martimort, were too imbued with Latin culture and respect for tradition ever to have dreamt of it. Certainly if you wanted to get Rome to agree to certain modifications of the use of the vernacular for the Scripture readings of the Mass and for the singing of songs at the entrance, offertory and Communion, it was useful not to appear to be too innovative. But we were dealing with something much deeper. We were caught up in the liturgy that we had known since our childhood, and in the heart of which was born, for some, their priestly or religious vocation. We found the twelve readings of the paschal office of Holy Saturday to be so rich, and discovered in them a synthesis of the mysteries of our salvation! We were not thinking of asking for anything. For us, history remained our *magistra vitae* [the mistress of our life].

## Wasn't anyone at all impatient?

The only area in which there was some impatience was precisely on these two points: getting the proclamation of the readings of the Mass into a living language (we got this through in 1956) and the same thing for the things the people had to sing. You can't imagine today how much we had to fight to get even to that point, not so much with the higher authorities but with the practitioners of Gregorian chant, who felt that the slightest breach in the Latin rampart would result in a torrent of devastation....

## At what point did the liturgical reform start to accelerate?

The Constitution on the Sacred Liturgy (*Sacrosanctum concilium*) was a turning point. The level and vigor of its norms were like a beacon, even if the concrete applications envisaged were fairly modest. The Council fathers did not make a case for a plurality of eucharistic prayers, and they mostly thought that the Divine Office ought to remain in Latin. The acceleration was due first of all to a deepening understanding of the teaching of the Council.... Furthermore, the implementation of this teaching took place at a time when history itself was accelerating, when culture was changing at a pace that the world had never seen before.

It was in this difficult context that the *Consilium* for the application of the Constitution, set up by Paul VI, had to start work. I was named a member of it in the spring of 1964, and working for it took up the major part of my life for the next ten years. I was put into fifteen of the working groups, and was asked to manage four of them, including the one dealing with the liturgical year.

We were immediately faced with a strong demand for change in every area, even some that we hadn't expected. We thought, for example, that even when allowing chants in living languages to coexist alongside Latin plainchant, the latter would always predominate. For our German friends, the Latin plainchant was a *thesaurus musicae sacrae* [treasury of sacred music] that could not be touched. This is why, in the Missal, we preserved the text of all the antiphons that had Gregorian melodies attached to them, contenting ourselves with merely translating them. In fact, what we should have done was create a real introductory *monitio* [instruction] instead of just translating the Latin text [of the antiphon].

When it came to the Divine Office, we were very surprised to find the monks, especially the Cistercians, asking for large-scale concessions in order to produce their own liturgy and celebrate it in the vernacular. They said, "When young people come into our monasteries, they mustn't find them to be nothing more than museums." This request was looked on favorably by Paul VI. Well before the Council, then-Cardinal Montini had taken on board the idea of using the language of the people in liturgy. One day he said, "It is the language of the heart, and you can't really pray to God properly except in the language of your heart." Monsignor Bugnini, secretary of the *Consilium* and linchpin of the reform, was also of the same opinion; and so it was that in 1967 permission to use the language of the people in the entirety of the celebration of the sacraments and the office was enshrined in church law.

Another surprise was that it was the Latin countries that most spontaneously welcomed the changes. Whereas in France, Germany and England there were certain little "islands" that organized themselves to remain faithful to the Latin, the changes happened painlessly in Italy and Spain. The great efforts that had been made in French- and German-speaking countries to get the people to participate in the Latin liturgy had not been replicated elsewhere. If an Italian was unwilling to respond *Et cum spiritu tuo* to the *Dominus vobiscum*, he or she was quite willing to respond *E con il tuo spirito*!

Jounel is convinced that the sociocultural whirl of change broadened the field of liturgical change, too.

The conviction that the people must participate actively in the celebration of the sacred mysteries was always at the root of the reforms; but because the bishops in some areas (e.g., The Netherlands) lost control, it was necessary for the *Consilium* to work even faster, providing firebreaks where needed. The existence of hundreds of newly written eucharistic prayers in Holland, Germany and then in France posed a problem that needed urgent resolution. Not only discipline but faith itself was at risk. Of one particular Dutch eucharistic prayer, Bernard Botte declared, "I do not say that it is in itself Arian, but an Arian could use it without difficulty." So it was a matter of urgency to propose alternative prayers to the Roman Canon.

## Did you sometimes feel overwhelmed by this huge amount of disordered creativity?

Yes. Things were moving very fast indeed. I remember during the Council seeing a cover of the magazine *Paris-Match,* which showed a Dutch priest giving Communion in the hand to a teenager. "This is unbelievable!" I said to myself. The idea had never occurred to me. I knew, of course, that this was in fact the practice during the first thousand years of Christianity, and I was very happy to cite to my students the texts of Ambrose and Cyril of Jerusalem on this subject. I felt that things had completely overtaken me. Was I secretly happy about it? Perhaps yes.

## In the Preparatory Commission for the Council set up by Pope John XXIII, you were the secretary of the subcommission whose task was to lay down the theological foundation for active participation by the faithful. This was an important point. Can you tell us how the reflection progressed?

Fr. Bugnini started off on the wrong foot. In this participation he saw the expression of the baptismal priesthood of the faithful, which put this priesthood exclusively into a worship context. This was not good enough, as the major texts of the Council make very clear. When St. Paul said, "Offer your body as a spiritual sacrifice" (Romans 12:1), he was talking about the entire life of the baptized and not primarily of participation in worship. With the help of work in this area by Botte and many other theologians, I was able to put forward a counter-thesis.

> Jounel's work, aided and abetted especially by Roguet and Bishop [Henri] Jenny [b. 1904], at that time auxiliary bishop of Cambrai, resulted in the first chapter of the liturgy constitution which, as Jounel puts it, "is of an exceptional theological density."

## How far were the *Consilium's* liturgical *schemas* used experimentally?

We need to admit honestly that there was no systematic form of consultation right the way through the work. It was only when the various rites were in an advanced state of being put together that they were experimented with. This was the case, for example, with concelebration.

**Thinking of the first intuitions and the main lines of the liturgical reform, what do you think is still to be done, and which area has shown itself to be the most fertile? What remains to be deepened in the Christian people, in liturgical teams, in dioceses, in parishes?**

I cannot forecast the future.... The thing that has worked best, it seems to me, is the recovery of the proclamation of the word of God as a structural element in all-liturgical celebrations. "The book is the chalice," said John XXIII. Everyone today is convinced of the truth of this. No sacrament is celebrated today without being preceded by a reading from the Word of God. This was an absolute novelty in the Roman liturgy, hence the importance of lectionaries for Mass, for the sacraments, for the Liturgy of the Hours.

Now those who worked on the reform did not at first understand how far they had to go. If we felt very strongly the need to expand the Sunday readings at Mass, it was only quite late on that one of us proposed that we should have a weekday lectionary as well. How many people remember today that there were no daily readings in the old Missal, apart from Lent and the octaves of Easter and Pentecost, i.e., only for eight weeks of the entire year? On the other weekdays, you used the readings for the saint's day, or those of the previous Sunday. How many of our people now drink at the well of the readings of the weekday, even if they can't get to church for Mass! No one could have foreseen the success that Sunday and weekday missals have had, nor publications such as *Magnificat*.

## This is a strong point. Are there any weak ones?

I have been too close to the liturgical renewal to be able to say with certainty what has not worked well. People say that the eucharistic prayers have not been a pastoral success, that people's attention wanders as we move into the Liturgy of the Eucharist. I'm not sure. It seems to me that, with the newfound thirst for stability and faithfulness to the tradition, many people attach themselves to the official texts of the church and do not give enough credit to individual initiatives. After twenty-five years of use [this interview was conducted in 1994] the Missal of Paul VI now constitutes the expression of the tradition.

Having said that, an enormous task is still ahead of us, which can be summed up in the word "inculturation." We know how important this was in the Synod of African bishops in the spring of 1994; and an instruction from the Congregation has recently formulated the essential orientation for inculturation in liturgy. We had already laid down the main lines of this document twenty years ago. Inculturation is not only aimed at non-Mediterranean countries but at all the places where there is life. This will be the task of a new generation of liturgists, and it is of primary importance for the future of the reform undertaken by the liturgists of Vatican II.

## What would you say to those people who don't want to know the Missal of Paul VI, and to those who, while respecting it, regret that it was imposed to the exclusion of the Tridentine Missal?

I would say to them that they use computers, that they live with the instruments of the culture of their time, and that they have no reason to get stuck on the 1570 date when the Missal of Pius V was promulgated. Why should the liturgy be frozen then, when it had been periodically renewed up to that date? These people lack historical knowledge. Monsignor [Marcel] Lefebvre was absolutely convinced that the ancient formula for confirmation goes back to the time of the apostles, when in fact it only dates back to the thirteenth century.

Jounel then went on to demonstrate how Paul VI followed exactly the same procedure with his Missal as Pius V had with the Missal and Breviary in 1570, Clement VIII in 1595 with the Roman Pontifical, Pius X with the psalter of the Breviary in 1911, and Pius XII with the Holy Week rites in 1955.

In all these cases, the previous usage was abrogated and replaced by the new. This is the church's constant practice.

But the confrontation between yesterday's liturgy and today's liturgy is not limited to the Mass. A huge change has taken place with the celebration of funerals, Yesterday, we had black vestments, the *Libera me de morte aeterna* [Deliver me from eternal death], and a collection of prayers which were certainly ancient and respectable but in which the resurrection of Jesus did not figure. Today, we sing "Keep in mind that Jesus Christ has died for us and has risen from the dead" or "On the threshold of his house our Father awaits us." When in the 1970s Father [Joseph] Gelineau told us to hope for singing by the assembly at funerals, that seemed like pie in the sky to us. Look what has happened, though!

## In all the work you were involved in, which task seems the most important to you?

Without question the renewal of the calendar of the saints and the liturgical year. But the most enduring thing will turn out to be the absolution formula for the new rite of reconciliation that I was put in charge of preparing and which is now in use throughout the world. My only regret is that the *Consilium* did not agree to the writing of similar formulae for children and for adolescents.

I have one especially juicy memory. Only a short time after the French bishops had approved the translation of this prayer, I was passing through Paris and went to the church of Saint-Ignace to go to confession. After listening to me, the Jesuit father (who had no idea who I was) said, "I'm going to use the new absolution formula. Listen to it carefully—it's very beautiful!"

## Did you use an existing text or did you write it yourself?

It's a long and complicated story. The renewal of the liturgy of penance was entrusted to Joseph Lecuyer, assisted by a group of historians and theologians, who included Louis Ligier and Cyrille Vogel. Two points occupied them first of all: collective absolution of sins without individual confession, and a possible plurality of formulae for absolution.

On the first point, they gathered together a dossier establishing the numerous indults granted by the Holy See, especially to missionaries, since the First World War. On the subject of the absolution formula, they were also able to produce a collection of depreciative formulae of the "May almighty God have mercy on you" type alongside those of the "And I pardon you your sins" type. (The early centuries had never known a declarative formula like the latter.)

This research work was only the first stage in the preparation of the revised *Ordo* for reconciliation. When they took their work to the Council fathers, they received a lot of counterargument. Cardinal [Pericle] Felici, former secretary of the Council, declared, "The question of collective absolution is not our business but belongs to the Congregation for the Doctrine of the Faith."

As for a diversity of absolution formulae, it was thought that only the *Ego te absolvo* [I absolve you] should be preserved. The primate of Ireland, Cardinal [William] Conway [1913–1977], remarked, "If you take away the *Ego te absolvo* from the priests, you will cause them to lose their identity. They will no longer know who they are!" I can still see the sheer disbelief on the face of Rembert Weakland [b. 1927], Abbot Primate of the Benedictines, when he heard this.

The work of the group of experts was suspended indefinitely—"The submarine has dived," as Monsignor Bugnini now liked to say—but the problem surfaced again abruptly three years later in 1972, when the Congregation for the

Doctrine of the Faith made public its proposed norms on the subject of collective absolution. Surprise became agitated excitement when on June 23 the pope told Cardinal [James Robert] Knox [1914–1983], Prefect of the Congregation of Divine Worship, that he intended to promulgate the new *Ordo Paenitentiae* so that it could be implemented at the same time as the juridical norms.

I was in the process of preparing to return to France. Someone caught me up at the airport to ask me to prepare the text of a note to explain to the pope that for better or worse the *Ordo* was not in a state to be submitted for his approval, but that it would definitively be ready in the autumn. Now Monsignor Bugnini decided to set up a new working group and on the spot named me as its reporter, giving me carte blanche in the choice of my co-workers. On the eve of the summer vacation, it was not obvious how one would find competent people and set them to work. In all good faith, I contacted some of my former students who were not among the official consultors of the Congregation. (Bugnini's enemies used this later as an argument against him, and they were correct insofar as this did not accord with the way of working of the Roman Curia.) As my assistant I chose Franco Sottocornola, a priest of the Parma Missionaries. An expert in history as in theology, polyglot, spiritual leader, a missionary to the depths of his soul, he lives today [1994] as a semi-hermit in Japan, where he is studying Buddhist monasticism. It was he who developed the absolution prayer for collective celebrations and proposed the title of Sacrament of Reconciliation.

The proposed new *Ordo* was put before the members of the Congregation at their plenary session in October 1972, but its final form required another year of delicate navigation among the various Roman bodies concerned.

The *praenotanda* [introduction] received particular attention, and the pope was delighted with it. The experts had agreed on a short formula of absolution, but the fathers of the Congregation were fundamentally opposed to it on several grounds. I went to bed that night very depressed, knowing that something else had to be found by nine o'clock the next morning. I awoke at dawn the next morning with a new text in my head, which was the one finally approved—not without two modifications. My idea was that the priest should use this forgiveness formula: "And therefore I, a sinner like yourself, absolve you from all your sins." The word "therefore" was rejected, as it was thought it detracted from the primacy of "I." In the text proposed, the priest had appeared more as the minister acting in the name of the church, bringing pardon and peace. Another phrase was also rejected—"a sinner like yourself"—even though it is part of the Eastern tradition.

## You also worked on the composition of the lectionary, especially for the Sundays of Advent and Eastertide. How did you approach this?

I had been interested in the problem for a long time, and in *La Maison-Dieu* in 1961 I had already sketched out a possible restructuring of the Missal readings. I expect this is why they included me in the group responsible for revising the *Lectionary for Mass*. The work was directed by Cypriano Vaggagini [1909–1999], a [Camaldolese Benedictine] monk of Maredsous, and Gaston Fontaine, a Canon Regular of the Immaculate Conception residing in Canada. The group included a number of eminent biblical specialists, among whom the Germans especially were shining stars.

Two trends would confront each other, while things still remained completely cordial. Some were very sensitive to exegetical realities, others to liturgical tradition and to pastoral implications. The exegetes were not shocked if a Gospel reading contained only a single verse provided that it included the entire pericope. Others could not visualize a solemn Gospel procession with lights and incense leading a deacon to the ambo for such a short reading of the Word of God. Sometimes the solutions reached were compromises. The upholders of the patristic tradition, for example, wanted Lent every year to include the three Gospels of the Samaritan woman, the man born blind and the raising of Lazarus. The pastoral people wanted other choices, calling to conversion or announcing the mystery of the Cross. You can see what happened in the end by looking at the current lectionary.

Studying past practice was only of secondary interest since it had been right away decided to have a three-year Sunday cycle of readings, something that the Roman rite had never known. This had already been tried-out successfully in some Protestant churches, for example in Sweden, and this was encouraging for our work.

The organization of the lectionary for paschal time was something especially dear to me. I produced a first version *ad experimentum* for France. I wanted above all to put the Acts of the Apostles back in pride of place as readings proper to paschal time, alongside the Gospel of John, following the usage of the Eastern churches, which goes back to patristic times. Some, however, suggested beginning the reading of Acts on Pentecost Sunday and continuing, making the following Sundays a sort of "Time of the Church."

While remembering my own modest contribution to the *Lectionary for Mass*, I'd also like to pay tribute to all those who worked on the other lectionaries, the Liturgy of the Hours, all the sacraments, *Book of Blessings*. Here we have what is perhaps the jewel of the conciliar liturgical renewal.

## What about the cult of the saints? This was an important part of your work for many years.

This was certainly my preferred area of work for the *Consilium*, and later for diocesan liturgies, and it's where I have the greatest number of memories.

It was not just a question of reviewing the list of saints inscribed in the Roman calendar but, above all, of setting the ways in which their feasts were to be celebrated, renewing the entire collection of prayers in the Missal and the Liturgy of the Hours, and making a choice of Scripture readings and hagiographies suitable for introducing Christians into the soul of every single one of the saints whom we celebrate throughout the year.

To establish the list of saints, we had at our disposal a fairly nebulous directive from the Council. We should only be putting into the General Calendar those feasts "that commemorate saints of truly universal significance" (SC 111). What were we to understand by that? A great deal of subjectivity was necessarily involved in the choices. We obviously tried to preserve saints who have marked the life of the church. On the other hand, there was a concern to "de-Italianize" the calendar in order to open it up more to the universality of Catholic sainthood in space and time. Thus it was that every century and every [populated] continent were represented. Allowing for optional memorials offered a certain flexibility in choice, and aroused a somewhat indulgent attitude toward certain saints whose hagiographical details are rather slim. I was especially keen that we should fix the ways in which a saint was commemorated in the Mass and the office. By only imposing the Collect of the Mass and the hagiographical reading in the Liturgy of the Hours for all those optional memorials, it seems that we managed to establish a balanced relationship between the temporal and sanctoral cycles. Twenty-five years of use will bear witness to whether that opinion is correct or not.

## Do you think that the General Calendar established in 1969 will last?

All you can say is that for the moment it is lasting, despite the flood of canonizations by John Paul II. Within thirty years of the publication of the Missal of Pius V, his successors had introduced thirteen new feasts into the calendar. Only St. Maximilan Kolbe and three groups of Far Eastern martyrs have been added since 1969. [This interview was conducted in 1994; further saints have been added since then.] In fact the calendar is nothing more than a choice. It is the Martyrology that gathers together the complete list of saints honored in public worship in the church. The compiling of the Martyrology was a great and far-reaching task. Begun in 1970, it is still not [in 1994] finished, despite the work of Jean Evenou. Just when people were thinking it was coming to an end, John Paul II began the project of a universal and ecumenical Martyrology for the Jubilee Year 2000. To do this, he set up a commission with a Ukrainian bishop as its president. We can only wish the commission good luck.... [The *Martyrologium Romanum* finally appeared in Latin in 2001—Translator.]

## What is the position with the cult of the saints from an ecumenical perspective?

As far as the East is concerned, there is no major problem. I personally would be happy to celebrate St. Seraphin of Sarov each year, and to join the memorial of St. Andreij Rublev to that of Fra Angelico. With the Protestants, it is quite different, especially for the Calvinists, since at the heart of their "protest" is a refusal to allow the cult of the saints. Anglican "comprehensiveness" has a calendar that does not hesitate to include John XXIII alongside Martin Luther King, but it's only a memorial (Canadian Anglican calendar). Before we inscribed Sts. John Fisher and Thomas More in the Roman calendar, we took the trouble to consult the Church of England via the Vatican Secretariat for Unity. Would it be appropriate to bring to mind such painful memories? The response was in fact quite positive.

## Was the new calendar well-received when it was first published?

That depends on which country you are talking about. Certain Italian newspapers stated ironically, "Thirty saints lose their halos," while the Neapolitans were indignant that the memorial of St. Januarius was now only optional. In the USA, sorrow was expressed over St. Christopher and even St. Rita (who actually did not appear in the old calendar). In Germany, people were astonished at the disappearance of St. Ursula and the Eleven-thousand Virgins of Cologne!

French newspapers were more objective. The Bureau of Statistics, which has the job of establishing the official calendar used by the post office, radio and TV, quickly got in touch with the CNPL in order to take account of the changes to dates and feasts of saints in the new calendar.

## Did you also participate in the preparation of the Rite of Confirmation?

Yes. I did a lot of detailed work on it, but time has blurred my memories a little. From the outset, the preparation team was agreed upon the essential kernel, i.e., the formula for chrismation, borrowed from the Byzantine liturgy. Dom

Bernard Botte had showed that it dated back to the fourth century.

Next there were two debates. The first was about the respective importance of the laying-on of hands and the anointing with chrism. Which was actually the sacramental rite, properly speaking? It is certain that, if there were no Eastern tradition favoring the anointing, it was the imposition of hands (or a single hand) that was considered as the essential of the rite, in conformity with Acts 8:17. Paul VI did not want to slice up the rite. Number 9 of the *Praenotanda* sets out the symbolism of these two complementary gestures, since the entire content of a sacrament is not necessarily expressed by a single ritual action.

The second debate was on the age for confirmation. The majority of the experts, but not of the bishops, wished to respect the ancient order of the sacraments of Christian initiation: baptism, confirmation, Eucharist. But there was a great deal of pressure from pastors to delay the age of confirmation to the teenage years or even later still. The pope leaned in this direction too, and the question was left open.

## You were a great admirer of Paul VI.

I first received his blessing, along with the students of the Institut Supérieur de Liturgie, on the piazza of St. Peter's on June 21, 1963; and I was very moved while watching the TV broadcast of the funeral liturgy of the dead pope fifteen years later on the eve of the Transfiguration. Perhaps I was even more moved because I was the author of the revised ceremonial for papal funerals, with its triple farewell: from the local church in Rome, from the Eastern churches, and from the universal church. This *Ordo* was developed in 1976 and had pleased Paul VI, who said, "I want to promulgate it as soon as possible because if I die first they won't even light a candle for me!"

As early as 1964, the pope had asked Monsignor Martimort and me what we thought of the way the pontifical ceremonies unfolded in St. Peter's. In my report I emphasized what seemed to me to be outdated and even inconvenient, stressing the fact that with TV coverage all the anachronistic stuff would be watched in shops and cafes. The impression given by a papal Mass required an exceptionally high standard of quality, both liturgical and aesthetic. It was no longer appropriate, as it had been at the time of John XXIII, for a master of ceremonies solemnly to unfold a handkerchief before the pontiff when he wanted to blow his nose. Even worse, it seemed shocking to hear the clattering as the Swiss Guards presented arms at the moment of the consecration. I was quite open about writing down everything negative I had noticed. I sent my text to Monsignor Martimort, thinking that he would soften the edges a bit, but he sent it on to Monsignor Bugnini just as it was. Bugnini hesitated before presenting such criticisms to the pope, but his colleagues urged him on, saying, "It's not you that he'll interrogate about this; you're only an intermediary." So he handed on my paper. I have a photocopy of the pope's annotations on this text. It is precisely alongside the most critical passages that Paul VI wrote in the margin, "*Bene, bene* [very good]."

I had also prepared the basics for the enthronement liturgy of a new pope. We could not know in advance if he would want to be crowned or not. Although Paul VI had taken off his tiara and placed it on St. Peter's altar during the Council sessions, he did not decree the abolition of this piece of insignia, and a crowning therefore remained provided for in the *Ordo* for papal elections. What I did was provide a simplified rite containing two possible choices, with or without crowning. John Paul I and then John Paul II both judged a crowning not to be useful. Some people regretted the passing of such a large symbol in the liturgical celebration.

## What are your most vivid memories of your work for the liturgical reforms?

I have two. The first is the very first Sunday Mass celebrated entirely in French in the parish where I was born. But the second is paramount: the closing of the Council. Monsignor Bugnini had given me the responsibility of putting together the rites. They had never been used since the end of the Council of Trent. Following the pope's wishes, they took place over two days, December 7 and 8, 1965. The first day, in the Vatican basilica, the most moving gesture was the kiss of peace exchanged between Paul VI and the Patriarch of Constantinople's delegate after the official renunciation by both churches of their reciprocal anathemas against each other. This kiss of peace was followed by a prayer of repentance and the communal recitation of the *Pater noster*. We had the impression that a new chapter was opening in the Christian history of both East and West. The next day, at the end of the Mass celebrated by the pope on the piazza in front of St. Peter's, it was the final dialogued acclamations between the bishops representing the five continents and the complete gathering of Council fathers. [Jounel had written these acclamations, basing them on those led by the Cardinal of Lorraine at the conclusion of the Council of Trent, December 4, 1563—Translator.] I was in among the crowd for this, as they had forgotten to give me a ticket to get into the reserved seats.

When the bells rang out immediately afterwards, I felt that I was living through one of the greatest moments of my life.

Pierre Jounel is a priest of the diocese of Nantes, France and former professor of the Catholic Institute of Paris. He served as a consultor for the Preparatory Commission for the Second Vatican Council and served on the commissions for sacraments and for sacramentals and music.

# Cardinal William Keeler

## Interviewer: Jerome Hall, SJ

**What was your capacity at the Council?**

I was a *peritus*; but also, at the Council's first session, I was assigned to the press panel that responded to questions from English-language reporters. Actually, I don't think that I ever got a question, because I was the youngest one on the panel, and nobody was that interested in canon law, either. But beginning with the second period of the Council, I was one of about five priests recruited each day to produce something we called the Council Digest, a summary in English of the addresses given that day. I was paired with another priest, so we each took notes on a set of talks—say somebody took the first, second, third and fourth, then we took the next four—and we would check each other's translation. We would translate and summarize the talk in English and we would check each other so that we would be sure that we would have a fairly accurate report of what was said. Immediately after the Council we'd go down to the National Catholic Welfare Conference (NCWC) office on Via della Conciliazione and type up our summaries, and they would then be put onto an old-fashioned mimeograph and duplicated and dispatched so that the bishops would have them before supper at their various places of residence around Rome. The Council Digest started with a circulation of less than two hundred—the American bishops—but by the end of the week we were up around nine hundred—the English-speaking bishops. Now English is the most spoken language in our church today. Somebody asks, "Qual'é la lingua più parlata nella chiesa d'oggi?" E la risposta é "Cattivo inglese!" ["What's the language spoken most in today's church?" And the reply is, "Bad English!"]

## How many sessions of the Council did you attend?

I imagine that really means "How many periods?" There were four periods; I attended all four periods.

## What was the most significant moment of the Council?

When Pope Paul VI returned from his visit to the United States and came immediately to the Council hall, walked up the center aisle, and delivered a very interesting and exciting report about his speech to the United Nations.

## Of all the documents of the Council, which one is the most significant one for you and why?

*Lumen gentium,* the dogmatic constitution on the nature of the church—it's the fundamental document of the Council. So many of the other documents are rooted in that one. Liturgy—although liturgy (*Sacrosanctum concilium*) came before it in time, it really has its roots in the theology of *Lumen gentium.* And ecumenism, certainly—*Unitatis redintegratio* is related to it. And many other documents, on the office of bishops and so on.

## What's the most important teaching that came out of the Council?

The affirmation of collegiality. Vatican I had put the spotlight on the office of Peter. The Second Vatican Council enlarged the light so that we looked at the other successors of the apostles.

## Who do you feel was the most significant figure at the Council?

That's a hard one to answer. In many ways, Pope Paul VI, who was very significant. Pope John XXIII, who called the Council, was pope when the questions were asked. Pope Paul VI was pope when the questions were answered. Other people had very prominent roles: Cardinal [Leo Joseph] Suenens [1904–1996]—although he was not the chair of a conciliar commission, I used to think that his interventions were worth several hundred votes because he spoke with such eloquence. Cardinal [Augustin] Bea [1881–1968], also, was a profoundly influential speaker at the Council; he marshaled real scholarship in the talks that he delivered. But there were others, too, who did outstanding work at the Council.

## What was the most significant statement from the Council and why?

Well, I go back and say *Lumen gentium* was the most significant, but under that I would mention also *Nostra aetate*, because it really changed the church's attitude toward the Jewish people. It was profoundly significant in that fashion.

## What has happened that you never imagined would happen?

The broad acceptance of the major liturgical changes. Initially, one wondered how quickly or well these would be received by the people. Now they were received, actually, very quickly, sometimes superficially. We still have an immense amount of work to do in order to help all of us understand what liturgy calls us to do and to be, but the fact is that the liturgical aspects of the various conciliar decisions went around the world very fast.

## What hasn't happened?

I say what hasn't occurred is the internalization of the theology of the Council. I have yet to see people in general, especially the popular press, acknowledge the contributions of *Lumen gentium* to the life of the church. That would also be true of the theology of liturgy. I don't think it's fully understood by many of the people.

## Is there any issue you regret that the Council did not address?

I can't say that anything comes to my mind, because we have to look at where we were in history at that time, and I think the Council tried to look at the issues that presented themselves then.

## What has been the most significant liturgical achievement, and what do we yet need to do to implement full, conscious and active participation?

That's hard for me to say because I think liturgical life is still evolving, and to say that we have achieved something in a final fashion is, I think, to be deceiving ourselves. We are still looking for the right way, especially in the English language, to try and capture some of the mystery and some of the depth of the great prayers of our liturgy. Music is getting better, we can say that. We went through a period in which the music left a lot to be desired.

## In your opinion, should there be a third Vatican Council, and what topic or topics would you bring to the table?

We are not yet ready for a third Vatican Council. We'd be more ready if we had more agreement with our friends in the Orthodox family of churches, because they are potential members of a Council. But there still has to be some distance traveled before we're ready to sit down at the same conciliar table with them. It would be a great day to see a return of full eucharistic Communion.

## What Council teaching was most difficult to implement in the local churches?

I would say again the teaching of full participation in the liturgy. It's difficult because many were not ready for a lot of the changes that were made. I remember eucharistic ministers, Communion in the hand, and people enormously upset by both of those steps; it took much explanation, and I'm not quite sure whether it's all yet been received by the church.

## Is there any special historical or cultural significance that Vatican II occurred in the 1960s? Could it have happened earlier, later, in your opinion?

The 1960s came after the end of the pontificate of Pope Pius XII, who really prepared the way for Vatican II with his great documents on the liturgy, on the biblical texts and on *Corporis Christi Mystici*, which for the first time brought the Scriptures into a formal discussion of ecclesiology in a very vibrant, vital way. I would observe that the Council occurred just at the time that the Vietnam War was beginning to make an impact, and I remember that there was some criticism of the Council, of the costs of it. But I discovered that the whole Council cost what it cost the United States to participate in the Vietnam War for eight hours. That's the kind of figures that one could have available. Now, that Vietnam War also had a profound impact on how the Council was received, because so many people were upset by that and by changes going on in the culture with the introduction of television and instant communications. I'd say that what we learned is that we could find out if we had a pain someplace in the system, but never get that pain in context. It was always a pain that hurt, but you couldn't see whether it was a cancer or a hangnail. It was just not possible because of the way in which the communications functioned then.

**Is there any shaping, formative memory that you find keeps on coming back to you?**

A beautiful memory was the daily procession up the aisle [of the basilica] with the open Book of the Gospels, which was enthroned. (I understand this went back to the Council of Constance, when there was the question as to who should preside: the pope, the ecumenical patriarch or the emperor; so they resolved that the Book of the Gospels would preside.) And then we'd say the prayer together to the Holy Spirit. That summarizes the Council for me. I have another vision of the final working session, December 7, 1965, when there were television cameras all over the place, and I said "My, what an enormous challenge this is." The final working session of the Council, in which the bishops voted on some things, could be transmitted instantly, but the message which is going into the television camera is not being transmitted, could not be.

**You had to be there?**

Yes.

**Is there anything else that you would want people to know?**

The thing that I would say, and I have said this often, is that I have read a great deal written about the Second Vatican Council, but what I read does not really catch the spirit or the detail of the Council, because it was written by reporters who were not part of the conciliar process. They were looking more for conflict and division than they were for what was going on, which was the development of a consensus as the bishops spoke and listened to each other. So what you have at the end of the Council are sixteen documents that represent a broad consensus of the bishops on key issues facing the church today, and the consensus was overwhelming in every case; but you wouldn't know that to read the news accounts. [The arrival at consensus] is the way it's been at our Councils—you look at Vatican I and you see that their definitions were so carefully crafted and so limited in order to have a consensus of the Council fathers. And I see the same thing in our World Synod of Bishops, or at least an effort at it.

William Henry Keeler was ordained a priest for the diocese of Harrisburg in 1955. He completed the License in Theology at the Gregorian University in Rome in 1956, and returned to the Gregorian two years later to study canon law. After receiving the J.C.D. in 1961, he served as a parish priest and as defender of the bond in the Harrisburg diocesan tribunal. Bishop George Leech brought then-Father Keeler to the Vatican Council. In 1964 Keeler became pastor of Our Lady of Good Counsel, Marysville, Pennsylvania, where he had served as an assistant pastor. He continued his work in the tribunal, becoming chancellor of the diocese and then vicar general. In 1979 he was ordained bishop, and served as an auxiliary until 1984, when he was installed as the seventh bishop of Harrisburg. In 1989 he became archbishop of Baltimore, and was created cardinal in 1994. Long active in ecumenical and interreligious dialogue, he is a member of the Pontifical Commission for Promoting Christian Unity and the Pontifical Council for Inter-Religious Dialogue.

# Archbishop Piero Marini

## Interviewer: Aurelio Porfiri

Transcribed by Marina Madeddu

**Could you tell us what you were doing during the Council?**

During the first part of the Council, I was still a seminarian, but in the last months of the Council, as a priest, I had the good fortune to work here in Rome, in the Santa Marta Residence in Vatican City. The various Council Secretariats were all located there, including the *Consilium ad Exequendam Constitutionem de Sacra Liturgia*, which guided the implementation of the liturgical reform. I began to work in the *Consilium* at the end of September 1965. Walking through St. Peter's Square on the way to Santa Marta every day, I would meet the bishops either going to the Council sessions in the morning or coming out at one o'clock. During this time at the *Consilium* in Santa Marta, we also met with the bishops of the Council who were members of the *Consilium*. So during that period I breathed the air of the Council, even though I never entered the council hall during its sessions. I remember once looking into the door of the basilica out of curiosity, but I did not more than that, because I was a young priest, only 23 years old, and I was still a little timid about this important event.

## And what do you remember in particular related to those years— a person, an event, an atmosphere?

Most of all, I remember the expectations for this great renewal in the church. Perhaps because I was young, I was so enthusiastic about the Ecumenical Council. There were many challenges facing the church. There was the question of the renewal of the liturgy: For four hundred years it had been fixed in its language and in rubrics. There was excitement about dialogue with the world and ecumenical dialogue. There was a strongly felt need for renewed contact with the word of God. The openness of the Council in dealing with these issues made for great enthusiasm, expectation and hope for renewal. I was impressed particularly by the Constitution on the Sacred Liturgy (*Sacrosanctum concilium*), not only because it was the first document issued by the Council but also because it set the tone for everything the Council did afterwards.

## Following the Council's reform of the liturgy there were great expectations for renewal, but also serious problems, among them a great opposition to the liturgy reform among certain groups. In your opinion, why did this happen? Was it because they did not understand *Sacrosanctum concilium* or because some people went beyond its spirit in applying it, or because of prejudice, or for some other reasons?

First of all, we have to take a closer look at the problem: the difficulties in the implementation of *Sacrosanctum concilium* at the time, and the difficulties that exist today. The first were serious, but they were all overcome, primarily because the liturgical reform was approved by all the Council's bishops (2,147 bishops voted in favor of the document, and only four against). All these bishops, especially those who came from afar, gave their approval to the reform. So the reform became possible.

The *schema* of the Constitution was the only one which was not rejected; essentially it was approved because it had been preceded by fifty years of the liturgical movement, of people's involvement in the liturgy, of scholarly studies, of experiences (e.g., [Lambert] Beauduin's experience in the monasteries, [Odo] Casel's work in theology, [Romano] Guardini's experience with young people). So the liturgical movement had matured and had already borne fruit in the reforms of Pope Pius XII. True, there were difficulties, especially on the part of those attached to the Tridentine liturgy. The institution most linked to the Tridentine liturgy was the Congregation for the Rites, which was founded in 1588 to defend the unity of the Tridentine liturgy. The Council of Trent had stressed unity because it was the most important problem for the church at that time; the church's unity and identity found expression in the liturgy through a unity of language and rubrics from which no deviation was permitted. So the greatest opposition came from that Congregation. At the same time, though, the Second Vatican Council was moving toward the concept of pluralism and toward an understanding of diversity within unity, a diversity expressed in a variety of languages and options for adaptation.

**After the Council many things were done away with, for example, candelabras and liturgical books, to say nothing of liturgical music. The Council never suggested throwing away the past to create something new, yet in some quarters the past was considered irrelevant. Did this attitude contribute to a sort of distrust in some groups at the Council? In your opinion, does this attitude belong to that period or does it still have consequences for today?**

Here, too, we have to understand clearly the situation, to pin it down. I have said that the Council was open to a new way of thinking and a liturgy capable of adaptation and more flexible rubrics. After four hundred years of being chained to the rubrics, there was a certain euphoria resulting from newfound freedom, but this was understandable. Pius X had earlier reformed sacred music, but this was still in the Tridentine pattern. The real reforms were those of Pius XII concerning Holy Week; they were marked by a new style closer to that of the Council. The real change in rubrics, especially in the complex rubrics for celebrations by bishops, took place with the Council and this created a euphoria for the new. The first years of the liturgical reform were characterized by great change. True, sometimes participation turned into "participationism," and change turned into "changing for the sake of change," "doing for the sake of doing." It is clear that in all this movement, in all this enthusiasm, the pace of change led to certain exaggerations.

## Could we call it "youthful impetuousness?"

A "youthful impetuousness" which was understandable because it had been pent up for so long. Especially in the area of church decoration, and sometimes also in architecture, it led to some unfortunate decisions. As for architecture, we realized after a number of years that, for example, insufficient space was being given to essential elements of the celebration. Some things had been improvised, for example, altars facing the people, the celebrant's position, and the ambo.

Then improvisation became the rule, and this was not good. For example, we did not really appreciate the ambo; there was a lectern and that was all. Nowadays we understand that we need a more significant symbolism for the place where the Word of God is read. There were many new elements as a consequence of the sudden changes.

As for music, we had beat [folk] music, the introduction of guitars. There, too, we saw some exaggeration at times. I remember the beat Masses in Rome, which were severely criticized by some groups and highly praised by others who felt that this music was able to bring back young people to the church, to the liturgy. Some traces of the beat Masses are still with us; for example, the "*Padre nostro* (Our Father)" by Giombini can be heard in Rome's parish churches, and I personally like it. Needless to say, the passage of time set the situation back in a proper perspective.

As for our present problems? Some people still keep looking back to the past and mistakes that were made; we have to stop crying over spilt milk, roll up our sleeves and create something of lasting value. It happened that at times the fixed elements of the celebration (the ambo, the altar and so on) were needlessly changed. True, sometimes music found expressions that were not always appropriate for the celebration, but it is useless to keep criticizing the past. We need to devote our energies today to improving the liturgy. Today we need to stress quality.

**You have spoken about adaptation, an important concept related to inculturation. *Sacrosanctum concilium* states that adaptation is allowed, except in the essential element of the eucharistic celebration. Can you tell us what is this essential element of eucharistic celebration that is not possible to adapt?**

To answer this, we need to understand the spirit of liturgy. If we do not understand the nature of the liturgy, we cannot understand what is primary and what is secondary. *Sacrosanctum concilium* set forth two fundamental principles for understanding the nature of the liturgy. First, there is the Word of God, not only as something to be listened to but as something to be interiorized, and also as the norm for understanding and renewing the liturgy. The liturgy is based on the Word of God. This relationship between liturgy and the Word is funda-mental for an understanding of the nature of the liturgy: Everything present in the Holy Scriptures is brought about or accomplished in the liturgy. This is important for understanding liturgy today. The second principle is that of a return to the tradition of the Fathers of the Church. This means that in every age the liturgy finds its model in the celebrations of the patristic period, in the liturgy as a celebration of Christ's paschal mystery in its entirety. When we return to the tradition of the Fathers, we discover the simplicity of the liturgy, its so-called "noble simplicity." All the other elements stand in relation to this.

## So what is the essential element?

The main thing is to understand that the mystery of our redemption is accomplished in the liturgy. What was brought about in the Scriptures is carried out today in the signs of the liturgy. An essential aspect of the liturgy is the Word of God, hence the structure of the Liturgy of the Word. Another essential element is the presentation of the gifts, hence the elements of the eucharistic prayer, the breaking of the bread and Communion. These essential elements cannot be changed, because they are in the tradition of the apostles and the Fathers of the Church who gave us the liturgy. Liturgy is not something to be invented ever anew. Even when it is renewed, liturgy continues to be something that we have received from the past. That is why we went back to the beginning: to have a simpler liturgy. The Council states that other elements, later "deposits" that obscured the original spirit of the liturgy, are to be abandoned, in order to rediscover the celebration. We have to be immersed in the spirit of the liturgy.

Together with this basic idea of the liturgy as the actualization of the mystery of our redemption, the Council stressed the inseparable unity between the descending movement of sanctification and the ascending movement of worship, the centrality of the paschal mystery, and the presence of Christ in his church and, in a special way, in the liturgy. The presence of Christ in the celebrating community is certainly one of the major themes of *Sacrosanctum concilium*: In the liturgy it is the whole assembly that celebrates. This is obvious: An assembly is made up of lay people, of those who possess the baptismal priesthood, and of those who also possess the ministerial priesthood; but they are the one people of God that journeys through history and makes its way toward the Lord who continues to work his wonders among us as in the journey of the Exodus. Certainly in this journey there will be moments of nostalgia, as there were for the ancient people of Israel, and moments of difficulty and trial, but God is always there to lead us. The liturgy and its signs help us to make our way toward the Kingdom.

**If you could sum up in few words the most important statement of the Council, what would you say? What really important thing did the Council leave us?**

I think it is the rediscovery of the church as the people of God, because here once again we see the great relationship between church and the liturgy. And in my opinion, in spite of what some theologians may say, *Sacrosanctum concilium* remains the most important document of the Council because it set the tone for the Council and for all the other documents. It presented a concept of the church that we find again in *Lumen gentium*, where perhaps it is set forth more clearly than in *Sacrosanctum concilium*; it showed us the church as a community which must be open to the Lord, a community of prayer and the praise of God. So in my opinion *Sacrosanctum concilium* was the heart of the Ecumenical Council, even as liturgical celebration is the heart of the church.

**For many years you have been Master of Papal Liturgical Celebrations. How have papal liturgical celebrations adapted to the spirit of the liturgical reform? What has been changed, what has been kept of the old style?**

The liturgical reform was proposed in a spirit of fraternal and expert collaboration among the center, the *Consilium* and experts from all over the world. Then, in a second stage, it was implemented in the local churches. This second stage of the conciliar reform also took place in papal liturgical celebrations. The adaptation was carried out by Monsignor [Annibale] Bugnini, who, for three years, from 1967–1969, was responsible for the Office of Papal Liturgical Celebrations. In those years the spirit and the form of the new liturgy entered into the papal celebrations. For example, I remember the altar *versus populi* (toward people) only in the Sistine Chapel.

I remember the first celebration of the new Rite of Baptism by Pope Paul VI in Colombia. The Holy Father's apostolic journeys showed the world that the papal liturgy was also being adapted to the new liturgy. Here certain ceremonial aspects were eliminated: the *flabella* (fan), the tiara and the great procession that preceded the pope's entrance even during the Council, which seemed more like the entrance of a worldly ruler than an image of Christ in the church. So there was a process of adaptation. Certainly the papal liturgy differs from other episcopal liturgies. For example, here in Rome we have the Conferral of the *Pallium*, which is a typically papal rite. We have canonizations, beatifications, celebrations of the consistory, important ecumenical celebrations, all of which take place only with the pope. These celebrations were all adapted, and some ancient and forgotten rites were restored, such as the *Resurrexit* rite on Easter Sunday [veneration of the *Acheiropita* icon by the pope] or the *Kalenda* [proclamation of the birth of Christ] at Christmas midnight Mass. So there is a richer liturgy in the celebrations here in Rome; but it is also a liturgy characterized by adaptation because the pope, in his worldwide travels, includes in his liturgies those elements that are expressions of the local churches wherever the pope celebrates. You can see this in every papal trip.

**There are those who say that many people who come to papal celebrations are there to see the pope and not to attend Mass. Do you agree? How can one involve people in this kind of celebration, when the presence of the pope is, in some sense, a media event?**

This is one of the problems with papal liturgies. Many people come to see the pope. Some of them come out of curiosity, but the majority of them are believers who see in the pope the sign of the communion and unity of the whole church. If it is true that at times more attention seems to be being paid to an individual than to the mystery, on the other hand this individual, the pope, helps us to discover the mystery of the church, and to discover, above and beyond our small assembly, a greater one, which is the communion of the whole church, with all the saints. Hence the almost palpable sense of communion which is evident in papal celebrations. Clearly, we need to work at putting the stress more on the celebration, on what happens inside, on what is invisible than on what is visible, because that is much more important in the celebration. It is the spirit, the presence of Christ in the liturgy, which influences all that we do.

**You have been all over the world with the pope, so you have seen many celebrations. In the spirit of the implementation of the liturgical reform, is there a celebration you remember most, or a country in which you found a greater reception of the liturgical reform, a greater zeal?**

It is very hard to make comparisons, because every country is different from the others. But I have to say that during all these years I have had moments of great personal and spiritual satisfaction, because I have seen the fruits of the Council in so many countries: participation, the sense of being church, openness to God's Word, the many expressions—including physical, bodily gestures as in Africa—and the joy of being Christian, of celebrating Eucharist, the presence of Christ. I remember the Holy Father's visit to the United States in 1987; that, for me, was also a chance to discover the quality of celebrations in United States, from which we in Italy have much to learn—for example, the artistic quality of buildings and of furnishings.

## Also the attention to music.

Most of all I noticed the attention given to music. In the United States there is a greater sensitivity to music than we have here, and this is an important element in helping to discover the mystery. Singing and music, when it is suitable, help us to transcend the immediately visible and to discover the working of the Spirit within us and in our midst. I was also impressed by the orderliness of the assembly, which reflected the ordering of the people of God in the celebration of the liturgy.

## Could you say something more about music? For example, what is the role today of Gregorian chant, which the church acknowledges as her own proper music?

Gregorian chant is nowhere in the world more present than in papal celebrations—partly because we are in Rome, but most of all because we have an assembly made up of different cultures and different languages, so we make use of those elements which can build communion. In the Ordinary of the Mass, Gregorian chant is still an element of cohesion, one that brings people together. For popular participation we tend to choose the simpler Masses.

## The more famous ones.

Yes. Unfortunately, it is hard to add other Gregorian Masses. Sometimes we try to do it, especially when there are large numbers of priests or bishops present, but it is not always easy. But it is still the main element in our celebrations.

## Outside of the Vatican, what is the role of Gregorian chant?

I think that with the liturgical reform it tended to be neglected; as a result of the sense of novelty and renewal, not enough attention was paid to it. There was a book, *Jubilate Deo*, which strongly urged the occasional celebration of a Gregorian or Latin Mass, or at least some parts of one, on Sundays in parish churches or at the least in cathedrals, in order to preserve this richness, which builds up the communion and the unity of the church. I have to say that, unfortunately, this element has been lost. It would be easier for us in Saint Peter's if all the people who came here knew Gregorian chant, because we would have a more united assembly.

**Could this also have been caused by the fact that for some reason (more in Latin countries than in the Anglo-Saxon and northern European ones) there was an opposition to using professional, trained musicians?**

Dilettantism did not help improve the quality of liturgical music. I agree with you completely. This is what happened everywhere. In the Anglo-Saxon and northern European countries, there is a deeply-rooted tradition of singing. We have to thank our Protestant brothers and sisters who preserved this great treasure, and so Catholics held on to it also. Even now there are some good sung Gregorian Masses, Masses celebrated with music of a high artistic quality. I am not saying that all Masses have to be celebrated this way, but at least some Masses still expressed a genuine, popular musical culture. Here in Italy, unfortunately, we were unable to preserve this musical tradition, since at the time of the liturgical reform most church music was late nineteenth-century music, with a number of devotional hymns to the Blessed Virgin Mary. This was fine for that time, but it did not have a strong tradition behind it.

**On the other hand, these devotional hymns to the Blessed Virgin Mary continue to involve people (especially in Italy), even today. Why is that? Does it have something to do with the way the liturgical reform was implemented?**

If we have to assign responsibility, we have to turn to those responsible for the liturgy: first, priests, and second, musicians. We need to work together to create that church of communion which the Council set before us. Priests, bishops and musicians must aspire to creating and working for a noble liturgy, to creating new forms together with old ones, forms marked by nobility and content, forms worthy of being offered to God's people. The people of God want to sing music of perennial value, not trendy or occasional pieces. We need to have the courage to provide more significant offerings. And there are good texts and good choral music. I think that time will improve the quality of our music. Here in Italy the problem is that we have lost our taste for church music: we sing in the streets, but not in church.

**In your opinion, could not the passage from Latin to the vernacular have been more gradual, in order to avoid the traumatic loss of a language that for centuries was the language of the liturgy?**

These are things we can think about with a certain regret, but today we are dealing with a quite different reality. Today Latin is a dead language, a language limited to a few experts. I do agree that most of all in cathedrals there should be, for example, on Sundays a Latin or Gregorian Mass, with readings in the national language, while the Ordinary of the Mass and the eucharistic prayer can be sung in Gregorian chant. I agree with that, but thinking of a return to Latin on a large scale is completely unrealistic.

**If you had the chance, what would you do in concrete terms to improve the active, full and conscious participation of believers?**

First of all, we need to pay attention to the problem of liturgical education, of teaching people to understand the nature of the liturgy—to go from "doing" to "understanding" and "experiencing." In the beginning, the liturgical reform was concerned with the translation of texts, explanations and so on. Today we must be guided by the celebration itself. Now that the reform is finished, we must think more of the essence than the "mechanics" of the celebration. This does not mean we should not be prepared. We need to be prepared, especially spiritually prepared. To do this we have also to pay attention to the quality of our celebrations. Today we can no longer improvise celebrations: we need quality in music, in signs. First of all, the signs are the assembly—when we gather, the assembly is the first sign of the church—the Word of God, the manner of reading the Word of God and how that Word is received by each of us. We need to emphasize the visible signs that speak of our identity and roots as Christians. If we do not see the baptismal font as the womb from which we were born as Christians, if we do not see the ambo as the place where we receive the Word of God, if we do not have veneration for the altar.

I have to say that sometimes I miss the early period of the liturgical renewal, which brought with it any number of disasters, but was at the same time filled with so much enthusiasm and hope for the liturgy. We need to return to the study of the liturgy. As I said before, *Sacrosanctum concilium* was possible because there had been fifty years of studies and experience of saintly men, some of whom I was fortunate to meet—[Balthasar] Fischer, [J.] Pascher, [Bernard] Botte, [Josef] Jungmann, [Cipriano] Vagaggini, [A.G.] Martimort—who dedicated their entire lives to the liturgy. So today we cannot lose the heritage of the past. If we want good liturgy, first of all we must study the liturgy and secondly, we must go back to the spiritual aspect, the aspect of enthusiasm, the aspect of the quality of signs. How? We should start in the seminaries. But that is the question: How is liturgy being taught in the seminaries? How are new priests being educated?

In a sense, the crisis of the church today is a crisis of the liturgy, because the liturgy and the church are two realities that are almost identical. If we do not see in liturgy the reference point, the source from which the church receives grace, strength and help, and if we do not see in liturgy the goal of all our activity, we are wasting our time. It is important that everyone be convinced of the relationship between the study of the liturgy and the life of the church. The Council said that the liturgy is the first and indispensable source from which the faithful can derive the true Christian spirit (SC 14). We need to put this into practice.

### Some people have proposed a third Vatican Council. Do you think this could be a possible solution? If so, which problems involving the liturgy could be faced first?

Until now we have been talking about the positive aspects of the liturgy and about the difficulties of the liturgy following the Second Vatican Council. In my opinion, if we recognize that these difficulties exist and that we have not yet communicated the vision of the Second Vatican Council to everyone, how can we think of a third Vatican Council? Remember the problems we had at the beginning of the liturgy reform, when everything was activity, movement, and change. Only later did we begin to reflect, discern. Can we really think that a new Council will solve the problem? In my opinion, it is important to continue to return to Vatican II, which perhaps we have neglected, and to implement not only its outward forms but also its profound insights and recommendations, and to participate in the liturgy with our lives. In the liturgy each of us celebrates, but to celebrate means to change and redirect our life; otherwise we are performing an empty rite. Unless there is this correspondence between life and liturgy, we will not have the liturgy desired by the Council.

### What is the liturgy's future? Where is liturgy going?

This is how I see the future of the liturgy: we are called to form real communities, to make participation in the liturgy an education in the "sense of the church," in the different ministries present in the people of God, to improve our ability to listen to the Word of God and to enter into the signs by which the liturgy speaks to us. Our liturgies should be marked by beauty and dignity, where its signs speak eloquently: the assembly, the Word, but also the environment of our churches. There is a space, an environment where Christians develop themselves; there is a place where Christians are born, and this is the church. Unless we make these signs, including music, a central part of our celebrations, we will not give Christians a chance to take a giant step forward, which can bring them to discover the beauty and the reality that is truly present in the liturgy.

Archbishop Piero Marini was born January 13, 1942 in Valverde, Italy, in the diocese of Piacenza-Bobbio. He was ordained a priest in 1965, and was private secretary to Archbishop Annibale Bugnini. Marini was appointed an official of the Roman Curia in 1998, the same year he was ordained bishop. He is the Papal Master of Ceremonies, Office for the Liturgical Celebration of the Supreme Pontiff, and travels with the pope throughout the world. He was appointed archbishop in 2003.

# Frederick R. McManus

## Interviewer: Sean M. McCarthy

In the daily exercise of our pastoral office, we sometimes have to listen, much to our regret, to voices of persons who, though burning with zeal, are not endowed with too much sense of discretion or measure. In these modern times they can see nothing but prevarication and ruin. They say that our era, in comparison with past eras, is getting worse and they behave as though they had learned nothing from history, which is, none the less, the teacher of life. They behave as though at the time of former councils everything was a full triumph for the Christian idea and life and for proper religious liberty.

We feel we must disagree with these prophets of doom, who are always forecasting disasters, as though the end of the world were at hand.

With these words, Pope John XXIII addressed the opening session of the Second Vatican Council. All who heard or read these words were given hope that the reform of the church was going to succeed.

Monsignor Frederick R. McManus was no exception.

In 1960, Monsignor Frederick R. McManus, a presbyter of the Archdiocese of Boston, was appointed a consultor for the Preparatory Commission for the Liturgy, leading up to the first session of the Council. The twenty-five consultors on the Preparatory Committee met several times in Rome from 1960 to 1962. In the summer of 1962, fifteen of the consultors were appointed *periti* (experts) to the Council and then assigned to a specific area or subcommittee. Monsignor McManus was assigned to the liturgy subcommittee.

As a *peritus*, Monsignor McManus had the wonderful vantage point of seeing the workings of the entire four sessions of the Council. He also served with others as a member of the Press Council serving the American press corps. Each day he would attend the Council session in the morning, and then spend some time meeting with the press corps fielding questions and searching out answers. The actual work of the liturgy commission (it met at the Catacombs of Priscilla in the outskirts of Rome) was done in the afternoon.

McManus praises the work of all the documents that emerged from the Council. The most important to his own heart is the Constitution on the Sacred Liturgy (*Sacrosanctum concilium*). Within this document there are groundbreaking moments: the shift to the vernacular, the call to a more active participation by all the faithful, the issue of inculturation, the restoration of the catechumenate, and the reform of all the rites. Not all of this was new; much of it was restoring to the liturgy our ancient ways of worshiping. Within this litany of titanic shifts, McManus devoted much to this endeavor in his role as a *peritus*.

The strength of the Constitution on the Sacred Liturgy according to Monsignor McManus, comes from the careful design of the document, which balances three items: 1) the doctrinal introductions to each section; 2) the areas that call us to do better that which we have been doing all along; and 3) the actual reforms and changes in the liturgical life of the church. It was done with great care and caution.

Monsignor McManus names several players who were key to ensuring the success of the liturgical reform at the Council: Josef Jungmann, who was able to cultivate votes behind the scenes; A.G. Martimort, who brought scholarly and pastoral perspectives to bear on the texts and the discussion; Bishop Paul Hallinan of Atlanta, the only American bishop on the commission; and Benedictine Father Godfrey Diekmann.

Not all was easy. There were many days of frustration and others of exhilaration. In a letter to Father Godfrey Diekmann (who had not yet been appointed to the commission), Monsignor McManus told of the fate of the *schema* on the liturgy:

> Having spent a ridiculous day of the usual ups and downs, I write to unburden my soul. The people here are more confused than ever. Hallinan is an excellent man and may well turn out to be a real hero. Vagnozzi told me yesterday with great glee that the liturgy constitution will have rough sailing.

The Germans are afraid that liturgy coming first may be fussed over too minutely even apart from die-hard opposition. But the decision to put it ahead of theology was evidently forced on the body of presidents by those who are utterly contemptuous of the theological *schema*. Karl Rahner, [Yves] Congar and [Henri] de Lubac are supposedly doing new *schema* as substitute.

Several months later, Monsignor McManus again wrote to Diekmann:

Generally speaking (and humanly speaking) I am hopeful so far as the *Patres conciliares* are concerned. My fears are mostly in our liturgical commission where the will of the pastoral bishops could be frustrated or delayed—and of course in the Curia, which would never implement the liturgical constitution. There seems to be a great hope that many of the bishops are having their eyes opened and that the passage of time is much on the side of acceptance of the liturgy constitution.

McManus admits to having been surprised at the battle over the vernacular—not that it happened, but how it happened. Those who were pushing for it were pejoratively labeled vernacularists. "At different moments the tide would shift in our favor, only the next day to hear of some defeat," he says. "Even after the first session of the Council, when it was clear to most that the vernacular debate had been won, there were some bishops who still didn't believe it."

"What most surprised me, and most others," McManus continues, "is the speed at which the vernacular took off. No one thought that it would happen so fast! It was as if the vote happened, and the vernacular was everywhere. It was wonderful! No one imagined it would or could happen that fast."

For McManus, there were several disappointments in the Council. While the Roman reform was good, it was full of compromises. McManus points to *Sacrosanctum concilium*'s attempt to deal with inculturation (SC 37–40). The approach of the commission and the Council was to leave the door wide open and see what could happen. "Since the Council, and most recently, our approach has been very weak." McManus continues, "The freedom to adapt culturally has all but been contradicted. It's a joke now. That's sad. What we have now was not the vision of the Council."

Another area of concern for McManus is found in *Gaudium et spes*. He offers that the Council did a good job on *Gaudium et spes*, but the commission working on it got underway very late in the process; it was rushed, and therefore their work was limited. He adds, "The document has good stuff in it but it could have been stronger, especially biblically and with regard to our contemporary situation in life. It needed more detail. Within *Gaudium et spes*, the topic of academic freedom is fostered. You don't hear this paragraph being quoted much anymore, especially in Catholic circles."

Looking ahead to the future of the church, aware of present difficulties within the liturgical movement, McManus is most hopeful. Asked about a future gathering of bishops in an Ecumenical Council, McManus states, "They will be addressing many of the same issues as they did before, but with more experience." His hopes for topics for future Council gatherings include the church's relation to culture. He says, "Take what the Asian bishops have done with this topic and go after that. There is wonderful work already being done by the Asian bishops."

Monsignor McManus also hopes the next Council will better address the "nature of the church." Topics such as subsidiarity, ecclesiology, the church's relation to other Christian churches, the whole topic of intercommunion—"all these need to be looked at again."

Another area that needs reexamining is the issue of inculturation. "Now more than ever we need to not be afraid of other cultures and learn from them. Back at the Council, the Melkite Patriarch, Maximos IV, gave a wonderful talk on collegiality in the East—how it worked, and how the West could learn from the East. He was all but ignored. He was right, though! This topic needs beefing up and we need to listen to our brothers and sisters in the East."

Frederick R. McManus, born in 1923, ordained in 1947 for the Archdiocese of Boston and later made a monsignor, was an instrumental player in the reform and the promotion of the liturgy in the days preceding the Council, during the Council and in the years following. He was invaluable in establishing the United States Bishops' Committee on the Liturgy (BCL). Along with Benedictine Father Godfrey Diekmann, Cardinal [Joseph] Cordeiro of Karachi, Cardinal [Gordon] Gray of Edinburgh and Archbishop [Denis] Hurley of Durban, McManus was one of the five founding members of the International Commission on English in the Liturgy (ICEL). He was helpful in the foundation of the North American Academy of Liturgy (NAAL) and the Federation of Diocesan Liturgical Commissions (FDLC), which named its annual award in his honor. Until recent years, McManus was the staff consultant to the BCL, being the link from the Council to the present day.

# Bernard Olivier, OP

## Interviewer: Philip Sandstrom

### What was your capacity at the Council?

I was an expert (*peritus*) at the Council. I was authorized at the request of the bishops of the Congo in Africa; I worked specifically with and for the bishops of black Africa. At the time of the Council I was professor of moral theology at the Lovanium University at Kinshasa (once called Léopoldville) in the Congo. I was also theologian-counsellor for the bishops of the Congo.

### How many sessions of the Council did you attend?

I was present for the second, third and fourth sessions.

### What was the most significant moment at the Council for you?

It was certainly the discussion on religious liberty, because it is a theme on which I had taught and published. A collective work in which I participated, *Tolérance et communauté humaine*, published by Casterman in 1952, had attracted the attention and disapproval of the Holy Office, so I was particularly delighted to see that the Council took up our ideas and used them.

## Of all the documents of the Council, which one is most significant for you and why?

The constitution *Lumen gentium*, because it presents a way of looking at the church that is at the same time both more modern and more biblical: The church is essentially the people of God. And more particularly, the place given in this document to the laity as a central fact of the church. For the first time the laity are defined in a positive manner and not just as non-clergy.

## What is the most important teaching that came out of the Council?

For myself, it is the concrete, lived experience of the Council. I could not fail to notice how the Holy Spirit leads the church, not by revelations—no bishop came in on a day and said, "Last night I had a revelation"—but by the very human and face-to-face confrontation, even conflict, of different opinions.

## Whom do you feel was the most significant figure at the Council?

There were a number of significant figures. Among the cardinals and bishops who emerged strongly in my opinion were Cardinal Leo Joseph Suenens [1904–1996] and Cardinal Giacomo Lercaro [1891–1976] (who would have been my candidate for pope). But also among the experts, Monsignor Gerard Philips [1899–1972] was one of the most effective. And it is necessary to cite some well known (and prior to the Council, suspect) theologians: [Dominicans] Yves Congar, and Marie-Dominique Chenu.

## What was the most significant statement from the Council and why?

For me there are two very important fundamental documents, *Lumen gentium* and *Gaudium et spes*.

*Lumen gentium* is important because it presents a theology of the church that is more modern and better adapted to the present times. Traditionally there was the idea, taken from St. Robert Bellarmine [1542–1621], of the church as a perfect society. It was perfect and visible; it was quite clear who was a member and who was not; and for many, the church was, before anything else, its hierarchy.

In *Lumen gentium*, there is a new image of the church: First off, it is a mystery. It is necessary to approach it as such. It is essentially the people of God, wherein the hierarchy is put in its proper context. The laity are considered full members of the church, and they are called to holiness. This gives a renewed and more faithful image for the church.

*Gaudium et spes* is important because this document tries to give a Christian vision of the world, and of the relations between the church and the world. There is respect shown for human values, for temporal values.

I would add, among the other documents, the Declaration on Religious Liberty (*Dignitatis humanae*). It affirms a fundamental human right. It gives some general norms to help our approach to many modern problems and emphasizes the decisive role of personal conscience in the resolution of these problems. Of course, the personal conscience must be well-informed, and not just whimsical.

### Is there any issue you regret that the Council did not address?

I was for twenty years a professor of moral theology, and I note the absence of a consistent Christian anthropology. We live torn between two anthropologies—the one Hebraic and the other Greek—and it is very difficult to reconcile them. For example, there is an ambiguity about the notion of "flesh" and the "carnal man," according to Saint Paul (cf. 1 Corinthians 3, Romans 8, and so on). The Council should have asked for a profound study of this problem, which many Christian moralists do not seem to grasp as important.

### What has been the most significant liturgical achievement and what do we yet need to do to implement full, conscious and active participation?

The most significant achievements have been connected with liturgy in the local living languages. This promotes the more active participation of the faithful laity. The expansion of the Lectionary also has made the Bible more accessible to them. But it is now necessary to look again and more closely at:

- the idea of the Sunday community, and the grave obligation to assist at Sunday Mass;

- the manner of the active participation of the faithful laity, with more detail as to their precise and diverse functions; and

- the possibility of varied liturgical styles, especially for young people, with an opening for a larger resourcefulness without sacrificing the essentials.

## What has not happened since the Council?

A schism, which many feared, has not happened. That of Monsignor (later Archbishop) Marcel Lefebvre [1905–1991] and his followers [the Society of Saint Pius X] took place much after the Council, and for other historically linked reasons.

## In your opinion, should there be a third Vatican Council, and what topics would you bring to the table?

If a third Vatican Council were to happen sometime soon, among the topics to bring up would be:

- bioethics, in the largest sense of the word: artificial insemination, embryos outside the womb, contraception and euthanasia. Notably it would be urgent to distinguish clearly between contraception and abortion; most of the documents of the magisterium continue to mix them up.

- from the pastoral point of view: a reorganization of the system of parishes based solely on geographic divisions, which does not respond to the conditions of modern life.

- a serious examination of the pastoral approach to divorced and remarried people.

- the problems connected with the access of women to the ministries.

## Is there any special historical or cultural significance that the Second Vatican Council occurred in the 1960s? Could it have happened earlier or later, in your opinion?

Thanks to the Holy Spirit and Pope John XXIII, the Council was called at a ripe time in history. Most of the trauma of the World War was over; there was generally peace, calm and prosperity; and there were many problems facing the church and the world—times were changing. Later came many upheavals and changes in politics, civil and scientific advances, and many other questions, which the church was better prepared to face, and is still facing.

Bernard Olivier OP was born in 1920 and entered the Dominicans in Belgium. He made his studies in Philosophy in Belgium and in France (Le Saulchoir, and the École Practique des Hautes Études de Paris). He received the Doctorate in Theology from Le Saulchoir in 1947. He has been Professor of Moral Theology at Le Sarte-Huy (the Belgian Dominican house of studies), at the Louvanium University (Kinshasa, Congo), and at Saint Louis University and Lumen Vitae (Brussels, Belgium). He was a *peritus* at the Second Vatican Council. He was the Provincial of the Dominicans in Belgium and was an assistant to the Master General of the Dominicans in Rome (1974–1985). In Belgium he was theological advisor to the National Commission of Justice and Peace (1968–1974) and to Caritas Catholica (1970–1974). He was International Spiritual Director for Équipes Notre-Dame (1985–1994). He has published numerous articles, and several books: *Christian Hope* (in several languages), *Développement ou Libération, Amour-Bonheur-Sainteté*, and about his experiences at the Council, *Chroniques Congolaises* (Paris, Éditions Karthala, 2002).

# Bishop Donald W. Trautman

## Interviewer: Conrad Kraus

**How many sessions of the Council did you attend?**

I was in Rome as a graduate priest studying at the Biblicum and also study-ing at St. Thomas Aquinas University. So I was present from 1964 to 1966—three sessions of the Council—and it was an exciting time for me to be present. At the Council I was assigned to a section of bishops; perhaps sixty to seventy-five bishops were in my section. I was responsible to give them the ballots, to pass out the information and *schemas*, to help them in coming to the microphone to address the Council, and to collect their votes on the various documents.

An Italian bishop who sat along side of me would fall asleep. He was a retired bishop and couldn't handle the long Latin speeches, so when it came time to vote I would have to wake him up. He would say, "How should I vote?" They had three choices on the cards: *placet* (I approve), *non placet* (I do not approve), or *placet iuxta modum* (I approve according to a certain degree, certain reserva-tion). And I would say, "Put down *placet*." So he was the one person I could coach to vote, and so in a certain sense I think I voted at Vatican II although I was not a bishop.

I would collect the ballots and take them to Cardinal [John] Krol [1910–1996], who was the general secretary. We would pass out all of the *schemas* and all of the documents to the bishops. My position—a menial task of acting

203

like a substitute secretary—gave me the opportunity to be in the first row of the Council to see all that was going on.

I remember how the bishops carried the Bible in procession every day down the center aisle of the basilica and how they would incense the Scripture. This was how they opened their sessions. I was two feet away from that procession; I had sixty to seventy-five bishops behind me, and I would walk them down the tiered level, talk to them, answer their questions, escort them to the microphone, pass out notes to them from the media: that was my job. But it gave me an opportunity to be on the ground floor to hear every single word of Vatican II. I saw up close the human dimension: bishops and cardinals waiting in line for coffee—a blind bishop being escorted each day into the Council by another bishop, and so on.

## What was the most significant moment at the Council for you?

I remember that the Council was deadlocked over the revelation *schema* that had been passed out and the Holy Father, Paul VI at that time, asked that the *schema* on revelation be withdrawn and be worked on again. I thought that was a powerful move. Pope Paul VI had great insights in that regard. There were churchmen with theology from the days of Trent who were lobbying against the reform of Vatican II. It was pretty much a showdown: The Curia officials had submitted *schema* after *schema* reflecting that mentality or that theological outlook. It was only the pope, by the power of his office, who said, "No—let's call it back in and send it back to the drafting committee and resubmit it to the bishops." I had heard the speeches in which a number of the prelates (especially from France and Germany) spoke up strongly against the prepared *schema*. Obviously the pope was hearing those same remarks as well. So I praise the Holy Spirit who was present at Vatican II; the Holy Spirit did breathe new life into the church. However, it was the presence of the pope who had the wisdom and courage to intervene and move the Council forward. Some church people did not want to read the signs of the times; they wanted to keep the church as it was (in a museum—a relic of the past), and the pope was saying "No—we must break out of the museum, face the modern world, and bring the church into the marketplace."

## Which of the documents of the Council is most significant to you?

Well, as we know, the Constitution on the Liturgy (*Sacrosanctum concilium*) was the first document that was finalized, and the theology contained in that document influenced many of the other documents. The Constitution on Divine Revelation (*Dei verbum*) is a key document as well, but we have to recognize that the Constitution on the Sacred Liturgy and the theology it contained certainly influenced the document on the church itself. It described the church as the people of God. The Constitution on the Sacred Liturgy talked about their active participation, which led to a deeper understanding of the church and to a new ecclesiology.

*Dei verbum* was a major document that the bishops worked on. Again, it set the theological framework for the Council. And keep in mind the big debate that took place on the Council floor, and the pope's intervention. Several of the Council fathers wanted to define revelation as merely tradition. The document finally described revelation by turning to Christ as the one source of Scripture and tradition. When they came to defining "tradition," they talked about tradition as "all that the church is," "all that the church has," which would then tie in the entire historical legacy of the past. There is a big difference between "has" and "is." The progressives fought to say that the tradition is "all the church is," not "all that the church has." Thus we found a helpful distinction between "tradition" and "traditional." "Traditional" referred to all that the church has been through the years, but "tradition" is God-given, and that cannot change. "Traditional" must change. This was an important debate, and once that was ironed out on the Council floor the document on revelation was voted in. This sent tidal waves of change. The progressives certainly had won the day, and this would influence the *schemas* of other documents.

## Who was the most significant figure at the Council for you as a young priest?

Certainly Pope John XXIII because of the sheer magnetism of his personality and his wisdom and courage in calling the Council. I recall also Pope Paul VI. I remember going to receive my gift from him for working at the Council. We knelt down on the floor and kissed his ring. He did not attend all the sessions, but he had representatives who were there. Paul VI intervened when the Council was gridlocked, and he had the wisdom to remove items from the Council floor and to send them back to committee so that a greater consensus would result. He gave direction, and that saved the day.

## Didn't you see Monsignor [Annibale] Bugnini around there?

I saw him there often consulting people. The real work of Vatican II in my mind did not take place on the floor. You have to remember that every night the Council fathers met to hear famous speakers: Karl Rahner, Josef Jungmann, and so on. They heard the best, and they got together in the evenings. They asked tough questions and there was truly a turnaround in those evening sessions. I remember well participating and listening.

I almost missed the opportunity to work at Vatican II. The request for certain priests to assist came to the graduate house at the North American College where I was in residence. I was writing my thesis—I had not finished my doctoral degree—and I didn't think I would have time. I always remembered some of my friends at the graduate house saying, "Don't miss this opportunity!" "You've been asked—go!" "Don't bypass that!" I worried that I would go back to Buffalo without my degree. Should I bypass the Council and work in the library on my thesis? But I was able to do both. Thank God I did go, and I thank those priests who persuaded me to take advantage of the opportunity.

I would like to go back to the evening sessions as a critical dimension of the Council. I saw the rapport of the bishops. They asked profound questions and openly dialogued. We saw bishops truly going through a change in thinking. You know, John Tracy Ellis prior to Vatican II asked the American bishops what they expected from Vatican II. He surveyed them about what they wanted to have accomplished at Vatican II, and for the most part it was only to be a tinkering with canon law. No one was thinking big about Scripture and tradition, ecumenism or thinking about vernacular liturgy or reform of the liturgy. Tinkering with minor things was on the bishops' minds. They went through a real change of heart that could have only been effected by the Spirit. The American bishops did go through a real renewal and then were in the forefront of issues like religious freedom. As we know, all the Council fathers except four signed the Constitution on the Sacred Liturgy. There was overwhelming support for everything in the documents. The ramifications have been most impressive and far-reaching. Our bishops accomplished that, but I assure you that when they went to the Council they were not talking or thinking in such a manner.

I traveled with Bishop [Stanislaus] Brzana [1917–1997] of Ogdensburg, New York, during a time between the sessions. We went up to see my alma mater in Innsbruck, Austria. He leveled with me quite a bit about the thinking of some of the bishops. I was honored that he gave me his Latin speech that he was going to give at Vatican II; he asked me to check the Latin, which I did. So I was in close proximity with a lot of the Council fathers, with their thinking, with the interventions that they were making, and with the real changes of heart at Vatican II. This could come about only from the gift of the Spirit and the dynamic leadership of John XXIII.

**You mentioned that the bishops went to Rome thinking they would just tinker with things. What happened that you never imagined would happen?**

Well, I think of the progress that I have seen in the liturgy. Now I would like to see us take further steps; but I think we have been able to accomplish the dream of the Council fathers. I'm not sure all the bishops really understood the ramifications of the documents, especially the Constitution on the Sacred Liturgy. But the principles are there. The principles have been lifted out now and put into reformed documents, which have brought about the vernacular and the full, conscious and active participation of our people.

That is most significant. What I have not seen, what is really left undone, is the whole topic of collegiality. This is left undone and we need to talk more about the expressions of collegiality and how they might be realized for the church. I know there have been efforts in diocesan synods and regional synods of bishops and things of that nature, but we have to give more time and effort to understand the concept of collegiality.

**Is there any issue that you regret that the Fathers did not address?**

Well, let's say maybe more emphasis on collegiality. They read the signs of the times for their day and they responded very appropriately. But if we accept that principle, maybe we should be talking about a Vatican III or other ecclesial structures that would help us address the signs of our times today. One crisis that we have in the church is that it takes a long time for the church to accept the impact from an ecumenical universal council of the church. I think we've seen the internationalizing of the Curia, but I am not sure that the spirit of Vatican II has prevailed in all the workings of the Curia. I respect them highly; however, the recent draft that came from the Congregation of Worship and Discipline of the Sacraments—about restoring altar rails, altar gates, and questioning the presence of girl servers, and so on—seems to betray a mentality not in accord with the spirit of reading the signs of the times or the spirit of Vatican II. Is Vatican II fading in memory as well as in influence? We need to reinvigorate the liturgical renewal.

## Which of these teachings is most difficult to implement in the local church—here in the diocese with you as the bishop? What seems to be truly difficult?

Beginning with the theological framework that comes from the document on revelation, I'm not sure that we fully understood or adequately explained that. For example, inculturation in liturgy—I'm not sure that it has been fully understood, even though we have the church in Zaire (Africa) reading the Scriptures before the Penitential Rite. I'm not sure we have fully understood inculturation for the local church. I see some churches pulling back from those principles. Inculturation is in the document on revelation, as well as in the Constitution on the Sacred Liturgy. I think both complement each other.

I think that the task for the diocesan bishop now is to preserve the faith and to hand on the faith in very difficult secular times. We can only imagine what the church would be like if we had not had Vatican II. It indeed "opened up the windows and let the fresh air in." After the Council we put the screens and the storm windows. In certain places shutters have been installed. I think we still have to let the light and the fresh ideas come in, and not to be afraid, because the Spirit is with us. The Spirit has breathed new life into the church with Vatican II. So for a local bishop, we need to keep the family of the Lord together as best we can in very troubling, challenging, secular times. And we need the theology, the liturgy, and the spirituality of Vatican II to accomplish that. There are areas where renewal has not really taken hold, and I am sure that is true in every diocese. We try to work with them as best we can. We have to recognize that we still have miles to go in bringing the spirit of Vatican II to all of our people.

## Do you think there is any significance that the Vatican Council happened in the 1960s? Could it have happened earlier than that or later than that?

Again it goes back to John XXIII who, when he announced the Council, shocked the people in the Vatican. He talked about it as a giant step forward, *un balzo innanzi*. He called it a leap forward. The inspiration of the Holy Spirit personally led him to say that we need to look at the signs of the times. John came from a very traditional background and through curial diplomatic posts. He saw that the church was not being respected in the modern world. He had the courage to say, "Let us call a Council to examine the signs of the times and take a step forward."

It certainly goes back to the inspiration of John XXIII. No one advised him to have a Council. It originated from John XXIII as far as we know. The Holy Spirit communicated to him "there is a need here...do it!"

## What would you say to the countless numbers of young people, young married people and especially people in our schools that have never heard of the Vatican Council or have never seen a Latin Mass?

Pick up the sixteen documents and read them. They are timeless. Read the documents—study the documents. Some parishes have stopped having sessions about Vatican II documents. Some say, "It's kind of old hat." I assure you we still need to reexamine those documents, study them together. That must be the moving force for the church in this new millennium.

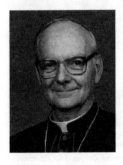

Donald W. Trautman, S.T.D., S.S.L. was born in Buffalo, New York, June 24, 1936. Pope John Paul II named Trautman, then auxiliary bishop of Buffalo, New York, to be the ninth bishop of Erie on June 12, 1990. He completed his theological studies under the Jesuits at the University of Innsbruck in Austria. In 1962, he received his licentiate in Sacred Theology. Ordained a priest in Innsbruck on April 7, 1962, he later pursued studies for one year at Catholic University in Washington, D.C. Bishop Trautman continued his postgraduate studies at the Pontifical Biblicum Institute in Rome, where he received his licentiate in Scripture in 1965. In 1966, he earned a doctorate in sacred theology from St. Thomas Aquinas University in Rome. During his time in Rome, Bishop Trautman assisted at the Second Vatican Council.

Bishop Trautman has been a member of the following committees of the National Conference of Catholic Bishops: Administrative Board of NCCB, ad hoc Committee for the Review of Scripture Translations, Doctrine Committee, Budget and Finance Committee, Pro-Life Committee, Migration and Refugee Committee, and Communications Committee. He was elected as the Chairman of the Bishops' Committee on Liturgy. During his three years of chairing that committee, he guided the Revised Lectionary and Revised Sacramentary projects.

Council fathers gathered in St. Peters basilica.

Pope John XXIII prays at the opening of the Council.
*Pontificia Poragraphis* by Fellciri.

The *aula* of St. Peters with Council participants.

Opening procession coming down the s*cala regia*, before
entering St. Peter's Square for the opening of the third
session of the Council on October 1963. Front: Cardinal
Francis Joseph Spellman [1889–1967] New York; Third
row: Fr. Russell Hardiman (without surplice), Cardinal
Gilroy [1896-1997] Sydney, Cardinal Grégoire-Pierre
Agagianian XV [1895–1971] of the Armenians.

Pope John XXIII.
Photo used with permission of Catholic News Service.

Church fathers at the Second Vatican Council.
Photo used with permission of Catholic News Service.

A group of Aussies at Second Vatican Council's first session, canonization of St. Peter Julian
Eyrmard, September 12, 1962. From left to right: Fr. John Hopgood; Bishop Francis Xavier Thomas
[1906–1987], Geraldton, Western Australia; Fr. Barry Jacobs; Fr. Russell Hardiman.
Photo used with permission of Father Russell Hardiman.

Canadian bishops with Pope P VI during the Second Vatican Council.
Photo used with permission of the Archdiocese of Halifax, Nova Scotia, Canada (file 31 #1345).

Council fathers, *Peritis* and observers at a eucharistic liturgy during the Second Vatican Council.

Concelebrants with Pope Paul VI; from left: Cardinal Patriarch of the Armenians Grégoire-Pierre Agagianian XV [1895–1971]; Cardinal Archille Liènart [1884–1973] of Lile, France; Cardinal Eugene Tissersnt [1884–1972]; Roman Curia, papal MC; Pope Paul VI; Monsignor Nasail-Rocca, papal MC; Cardinal Maximus IV [1878–1967], Saigh of the Melkites/Patriarch of Antioch; Cardinal Norman Thomas Gilroy [1896–1977], Sydney Australia (Father Russell Hardiman [Australia] behind him). Surrounded by members of the assembly.

Five founding members of the International Commission on English in the Liturgy (ICEL) at Edinburgh (1978): Godfrey Deikman, OSB [1909–2002]; Cardinal Joseph Marie Cordeiro [1918–1994] of Karachi, Pakistan; Cardinal Joseph Gray [1910–1993], Edinburgh; Archbishop Denis E. Hurley OMI [1915–2004] of Durban South Africa; and Msgr. Frederick McManus [b. 1923].

Bishops at the Second Vatican Council, left to right: Raymond Hunthausen [b. 1921] Helena, Montana; Hilary Hacker [1913–1990], Bismark, North Dakota; Bernard Topel [1903–1986], Spokane, Washington; Sylvester Treinan [1917–1996], Boise, Idaho; and Jospeh A. Rosario, MSFS [b. 1915], Amravati, India, in front of St. Peters in Rome at 8:45 a.m. on way to Council session, October 1962.

Photo used with permission of the diocese of Helena archives.

Bishops from India and Africa at the Council. Second from left: Archbishop Leobard D'Souza [b. 1930], bishop of Jabalpur India.

Photo used with permission of Archbishop D' Sousa.

Recessional procession at the Mass in which Paul VI declared Mary Mother of the Church, February 11, 1964. Paul VI with dark miter; forward from the Pope on the right, the third cardinal is Cardinal Gilroy of Sydney with Russell Hardiman on his left.

Photo used with permission of Russell Hardiman.

Left to right: Monsignor Thomas Tobin, pastor of All Saints Parish, Portland, Oregon; Mrs. David Powers, Monsignor Tobin's older sister; Father Edmond Bliven; and Pope Paul VI. Papal audience October 1962.

Photo used with permission of Fr. Edmond Bliven.

Paul VI entering a Council session on the *sedia gestatoria*.
Photo used with permission of Catholic News Service.

Bishop Hunthausen, Helena, and Bishop Topel, Spokane,
prepare to leave for Council sessions.
Photo used with permission of the diocese of Helena archives.

Loretto Sister Mary Luke Tobin chats with a bishop
between Council sessions.
Photo used with permission of the Sisters of Loretto archives.

Members of the Prepatory Commission on the Sacred Liturgy meeting during the Council.
Photo used with permission of The Liturgical Press.

Jesuit Father Joseph Gelineau and Paul Inwood on the day of the interview for this book,
July 3, 2003.

Photo used with permission of Paul Inwood.

Loretto Sister Mary Luke Tobin (age 96) and Michael P. Mernagh on
the day of the interview for this book, March 21, 2003.

Photo used with permission of Michael Mernagh.

Holy Ghost Father Lucein Deiss [b. 1921] at the organ
on the day of his interview August 16, 2003.

Photo used with permission of Paul Inwood.

# PART 3

# Theologians

# Lucien Deiss, CSSp

## Interviewer: Paul Inwood

Transcribed and translated by the interviewer

**What was your role at the Council? Were you a participant yourself?**

No, I was a liturgy specialist, a consultant who gave answers to the questions posed by the Council. I worked in liturgy for many years before the Council and published various books, et cetera, as well as a lot of liturgical music.

**During the Council itself, were you in Rome or in France?**

I was in France, but in my capacity as a liturgy consultant I was constantly being contacted by the commission set up by the Council. The bishops consulted a huge number of people.

**You're talking about the *Consilium*. You were a consultor to the *Consilium*?**

Yes, but not officially. I don't remember the exact title they gave people like me, but they were constantly in touch with us.

**Did you have a specialty, like Father Gelineau, who worked on the eucharistic prayer?**

Gelineau and I worked together, but not always with the same results. There were different working groups.

## When we last spoke, you told me that you had worked on the Breviary.

Yes, I did a lot of work on the Breviary. I worked on everything connected with the Breviary, especially in preparing for its reforms—what should be done with it. I wanted to reform the Christian way of prayer. My work was more of a general nature, not the really detailed stuff.

## So you didn't, for example, write new texts?

I didn't write new ones, but produced texts based on Scripture, many of which were used but were, of course, unattributed. I also did quite a lot of correcting of things that I didn't like in other people's work.

I did a lot of work on the texts of the Mass, particularly as regards the psalms and their relationship with the readings. Almost all the psalms that follow the first reading in the Liturgy of the Word were my work. It was I who made the selections. Not all my recommendations were adopted, but I worked on all of them.

## You worked with Fr. Gaston Fontaine [compiler of the lectionary]?

Yes, I worked with him. He was closer to Rome, more "Roman" than we were, even though he was a Canadian.

## You're not Roman in spirit yourself?

I know a bit about Roman liturgy, since I studied there for a long period of time.

## In your opinion, have the liturgical reforms been a success, or are there still things left to do?

It's not possible to give a global answer. It all depends exactly what you're talking about. Some things did not go well, and others were successful.

## Can you give an example of something that missed the mark?

I think the reform of the Breviary was far from perfect. It was produced for the priests rather than for the faithful.

**What about the Mass? Has it been a success? Do you think we have really achieved a true participation by the people?**

It all depends on your point of view. I think it would not be logical to say yes, or to say no. It's very complicated, and depends on where you're coming from, and which section of the people you're talking about. For example, some countries were not very interested at all in the reform of the liturgy, and by and large have not implemented it.

**And what about those in Rome?**

Some of them were not on the ball either.

**Was there anything that you were hoping for from the Council which in fact did not happen? Were there reforms that you would like to have seen which did not take place?**

Very many of them, but I can't tell you what they are. There are far too many. I think we could have gone about it differently. In my view, it would have been better to let each language group make its own decisions; but perhaps in retrospect it was best that decisions were taken at a global level, since that made it easier for Christians at grassroots level to accept them.

**Are you of the opinion that the bishops themselves are capable of making their own decisions about what is good for their people?**

No, I don't think it's the bishops' place to make these decisions. I think they should be approving or rejecting decisions made by those who work under them, who are working on behalf of the people and reflecting their desires.

**These decisions ought to come from the people themselves?**

I don't think the word "people" is the right one. I think these decisions should be rooted in Christian pastoral practice.

**That's a nice philosophical distinction! Do you see a need for a third Vatican Council?**

I really can't say. I'm not a prophet! I think the church should stop making decisions for the time being, let things germinate and grow a bit in order to see how they are going and where further work is needed. There are some things that were decided upon by Vatican II which were not a good idea—I can't now tell you what they were—but there were many excellent things, too. Some things were reformed, others were "deformed"! The liturgical life is not something definitive. It's in a constant state of flux. In my view, there is no such thing as a definitive reform of the church.

## It's always something that is moving along all the time.

Exactly. Not just in the liturgy but throughout the life of the church.

In my opinion, the reform was not perfect, but then I don't think there's such a thing as a perfect reform. Things are always on the move, and we have to accept that. For myself, I think I got what I wanted.

## There wasn't anything that you didn't succeed in getting?

No, I don't think so. As it is, we have not yet managed to implement properly everything that I succeeded in obtaining in the reforms.

## Are you still writing music yourself, or has composing ceased for you?

I'm still writing, and not just writing but thinking and reflecting. But I'm no longer publishing anything. There's a lot of stuff on my desk, but I don't think it will ever see the published light of day.

When I was writing and publishing material, I never had the idea in my head that this was for the universal church. I always wrote and published for my own community.

## When your *Biblical Hymns and Psalms* were translated into English for the American (and later the English) market, did you do the translations yourself, or did Gloria Weyman help you, or other people?

The translations came from all sorts of places. Gloria Weyman did not do any texts, but she was a critic who could tell me if a particular text was good or not so good, and was able to say if it was suitable for the people or not. Her primary profession was as a liturgical dancer, not a textualist.

In more recent times, there have been quite a lot of songs that were published first in English and then translated into French! This is because the English-speaking world was asking for things which the French speakers were not asking for.

## And so the hymns and canticles live on....

Yes, but I don't think we're going to be stuck with hymns for century after century, except perhaps for the Office.

## Do you find it interesting that we now have hymns in the Mass, when before the Council the Roman Rite did not contain any hymns as such?

I'm more interested in the different rites we have in the Mass, and the way in which music can help bring them to life, whether hymns or other forms.

Going back to before the Council, my specialization was in Latin and Gregorian chant. Some people think that, because of what I did later, I must be against Gregorian chant and Latin. I want to say that this is not at all the case. I wouldn't have received a *Grand Prix de l'Académie du Disque* for my first Gregorian chant recording if I had been out of sympathy with it. This was the music we used here in the seminary [of the Spiritan Fathers in Paris] every day for our liturgies. When I came here, I did not need to put a liturgical reform into practice, since it was already under way. We had 150 seminarians between the age of 20 and 30, and I was allowed to do whatever I liked musically in forming a top-class *schola*. This was how I was able to produce such good recordings.

## They were recorded in the main chapel here?

Yes. I was also able to have the large organ in the chapel completely refurbished. It was a condition of my agreeing to come to work here.

[Father Deiss then took me down to the little Oratory and showed me the smaller organ there. He is now suffering from a form of Parkinson's disease and his mobility is seriously affected; any distance of more than a few feet is accomplished in a wheelchair. Playing the organ is now a very difficult activity for him.]

*Lucien Deiss, CSSp*

Spiritian Father Lucien Deiss, is a pastor, liturgist, author, lecturer, Scripture scholar and composer. A native of France, he was born in 1921. He was heavily involved in the liturgical reform of the lectionary during the Second Vatican Council and was a member of the *Consilium* on liturgy. A specialist in biblical exegesis, he formerly occupied the Chair of Sacred Scripture and Dogmatic Theology at the Grand Scholasticat des Pères du Saint-Esprit in Paris. Father Deiss served as a member of the Committee for the French Ecumenical Bible and was formerly liturgical editor of the magazine *Assemblée Nouvelle*. As a missionary priest, he gave retreats and worked with the poor in several nations of the world for many years, including Africa, Haiti and Taiwan.

# Joseph Gelineau, SJ

## Interviewer: Paul Inwood

### What was your role at the Council?

My role was essentially in the group—the *coetus*—working on the reform of the Mass. My work on the musical aspects was fairly marginal because I had some rather savage opponents. Now [Archbishop Annibale] Bugnini [1912–1982] was very clever; he was a diplomat. He asked my opinion in private, and then put me in the working group on the Mass.

### Was this during the Council itself?

I didn't attend any sessions of the Council as such, but as soon as the Council fathers approved the Constitution on the Sacred Liturgy, I was invited to be part of the Roman committee that was set up in its wake.

### The *Consilium*?

Yes. The group working on the Mass was one of about twenty. My group had a lot of big names on it—Monsignor [Johannes] Wagner [1908–1992], who was the head of the Liturgical Institute in Trier, [Aimé-Georges] Martimort [1911–2000], [Balthasar] Fischer [1912–2001]—and many others, who had already been working on liturgical reform before the Council, from the liturgical and pastoral point of view—i.e., with a view to the participation of the faithful. My particular role in this group was working on new eucharistic prayers. My group started work while the Council was still in progress.

## You were not a *peritus* at the Council itself?

No. The *Consilium* was a council of the Congregation of Rites, set up by the bishops in the wake of the Constitution on the sacred Liturgy to manage the liturgical reform.

## For you, the most significant document to come out of the Council was the Constitution on the Sacred Liturgy.

Yes. It happened so quickly and was done so well. Of course, there were great battles in the course of it, but the vast majority of the bishops voted in favor. Bugnini was the pivotal person in all this, and the greater part of the text was prepared by Martimort and Wagner.

## Was the Constitution the most important document to come out of the Council or were there others?

They were all important, and very different in nature. But the most concrete was the Constitution on the Liturgy, since it touched the practices of the faithful themselves, whereas many of the other documents were of relevance to theologians and pastors and were of a more reflective nature. The liturgy constitution was unique in that it affected every Catholic throughout the world.

## Were there other documents that you would have liked to see the Council produce?

No. I was not in the theologians' circuit, so I was not expecting anything yet hoping for everything. I trusted in the working of the Holy Spirit! I have no regrets about the Council itself. Obviously I regret that the group working on the Mass was not able to do everything I had hoped, but you can't expect the impossible! But what it achieved was already marvelous; even though there remain things still to be done.

## The main achievements of the Council—are they the introduction of the vernacular, or the participation of the people, or what?

These are two pillars that were already well on the way before the Council. I already knew this in France before the Council. The people needed to be able to participate, both by singing and by being able to understand, rather than just reading translations of the Latin. The third pillar was the priority of the Bible, a rediscovery: the people knew nothing of the Bible up to that point. These were the three principal areas.

Obviously there were others, such as the reform of the Easter Vigil, put in hand by Pius XII well before the Council—the German liturgists had persuaded him that he needed to do something about it. Despite this, the question of language had not been broached—in fact, there were enormous rearguard actions against the possibility of using living languages in the liturgy, especially from those in the *Musica Sacra* domain, who saw a threat to the use of the Latin chants which were so dear to them. This sort of consideration was not taken very seriously by most of the bishops around the world.

## What still remains to be done in the liturgical field? Is there a retrenchment or are we still moving forward?

The further forward we go, the clearer it becomes that the most profound and the most important things are still to be done. This cannot be achieved by a decree coming down from Rome or a group of specialists, however competent they may be. What we have is a liturgy approved by Rome, which is supposed to be usable by all Roman Catholic churches throughout the world. The greatest movements— and we have seen this in the meetings and work of *Universa Laus*—have come in the wake of the promulgation of the use of the vernacular: people wanted to be able to sing anything they liked. I was not too worried by this because I knew it would not go on for too long. People went off in all kinds of directions—pop music, neo-Byzantine music, etc.—but collections were produced [in France] which contained the best that was being sung in the different styles.

As you know, the underlying question did not go to sleep—and it couldn't. The bishops from missionary countries came up with the conviction that it was not enough to begin from the starting points of the Christian liturgical tradition, good theology and the rediscovery of the Bible and patristic studies. It was necessary at the same time to use genuine culture as a starting point as well—the culture of each language zone or country or region. Without this, the liturgy remains a kind of intervention, but not something with a real life of its own. There were a few timid exceptions to this lack of cultural insight—in Africa there was the...

## The Zaire entrance rite?

Yes, that was it, and also similar experiments in the West Indies. Doing this kind of thing meant that there was a whole process of entering into a celebration: through silence, through watching, through instrumental music and singing as a way of arriving gradually at the proclamation of the Word.

## A sort of preparation, then.

Yes, indeed. This kind of preparation already existed in Jerusalem at the time of Egeria (or Aetheria, as some call her) [Egeria was a pilgrim in the late fourth century who described the liturgy in Jerusalem]. She makes it very plain that in advance of the celebration itself, a lot of people were already there—first of all, the monks and nuns (for they did not remain in the convents and monasteries on Sundays; that would have been unthinkable). They began to sing psalms as the people gathered, and the singing continued—psalms and antiphons. Then some of the clergy arrived, and each person came, according to what s/he had to do in the liturgy. This was all in the context of preparing for a specifically Christian liturgy—the proclamation of God's Word, plus celebration of sacraments (Eucharist or other sacraments), if this was to take place. Prior to that, one could not dream of carrying out a liturgy which touches people to the depths of their being if there is no point of departure already: a time of waiting—not necessarily something precisely formulated, but a time of waiting that can also do something good for the people in terms of their religion, their piety, their faith. It is clear that the entire West functioned in this way during the Middle Ages, right up to the Counter-Reformation. In other words, it didn't matter what the priest said, since the people understood nothing of it, and the deep symbols of the liturgy were not necessarily those which affected people the most. The proof of that is that the primary symbol of the breaking of bread did not exist for the people since they did not receive Communion.

## So what was the deep-rootedness of the people?

Well, when catechizing the barbarians, the starting point was their sense of the sacred, and their very real sense of vibrating with the sacred. It is striking that in France all the old Celtic high places were Christianized. In other words, all the mountains became the Notre-Dame mountains, the caves became St. George's caves, the wellsprings became St. Martin's springs with healing properties, etc. Everything was grafted onto the symbols of a religion that already existed. There is no problem with that, since a symbol does not have a precise meaning—it opens a doorway, and after that each person gives to the symbol the meaning that s/he wants. One can say that the conversion of the barbarians and the church of the Middle Ages were founded on this, right up to the Reformation and the Counter-Reformation.

What is nevertheless quite remarkable is that nothing that was done as a result of the Council of Trent—and in the progress in understanding the Bible, theology, etc., in the discussions between the different Christian schools of thought—has touched on this question of symbols. It's very strange. In a country like France, you can state that currently only 8–10 percent of Catholics practice their religion; but the majority are baptized, a large number still return to ask to be married in church and a still larger number come back to church to be buried.

Now, when I was parish priest of a number of small parishes, with very few people practicing, I made an empirical discovery, not knowing what was in store for me. This was quite the opposite of what lots of priests were saying and what I even thought myself—what to do with these people? They never come to Mass, they are scarcely catechized, are they really serious about all this? Except in the case of the baptism of babies—which I attempted to evolve by a strategy of infant baptism in stages, so that it's the young people themselves who choose, and not everything is determined in advance—in every other case I placed my trust in those who were asking for something from the church—marriage, special Masses, etc.—and in every case starting from what I call their sense of the sacred. Before I was a parish priest, I would not have believed that this sense of the sacred existed so strongly.

I remember one day interviewing a boy and a girl who wanted to get married in church. I did not know them; I had never seen them before, or their families. I asked them why they wanted to get married in church. A long silence ensued. I said to them, "When I marry you I will ask you before God and all the people gathered together to exchange your consent. So—when I say 'before God,' what does that mean?" The boy's reply was not helpful at all. "My father doesn't believe in all that; my mother says that if a loving God really existed, there wouldn't be so much unhappiness in the world...." So I asked him if he believed in God himself. "No," he admitted, "not at all." So I said to the girl, "Is it the same with you? Because, if it is, I won't be able to do what you have asked me to do." She replied,

"Well, my father also thinks it's all a load of rubbish; he doesn't give a damn." "And what about you yourself?" She thought for a moment, and then said to me, "I want to get married in church because marriage is a sacred thing." I did marry them in the church. It was curious, because I was not anticipating this expression "sacred" from someone who was not a worshipper or even of any particular religion; and it knocked me sideways because it is not a question of knowing what their religious culture is, nor whether they are practicing or are familiar with the Bible, but whether they have within them a dimension of the transcendent.

So, I think that the first thing to accomplish in a liturgical assembly is transcendence. For me, there are clearly two contradictory images: the Sunday Mass, and the fact that absolutely nothing happens. You can do all the explaining that you like, read the Bible, but the fact is that they don't really understand. You put on a eucharistic liturgy where the essential thing is lacking.... Now on the other hand, I can go to Taizé and I see young people of all ages, of every culture and every language, who are united in a single and very intense experience of community where everyone is drawn in. Some are kneeling, some are prostrating themselves, and some are sitting. Some are singing, and some are not, but the acid test is that when there is a silence, you can cut it with a knife, it is of such a density.

## You can almost touch it.

Exactly. So if you don't start there, the liturgy never gets off the ground at all. From a very practical point of view—and I'm not talking about Africa or Asia, which is something else altogether, but the Western countries, including North America—it seems to me that we absolutely have to rediscover in the liturgy the way to enter the world of the sacred that is the basis of all faith and all revelation. If the Mass does not begin at the bottom, it doesn't begin at all.

Now, in the rite of Mass there are five processions, but in many parishes there is no procession at all. To give another example, your emotional "core" only moves when your physical core also moves. So we're talking about the feet, the ears and the eyes. We need to touch the depths of human beings at the point where the sense of the sacred is launched, which is about that which is invisible, untouchable, incomprehensible—and yet one shouldn't get worked up about that. If you ask the people who come what they believe in, they remain silent. So, in my opinion, this is what remains to be done, to be reconstructed—what actually needs to be constructed for the first time in the "old" countries that are now, in fact, nonreligious societies, but nevertheless still retain these fundamental basics.

**I remember hearing you say in 1973 at Wood Hall that one cannot easily celebrate with a liturgy which grew up in the Mediterranean basin but which may not be relevant at all to other non-Mediterranean cultures—and it seemed to me at that time that you were talking about decentralization.**

Yes, I was talking about the Roman liturgy that we have inherited. With the conversion of the barbarians, there was no question of inculturation of the liturgy as such, except on the monastic side of things. People were content to reproduce the rites that emanated from Rome. But everything took place in the field of devotions—hence the importance of places of pilgrimage. In the region where I was a parish priest, which had been a non-practicing region for a very long period, there were heaven knows how many places of pilgrimage and days of pilgrimage. Everybody came, from all the neighboring villages.

The same thing applies to religious chants. This is a very important phenomenon. These are chants that came to birth spontaneously—i.e., not liturgical chants, which were in Latin, and Gregorian chant, or even polyphonic; these were elitist, not for the assembly of the people. In the midst of the people were born these chants that were of all kinds—those that told of the life of Jesus, the miracles, etc. I remember meeting an old Italian woman who sang the whole of her religion by heart. She couldn't read or write, but she could cantillate the whole of her religion by heart. And these popular hymns, which were often pilgrimage hymns, are typically hymns about feast days such as Christmas. And this is not necessarily something in the past. In my own experience, in the parishes where I worked, I used to try out different kinds of hymns to see which the people would really get involved in. I discovered that the ones that people really got into were the extremely popular ones....

When I sang an old Breton chant at burials, there was a kind of shock. People really got into it; they were taken up by it. One solution is to adapt melodies to texts that are imposed from above. With psalmody, that can work, but I don't think it's possible with popular songs. The words and the music have to be created at the same time; the words and music need to mesh together and, moreover, touch the depths of people's spirits.

Like many others, I would have believed that all the old songs, the old Christmas carols, and so on, were passé, finished, and that what really touched young people was contemporary music. But my pastoral experience has been that it is not like that at all. It's very easy to do great things with a choir, for example, that sings very well and has a repertoire of pieces of great value—but to touch the

225

heart of the people is not so easy. None of the pathways that we tried were successful, in my opinion. What I see is that the things which have survived in the liturgical reform from the 1950s are certain antiphons that go with the Gelineau psalms and the hymns of Jef Marthouret. I remember very well the songs he published in liturgical journals even before the era of *L'Église qui chante* [The singing church]. In any French parish you care to name, on All Saints' Day, you can hear Marthouret's *Dieu, nous te louons, d'ailleurs nous t'acclamons* (God, we praise you, and we acclaim you), because he had the knack of tapping into popular feeling. He wrote pieces that all the Catholics of that time were able to learn, but which have remained alive even in the generations that followed. When you put something like that before the people, they get into it.

Jacques Berthier was another composer who knew how to "play the popular card"—his most popular pieces were those where he did this. He did it with the music of Taizé, and with lots of other pieces that people commissioned from him. At the same time he ran the risk of being considered "unworthy" by his contemporaries in the classical music world. His roots were not "absent"—I think they exist everywhere in our contemporary culture.

To find what can really touch the depths of our young people today, it is not necessary to tap into contemporary song forms. That isn't necessarily what works best, and this is why I have produced "Bible songs" for children, songs that use translations of Bible stories with very simple cantillations that are always inspired by the rhythms and melodies of popular songs. The children pick them up straight away and know them by heart immediately.

All this is to say that when you want to inculturate today's liturgy, you really have to go and look for the roots of humanity. Whatever country you are in, the culture there has its own history, which needs to be looked for. Perhaps you have to seek out the things that seem to have disappeared, but that are actually still there; they are what I call the entry points to the world of the sacred. And on this basis you will be able to proclaim the word of God. Above all—and this varies from one culture to another, whether there is bodily movement or not (and this depends on how close you are to the Equator or the North Pole)—being able to do this means not being merely satisfied with what is seen by the eyes or heard by the ears: the entire body needs to be involved in it. I myself have learnt through experience the importance and the efficaciousness of processions in instilling an ambience of the sacred in an assembly. Of course, there are many other things you can do in the context of the Mass.

In my opinion, the Liturgy of the Eucharist seldom gets underway. There's a black hole there, and the reforms did not succeed in solving the problem. We didn't know what to do. We said, "Ah, well, we can sing a song that gets things going," but in fact this hasn't happened. We actually don't have any such chants because in the Roman liturgy the Offertory chant is not a song for the opening of the Liturgy of the Eucharist: it is a song which accompanies the procession of the…well, actually the collection! In order to do a procession of the gifts, my experience, now dating back over twenty years, is that at the moment when you bring up the gifts you have to have a song of a certain breadth and depth so that at the point when the priest says or sings, "The Lord be with you," there is something there to receive this greeting—it doesn't fall completely flat. If you take up the collection, if there is a piece of background organ music, no one really knows why suddenly they are hearing, "The Lord be with you." "And also with you." You're not actually beginning the action of the Eucharist. In this regard I've always envied the Eastern liturgies. The high point of the Byzantine rite is the *cherubicon* chant—that is to say, it is an entry into the Eucharist, not just a musical entry but a physical, bodily, spiritual entry. It is on that basis that you can launch the eucharistic prayer.

**You were just speaking about a chant of a certain gravity [breadth and depth]. I remember in 1978 hearing you speak about a great outburst of praise that would be followed by the act of thanksgiving in the first part of the eucharistic prayer.**

Exactly!

**And is a chant with a certain gravity the same thing as this outburst of praise or is it something more dignified?**

I think gravity means size rather than mood.

Going back to bodily participation, for us it's still something rather pitiful. Thanks to St. Pius X, a century ago now, little by little the majority of the people coming into the church for Mass receive Communion. But there are things in this area which I have not managed to overcome as a pastor, because the liturgy is ruptured at this point. For example, the kiss of peace would be far better placed before the Liturgy of the Eucharist, as it once was, as a gesture of reconciliation and understood as such: "Before you bring your gift to the altar, go and be reconciled." But in the Roman rite, it has not been clear what is going on here. You have the kiss of peace and then this little *Agnus Dei* chant—"Lamb of God…grant us peace"—

which is in no way a genuine fraction song. Thus the kiss of peace is concealing the strong atmosphere that you can perceive following the Lord's Prayer, for this is still an important moment which touches many of the faithful—this fundamental prayer.

If you say the Our Father slowly, or cantillate it, the kiss of peace breaks the mood and it's impossible to get it back. After the kiss of peace, you begin the *Agnus Dei*, the priest breaks one or two pieces off the host—and that's it. The fundamental symbol is the sharing of bread—yes, it's really that. Jesus said, "Take this and share it among you." If Jesus had wanted to make the washing of the feet the primary symbol, and John the Evangelist had put it into the Gospel instead of the Eucharist—well, that would have had a great impact, as it still does as a gesture. But with the breaking of bread, nothing happens because nothing is seen to happen. We break a few hosts and distribute them among different ciboria, and that's all. It's not enough. We don't take the time that's needed. I've experimented with fraction songs that express the mystery of the sharing of the bread, etc., and that take time to do it. This in turn gives time for the ministers of Communion to approach....

And then there's the way we come up to Communion. It's not a true procession in the sense that most of the time it's an individual gesture that is taking place. We don't actually *share* bread. I remember when I was still a young Jesuit at an ecumenical meeting in Germany and was present at a Eucharist where they distributed "tablets" of bread to be broken into twelve pieces, and we broke and shared the bread. There, the symbol of sharing was very strong; you couldn't avoid the symbolism. Of course, sharing in the cup is a different problem.... What I'm trying to say is that individualism holds center stage at the time of Communion. There is no real sharing. The cup is not circulated.

These are not just a few examples by which I wanted to show that if there are still important things that need to be improved in the liturgy as revised by the reforms of Vatican II, this is not for ideological reasons nor is it for the pleasure of making adjustments. It's because it's absolutely essential that we once again find the pathway that will enable us to get in touch with the deepest things that are within human beings. It's quite certain that really sharing bread can touch people deeply. So can processions....

Then there's the whole question of acclamations and litanies. You hear people saying, "We're not black people; we don't acclaim like that." My answer is that this isn't what's important. We must not confuse the style of doing it and the anthropological reality that is implied by a gesture. The style can vary. You can move your body a lot or only a little. The point is that the whole body needs to be involved, even if this may not be very visible on the outside.

I don't think we'll ever really be able to do litanies properly unless there is a real processional "reality," a great sense of power, of strength—for example, the procession to the baptistry at the Easter Vigil, with all the names of the saints being sung. The actual form of acclamations—well, actually, we acclaim very little. Our Amens are often quite pathetic. The Great Amen at the end of the eucharistic prayer should really *crown* what has gone before. It's at this deep level, I believe, that we need to work towards the inculturation of the liturgy in every country, in many and very different ways, while safeguarding the model proposed—or imposed—by Vatican II. In my opinion the main lines are right, but not everything has yet been given its full value. Often enough, we just recite the texts and make the minimum gestures prescribed by the liturgy; but this isn't a real liturgy unless and until each person in the assembly not only feels uplifted by it but also senses that each person is lifting up the others and being lifted up by them. From time to time, singing can achieve precisely that. Certain songs succeed in doing that. But that isn't enough. You mustn't break things up. There needs to be an immense wave....

## A sense of progression?

Yes, a sense of progression, which I think is certainly implicit in the structure of the reformed liturgy of Vatican II. There aren't too many things in it that I personally regret. However, I do regret that the beginning of the Mass is overloaded and incoherent. There is no time to do a real litanic entrance procession, such as there is in the Eastern liturgies. The *Kyrie eleison* is rather shabby, especially in its abominable French translation: "Lord, take pity [on us]." Even from a phonetic point of view, it's really awful! No rhythm, no sonority. And having the *Gloria* every Sunday is too much. We need an entrance rite that has more life, more of a sense of direction, which focuses on the processional cross around which people gather, and which concludes with the prayer of the priest.

I do not have much to say about the Liturgy of the Word, because it's really very beautiful. Nevertheless, it too is overloaded, too intellectual. Often the commentaries that are given mean absolutely nothing to the people. The readers read too quickly. It would be better to read less of the Bible, and read it very slowly, and even (as I did in my parishes) only have a single reading and read it at least three times, even to cantillate it the third time (after a number of other things have intervened) so that in a sense you are "eating" the text.

The psalms are very important for me. At the time of the reforms, everyone was in agreement that a psalmist should sing the psalm verses. Very quickly I noticed that the people were really not entering at all into the prayer of the psalms. They didn't understand them, and couldn't follow them. The people's refrain, which certainly is known and understood, is repeated too many times, in my opinion. It gets very wearing after each stanza. In order for the psalm text to be "eaten" or really chewed over by the people, a different form of psalmody is needed. In the little parishes where I worked, I saw that it was extremely simple to achieve this, even with young children and uneducated people, by using a good model whereby the psalm was sung slowly, with breathing space. It created a sense of to-and-fro, and the people "ate" the words. With twenty years of experience behind me, I can say that there was great power in that. So don't waste time by having the verses sung by a solo singer. The sense of the psalm is lost if you yourself don't actually enunciate the words "I cry to you" or "Lord, come to my aid." Even though people don't realize it when they're saying the words, they'll come back to them, precisely at the moment in their lives where they *feel* "Lord, come to my aid" or "Do not forget me, Lord." From this point on, people no longer say that they find the psalms difficult.

Once again, in my opinion, the Liturgy of the Word works well. However, I do ask myself one very fundamental question, which was not asked at Vatican II: what about the catechumens? In a country like France, we have 2,000 adult baptisms each year at Easter. Now, what is really serious and not generally realized is that the assemblies do not welcome the catechumens as catechumens. They don't understand that the liturgy has to be carried out in such a way that the catechumens are an integral part of the assembly present. So I have been led by the presence of catechumens to simplify the Liturgy of the Word, to read the texts over and over until they sink in, until they are grasped by them (and the same with the songs we sing), and then finally we say goodbye to them, we dismiss them. We certainly do not keep them around for a large part of the Mass. What could be more horrifying than to remain at a ceremony where you hear the words, "Take this, all of you, and eat it—but not *you!*"? That's very serious. This is the one thing in the Liturgy of the Word that I think is revolutionary in the good sense of the word—in other words, it must make us re-examine the role of the proclamation of the Word, starting from the texts, the chants, etc.

Regarding the Liturgy of the Eucharist, I've already said a certain number of things, and so I'll only say one to conclude this section: it was my achievement [in the post-Vatican II reforms] to have succeeded in having an additional acclamation included in the center of the eucharistic prayer—the memorial acclamation. We actually wanted more, but we said to ourselves that we were more likely to get it past the bishops if we limited ourselves to one! Unfortunately, the memorial acclamation is not in the right place. It was envisaged as a prolongation of the anamnesis pronounced by the presiding priest, and should not have formed a hiatus between the institution narrative and the anamnesis. "Do this in memory of me. This is why, Lord, we...." And so it is to this remembering of the Lord's death and resurrection that the people should be responding as if they were truly involved.

The reason [why the memorial acclamation is in the wrong place] is very well-known, and may even seem a little foolish. Paul VI (who was a great help to us, as the good Lord knows) had certain things which were very close to his heart. For example, he insisted that the *Orate, fratres* be retained, even though this is not exactly the ideal way of entering into eucharistic praise! And he also insisted on the retention of the words *mysterium fidei* in the institution narrative. We didn't know what to do. It was my idea, perhaps a bit idiotic, to make of these words the lead-in to the acclamation. What I did not realize was that this would have to be inserted just after the institution narrative. There are a few missed opportunities like that, but it's not too serious. It's not really very revolutionary, but I personally have always had the memorial acclamation sung *after* the presider's *anamnesis*, and no one has ever complained!

But I would make a strong plea for other interventions for the assembly in the eucharistic prayer. Apart from anything else, this makes sure that the presider does not have his nose stuck in the book all the time. (It's frightful!) The people need to raise praises that mount to the skies; and at the moment they don't have this role, unlike the practice in the Eastern liturgies. In the Coptic liturgy there are seventeen interventions by the assembly in the institution narrative. It's extraordinarily good! There you have a very deep participation by the assembly. I myself have arrived at the number seven for the acclamations [in the eucharistic prayer]. I haven't changed that for a long time because the people had got used to them and made them their own. Thus, there's an extra one in the part of the prayer following the *Sanctus*, there's an Amen or another acclamation after each of the two parts of the institution narrative, the Memorial Acclamation, two epiclesis interventions, and a concluding Amen that will be somewhat more substantial than just two notes!

## Do you find this still works if the priest does not sing at all?

It's certainly a problem. But there is the solution of the *ekphoneses* [which I have spoken about in *Liturgical Assembly, Liturgical Song*, Pastoral Press 2002], for I myself am quite opposed to the cantillation of the entire eucharistic prayer, i.e., a presidential monologue with no acclamations. It's unthinkable. I don't know if it has ever existed. If it does in the Eastern liturgies, I don't know how it works. But in the East they do use the practice of *ekphonesis*—they will be praying a text quietly and then all of a sudden everyone hears a voice raised at quite a high pitch. I've provided *ekphoneses* for all the assembly's interventions. It's not difficult to do one. If you don't know how to sing, use two notes, or just raise your voice.

## It's an audible signal for the assembly?

Yes, a very strong one. In some cases, it can be a deacon or an assistant or a cantor at the altar who does it.

## Do you dream of a Third Vatican Council?

No, I don't think that would be possible at the moment, for a variety of reasons. Gathering together three thousand bishops is almost unthinkable. Intermediaries are needed. What I fervently hope for is that the successor of the present pope—and this isn't a criticism—will have other preoccupations than those that have been dear to John Paul II. I don't think, for example, that he has realized how important it is for the liturgy to be really inculturated in every civilization across the globe. You can see this from the way in which he himself has celebrated liturgically as a bishop. And plenty of other people besides myself hope that the next pope will start off by gathering together a certain number of important bishops from around the world for a synod, saying to them, "What do we need to change in the church?"

## So Vatican II was a child of its time? Is there any significance in the fact that it took place in the 1960s, a time of historical and cultural significance—for example, the 1968 student revolutionary protests in Paris, etc.?

Yes, and we are in a different era now. Bishops themselves are protesting because they can't do what they want to do regarding liturgical translations for their countries because everything is revised by Rome; and things are imposed on them by people who are not even familiar with the language(s) in question. This is intolerable.

## For us the situation is identical…and with the ordination rites as well.

We therefore have to hope that something will move in the Roman congregations. We really need it to. The Holy Spirit needs to blow, certainly. The next pope will certainly be important, but on the question of inculturation—in other words, the face that the church and its liturgy in particular must give in every land and culture in the world—only the people who live there, the bishops who work there, know how this is best done.

There are, of course, still questions that concern the whole church. Many bishops asked for a very simple and clear résumé of the Christian faith. What we got in the end was the [Roman] Catechism, which is completely indigestible. Everyone buys it and nobody reads it… at least, that's what I see happening. Moreover, it contains a whole series of directives that are completely outdated. So we will also need to work over that again to see what our basis for action is going to be. And I think for the question of the liturgy, it will be absolutely vital—and revitalizing—that, in a new system for the Roman Catholic Church, there should be groupings of bishops by culture, and not just bishops but priests and lay people, too, who will be able to rethink the question of the liturgy as laid out by Vatican II; for I think the basic pathway was sound. So, I'm not asking for a further reform of the liturgy: I'm asking for an inculturation of what is at the basis of the Vatican II reforms. And I'm absolutely certain that it will happen.

## We'll need a lot of patience….

Well, I won't live to see it.

[Note: Père Gelineau suffered for three years from Horton's syndrome, which produces continuous pain. Although now cured, he is left with fatigue and cannot work for more than an hour or so at a time without resting. The interview terminated at this point.]

Joseph Gelineau, SJ, was born in 1920, and ordained a priest in 1953. He has spent a lifetime working to promote the place of quality music in the liturgy. The composer of the first psalms for use in the reformed liturgy in France, author of several books on liturgy, and for twenty-five years a professor at the Institut Catholique in Paris, Père Gelineau is one of the premier pedagogues on liturgical prayer, combining his extensive pastoral experience with an impressive scholarly background.

# Edward Schillebeeckx, OP

## Interviewer: Carl Sterkens

**What was your capacity at the Council?**

I was a private theological advisor to the Dutch episcopacy. Cardinal Bernard Johannes Alfrink [1900–1987] tried twice to let me be appointed as an official *peritus*, but (as we heard afterwards) Cardinal [Alfredo] Ottaviani personally prevented this, leaving the pope unaware of both the proposal and Ottaviani's decision. The reason for the refusal seems to have been a public, official Letter of the Dutch Episcopacy to the church in The Netherlands, dated November 24, 1960. In this document, about two years before the Council started, the bishops declared themselves in favor of an *aggiornamento*, or renewal of the Catholic church; in their colophon they explicitly mentioned my name as the main "ghostwriter" of that letter. This was correct. This Dutch episcopal document was translated into the major European languages and became very well known in The Netherlands and abroad. The Italian translation was prohibited by the Vatican, but was sold in secret and in great numbers. From that day on, the Vatican watched me closely, as I would soon find out. After the Council, the Cardinal-Prefect of the Congregation of Christian Faith four times required me to defend the orthodoxy of my thoughts and writings; luckily it never led to an official *fiat* or condemnation.

In the year preceding the Council, I wrote a personal document with critical remarks upon the pre-Vatican II drafts (the so-called "pre-schemata" or *schemas*) made by the Theological Commission of the Congregation of Faith in Rome. The document's title was *Animadversiones, Remarques sur la première série de projets de Constitutions et de Décrets sur lesquels le Concile aura à se prononcer* (45 pages, Nimègue, August 1962). I wrote this document for the Dutch episcopacy. Not only has this document been translated into many languages, even into rather bad Latin, but it was this document that helped me to attend the Council in the first place. The active Bishop [Wilhelmus Marinus] Bekkers [1908–1966], of the 's-Hertogenbosch (Bois-le-Duc) diocese in The Netherlands, arrived in Rome for the Council; he took the initiative of copying my recommendations and handing them out to more than two thousand bishops. Cardinal Alfrink asked me to go with him and the Dutch episcopacy to the Council as one of three selected *periti* (one canonist, one ecumenist, and I was the systematic theologian).

At the beginning of the Council, this document (next to the official *schemas*) seems to be the first that was passed to all the bishops present in Rome. It influenced many bishops, directly or indirectly, as we afterward heard from many of them.

Another way I would have influenced the bishops was by giving weekly conferences for the Dutch-speaking bishops of The Netherlands and Belgium, bishops in the missions of Congo and Indonesia, and for many other episcopal conferences—of Asia, Africa, Canada, the United States and, last but not least, South America (CELAM).

On one occasion, I could have, as a member of an official commission, directly influence one of the documents of the Council. Dutch and Belgian bishops (with their Dutch and Belgian theologians) were responsible for preparing the first drafts or *schemas* for the chapter about marriage in *Gaudium et spes*. It was a well-written and balanced draft. Alas, Pope Paul VI intervened personally in our commission. Four topics were withdrawn from our draft commission; these topics were about family planning, remarriage after civil divorce, and so on. These themes seemed to be reserved to the pope and were not to be discussed by the conciliar assembly.

## What was the most significant moment at the Council for you?

The most significant moment at the Council was November 1962, when, by an intervention of Pope John XXIII, the *preconciliar* drafts were completely withdrawn as the basis for the official discussions in the general assemblies of the Council.

## What happened?

In the first three months of the Council, there was a fierce fight going on between the bishops of the world and those of the Roman Curia. At stake were the *schemas* (drafts) prepared in Rome by the *preconciliar* commissions installed by the Curia. During the daily assemblies of the Council, many bishops criticized many of those drafts. This situation led to the urgent problem of whether or not these drafts could or should remain the basis of the discussion of the Council itself. In November 1962 the bishops voted about the present *schemas*; the *Praesidium* of the Council decided that a vote upon this problem by the Council's plenary assembly could bring the solution. The votes against the proposed texts were more than fifty percent, but a little less than the necessary two-thirds majority. In fact, legally, the pre-Vatican drafts remained *in possessione*. As a consequence of the votes, the drafts remained the basis for all further discussions of the Council.

Nevertheless, the day after the voting Pope John XXIII intervened personally, saying that with so many votes opposing the proposed schemes he found it morally more humane to withdraw all these drafts instead of submitting himself to a formally legal situation. This papal decision seemed to be the best solution at that very delicate historical moment of the Second Vatican Council.

A new theological commission, representing proportionally the votes against and in favor of the refused *schemas*, opened the possibility of preparing new drafts which better represented the opinions and convictions of the majority of the assembly. That was, for me and many others, one of the most significant moments of the Council. It was a courageous papal decision, a real consequence of what John XXIII in his opening address meant by his "*aggiornamento* of the Catholic Church" and his call against troublemakers and "prophets of doom."

This moment stood in sharp contrast with our common, more negative mood when we arrived in Rome; the climate then was not very optimistic. Jesuit Father Karl Rahner, to whom I spoke many times in Rome, even refused at that time to discuss the start of a project that would later become known as the *Concilium* project: an international theological review that would have the task of explaining and pastorally applying the coming texts of the Council. Rahner's first blockade of this project was based upon the reality of the situation: pre-Vatican *decennia* and of the "Synod of Rome," in which the synodal drafts prepared for that local Roman Synod were automatically, without any criticism, accepted by the Synod itself. In such a situation, Rahner said, we would not have the freedom to say what, as theologians, we have to say in such an international theological review.

But after the fundamental turn of November 1962, Rahner came back to the pioneers of that *Concilium* project and enthusiastically said, "Yes! After this turn I totally agree with your plans." He saw a very good future for the *Concilium* project, not as an authoritative interpretation of the coming results of the Council (that was, indeed, not the intention of the initiators of the *Concilium* idea), but as theologians with the freedom to have their own say. Without being the ecclesial magisterium, theologians have their own level as scientific magisterium, in service of humankind and the church as "the congregation of God."

## What was the most negative moment at the Council for you?

I think the week that in the press was called "the black week of the Council." On November 16, 1964, the *Nota praevia* was published by "higher authorities"—not by the Council but imposed upon the Council. This document interpreted the collegiality of *Lumen gentium* in a much more tightened way than did the theological commission (according to its answers to the proposed amendments of the Council fathers). The commission explained what really is the meaning of the collegiality of the world episcopate in reciprocal relationship with the pope, who exercises the Petrine ministry *within* the college of the bishops. The General Assembly positively gave its votes in favor of this explanation. The *Nota praevia*, on the contrary, actually combined collegiality with the possibility that the pope himself could rule the church either alone or together with the world episcopacy. The monarchical papal regimen in earlier times was not disavowed; it could restore the extreme centralization of the Roman Curia as a power higher and above the episcopacy spread over the whole world.

## Of all the documents of the Council which one is most significant for you and why?

I would not say it is the most important document of the Council, but the most surprising document, by far, is the Pastoral Constitution, *Gaudium et spes*. It breaks with many preceding papal documents from the nineteenth and twentieth centuries against liberalism (in the sense of religious freedom and the freedom of conscience), social engagement for the poor and the marginalized people. The Council [in *Gaudium et spes*] stated that the Spirit of God is also working in secular emancipative movements. Here, modern liberalism is not to be understood in the popular North American and Western meaning of being free from possibly everything, but in the historical meaning of some positive achievements of the Enlightenment, the North American and the French revolutions, without defending the violence that accompanied these new human and humane values which previously were condemned by the church's hierarchy.

*Lumen gentium* acknowledged that the Holy Spirit cannot work only in the Roman Catholic church or in other Christian churches, but also in secular groups or organizations. This document revolutionized the way the church thinks about salvation and the Spirit outside the boundaries of the Roman Catholic church. *Gaudium et spes* is to a certain extent the Catholic answer to the French *Liberté, Egalité, Fraternité*. In that sense the Council was, actually, an overtaking maneuver—the church catching up to certain human rights and new modern values.

But all these conciliar "renewals" were prepared for: before the Council by some theologians; during the Council itself by, for example, Pope John XXIII's encyclical *Pacem in terris* (1963); by the conciliar Declaration on Religious Liberty (*Dignitatis humanae*), the ecumenical decree (*Unitatis redintegratio*) and the Declaration on Non-Christian Religions (*Nostra aetate*). These were the most important documents of the *aggiornamento* of the Roman Catholic church and its engagement in worldly, humanly existential and societal problems—no longer as an ecclesiastic annexation of worldly power (as in earlier times), but in a sacramental model (*Lumen gentium*), i.e., in critical service to humankind in its struggle with world problems.

The shortcoming of *Gaudium et spes* is a certain lack of cultural-social criticism. Historically it is, actually, rather ironic. The document that accepted such modern, liberal, new social values as freedom of conscience and of religion was published in 1965; only three years later these same values were questioned by the upcoming fundamental societal-cultural criticism, which found its first climax in the worldwide student protests of 1968. I am afraid I have to say that the church reacted too late; there was some social criticism in many societies before the Council, but what happened from 1968 until about 1970 was neither diagnosed nor foreseen by sociologists at the time of the Council.

The big impact of *Gaudium et spes*—let alone a whiff of secular optimism (in those years a very dated mentality in the Western world)—was that it broke with the struggle between medieval Scholastic and modern neo-Scholastic traditions. *Gaudium et spes* overcame the medieval Augustinism that neglected the peculiarity and autonomy of the social, political and secular sectors of the world and its societal structures, which nonetheless the medieval Thomas Aquinas defended as philosopher against medieval Augustinism.

## What's the most important teaching that came out of the Council?

The most important teaching comes from *Lumen gentium* on the collegiality of the bishops (as I said above). *Lumen gentium* also implies conferences of bishops and pastoral synods with both priests and lay people; but after about ten years its practice in most of the ecclesial dioceses was gone. Jesuit professor Joseph Ratzinger, as a theologian at Vatican II, was enthusiastic about the Council's renewed patristic collegiality; he even wrote a very important article about this topic in the first issue of the review *Concilium*.

At the end of the first session of Vatican II, a lot of people thought that the principle of episcopal collegiality would make an end to the days of extreme power in the Roman Curia. The common thought was that the college of bishops stands above the cardinals of the Curia; this expresses the general feeling of the first two sessions of the Council. Sometimes it seemed as if the bishops had gathered in Rome to reduce the power of the Roman Curia as an organ above the collegiality of the bishops spread over the whole world. This "military" vocabulary droned through the halls and conference chambers of meetings of some theologians and bishops, who discussed the policy of tackling some problems in the *aula*. Once during a regular meeting of theologians, among whom was (the later Cardinal) Ratzinger, I heard Cardinal [Gabriel-Marie] Garrone [1901–1994]—at that time the archbishop of Toulouse, France—urging some colleagues to abandon their "military" vocabulary. I agree, strategic thinking was characteristic for the atmosphere outside the *aula*. But—as I told you before— then came the "black week" in which the *Nota praevia* was published, which interpreted the reciprocal papal and episcopal collegiality from *Lumen gentium* as what I would call hypersensitively "pope-centered."

## Whom do you feel was the most significant figure at the Council?

That is hard to say. I think Pope John XXIII, with his statements at the opening of the Council. The pope made a difference between the Gospel and the cultural forms and articulations in which the Gospel is embedded and handed down. His address to the Council as the solemn opening of Vatican II was a sign of clear longing to open himself and the church to the Holy Spirit: "Open the windows!" This was a major eye-opener for all the bishops, but especially for those from the Third World. Traditionally they feared to utter what they were thinking, for in their dioceses the praxis of the church differed seriously from the rules of the same church. Now they heard from theologians that they shouldn't change their Christian ways, but that the whole church should change its way. *Aggiornamento*—open the windows!

Of Pope Paul VI, I have more personal memories. As I said before, Cardinal Alfrink tried two times to let me attend the sessions as an official *peritus*, but Cardinal Ottaviani prevented this. Near the end of the Council, in a private conversation with the pope, Cardinal Alfrink personally complained about this refusal. The pope knew nothing about Ottaviani's refusal and suggested that Alfrink let me ask for a private audience, which I did on December 4, 1965. The conversation took place in French, insofar one can say that it was a conversation; every time I tried to say a word, the pope interrupted me. At the end of the audience, which lasted for a little more than half an hour, the pope gave me a rosary with the words "for your father." I was so confused, but also shocked about the implicit absence of "mother," that I too spontaneously replied, "And what about my mother?" The pope gave me silently a second rosary! For myself I received a Greek-Latin New Testament. About one year after the Council was finished, I got a book from the Vatican: the official publication of the documents of the Council (Vatican City, 1966) with the inscription *Donum summi pontificis* (gift from the pope). This I found a nice gesture from the pope: all official *periti* had received such a copy. Apparently Pope Paul VI wanted to make up for Ottaviani's silence.

### What has happened that you never imagined would happen?

The turn in the Council's direction after the intervention of Pope John XXIII in November 1962. I never imagined that the pope would go against the rules of the canon law after the votes on the original *schemas*. Although the votes on the refusal of the *schemas* did not get the legally required two-thirds majority, he refused to maintain these *schemas* as the basis for the debates in the *aula*. This gesture paved the way for renewal as result of the debates in Vatican II.

### What hasn't happened?

The greatest shortcoming in the teaching of the Council was the lack of systematic reflection about God. During four sessions (1962–1965) the Council was speaking about and discussing itself, the church (indeed, that was more than necessary), but it didn't speak about God. Meanwhile the Christian faithful outside the Council were in a state of confusion with regard to religion with God or religion without God. Four years before the Council would start, I was installed [in January 1958] as professor at Nijmegen in The Netherlands; my inaugural lecture was on the quest for God as an urgent problem not only for humankind but also for the Christian faithful ("In Search for a Living God," May 9, 1958).

Vatican II, on the contrary, took the reality of God for granted, hence "presupposed" to all what this Council had to say—and rightly so. But at that time (in Europe, anyway) the Christian faithful were already concerned about the traditional images of God. Religious Christian faith was at that time not self-evident anymore. In this respect the discussions in Rome during the Council were rather alien to many of our Christian faithful, and Vatican II didn't strengthen of their faith in the living God. To be honest, the Council aroused more hope and trust among the faithful in the *aggiornamento* of the church itself. This yields a great benefit, although about twenty years later, this hope and trust (on the intra-ecclesial level) changed and became a great frustration for many Christian believers. In the same period, the impact of the reigning Pope John Paul II on the extra-ecclesial level (the world), concerning social, economic and multicultural questions and, above all, his care and interventions for peace, were wholehearted and positively accepted by the same Christians.

Ironically, we live in a secularized Western world that has never been more filled with religions, religious phenomena and movements. At the same time we are confronted with a deep crisis about the belief in God's own reality and, on the other hand, many Christians are skeptical of a so-called absolutism of Christian claims, in which one's own religion sometimes is identified with the living God. Among believers in a personal God—Jews, Christians and Muslims—a tendency to radical fundamentalism is threatening the social and humane acceptability of faith in God. Neo-conservative Christians, above all in the United States, rule the air waves at the moment; and some Catholics are not aliens on this terrain of direction. The privileges of *Opus Dei* and its behavior are, for many religious people, a thorn in the side. Many Christians no longer experience Christianity as a joyful, hopeful Gospel, a liberating and redeeming way of life, but rather as a kind of sophisticated, hairsplitting, detailed system of [in their articulations] everlasting doctrines and subdoctrines that camouflage the "hierarchy of truths" so fortunately emphasized in Vatican II. In such an atmosphere, the institutional side of Christian churches is in imminent danger of a religious ideology in which there is no distinction between "God" and "own religion," with its dimensions of contingent and culturally conditioned embedding.

Another rather negative aspect of Vatican II is the fact that this Council was a remarkable, sometimes diplomatic "Council of compromises." The final writer, for example, of the Dogmatic Constitution (*Lumen gentium*) was in fact not only a good theologian, but also a diplomatic, political member of the Belgian Senate. To a great extent, such compromises were the result of an elegant and stylish respect for the majority in the Council vis-à-vis the little minority. The members of the Council had to make some compromises in order to save the essence of the new views defended by the majority and seriously attacked by a scanty but tenacious minority. In the solemn last votes about all the Council documents during the closure of the Council, only a quartet—say, four—of the Council's members refused some documents. After the Council, that was the beginning of a break with the Roman Catholic Church, by what is called the Lefebvrists—the conservative schism of Archbishop [Marcel] Lefebvre [1905–1991].

But the reverse of the model of those compromises was that we now are sometimes confronted with some ambivalent hermeneutics. Some Council texts can be interpreted in the line of the minority, but the intention of the Council, explained in the official amendments of some claims of the minority or of other even more "progressive" members, was very clear for the majority of the assembly. In post-Vatican trends, many theologians were convinced that some measures and decrees of the Roman Curia reflected clearly the minority side of ambivalent articulations in the texts of the Council, without a fine feeling for the spirit and soul of Vatican II.

As a surprise, I learned during Vatican II the enormously different and incomparable situation of being present in real life with bishops and cardinals and many other people, including the media, during a Council, as distinguished from studying ancient and faraway councils (for example, Ephesus and Chalcedon). In the first case you are feeling the emotions, the frustrations, and the elegant but serious fighting of the members of the Council. This atmosphere overwhelmed me. In the second (historical) case, you had to find out yourself and recreate from silent texts the atmosphere of what really had been at stake and what was (at that time) the dynamic that was bearing on the deepest religious and humane longings of all the members.

I remember a little friendly struggle during the Council with Monsignor [Gerard] Philips (professor at Louvain), the secretary of the newly appointed (November 1962) theological commission. I told him my doubts about some diplomatic texts in *Lumen gentium.* He said, "After the Council the secretaries of the diverse conciliar commissions will interpret the texts in the spirit in which we have formulated them, and which we in fact have explained in a very open way in the official Amendments [the answers of the "reporter," the official relator of each commission]." I replied, "Believe me, when the Council is finished, we will encounter many troubles with the lack of clearness of some Council documents. Their formulations are too diplomatic or too capable of multiple interpretations.

Above all, after the Council, I think the Roman Curia will regain its power after some time over what the theologians (with the bishops in your Theological Commission) have explained in the official Amendments [answers]. Directly or indirectly, the Curia will interpret the texts." He firmly did not agree. But after the Council, what I feared became true. Nowadays the impression is given that only certain members of the Roman Curia are authorized to legitimately interpret Vatican II.

## Should there be a third Vatican Council? What topic(s) would you bring to the table?

I think that the interval between the Council of Trent and Vatican I, and the later interval between Vatican I and Vatican II, are really too great. If there is a remarkable sociocultural change in a temporal epoch, the church stands in need of a Council. In that respect I plead for a Vatican III. But I am not sure about the "here and now" as the most opportune time of a new Council.

## Can you tell me why?

During the post-Vatican II period, the Roman Catholic Church became to a high extent a very polarized church. Many bishops think that the polarization is fading away. That in my opinion is a bad mistake. The polarization has already gone "underground": it strikes at roots, but is not "fighting for Christian freedom" anymore. It is indifferent to the church *as institution*, and that is not normal for a living ecclesial community, for a church. That institutional aspect belongs to the essence of the ecclesial community (as it belongs to the historical reality of every community). There is more. The result of the ecclesiastic policy of the church—above all, the policy on nominating bishops—has broadened the polarization in the midst of the episcopacy in many countries, all over the world. The relation between the *institutional* church and the great traditions of the *Catholica* and the Christian *ecumenicity* have remained for many years on standby.

In such a tense situation I would not be in favor of a new Council, here and now. We stand in need of a transitional time and a transitional pope, as was the (nevertheless) conservative Pope John XXIII. Pentecostal gifts don't leave either the church or our world! And those gifts of the Holy Spirit strengthen my hope and Christian gratuitous optimism.

The most important topic I would bring to the agenda of any new Council would be that of the reality of a real God. What is to be done about our talk *about* or, more urgently, *with* God? The Gospel is a way of life, the path of humankind's life on the way to God. If you want to name our nameless God, you cannot do otherwise than to name him in very human articulations, which are not stamped measures to express God's identity. That is the deepest meaning of what we call "infallible, solemn declared dogmas." They stand under the proviso of God's mystery, who (or which) is not identifiable. At stake is the real ortho-doxy as direction-post for "going the path of God": following the human mani-festation and way of life of Jesus of Nazareth, warranted by the humanly risky faith in God who raised the crucified Messiah.

## What has been the most significant liturgical achievement and what do we yet need to do to implement full, conscious and active participation?

The Council spoke about active participation and inculturation. But when you read contemporary documents from bishops or the magisterium about the liturgy, you can see a certain pattern of overemphasizing the minority of "liturgical rebels." These are being generalized in the liturgical renewal on the whole. Since Vatican II, sacramental liturgical practice has assumed widely divergent forms. In some countries (including The Netherlands), the verbal aspect of the liturgy—denoted by the traditional patristic term *legomenon* (to a little extent rooted in the Hellenistic mysteries, but actually rooted in Jewish liturgical usages)—is emphasized. At the same time, the aspect indicated by the equally ancient word *drómenon*—festive, even dramatic enactments forming an expressive whole of gestures, postures, light, the space in which the liturgy is celebrated, and so on—is kept subdued, sometimes eclipsed by treating these things as inessential extras. In Africa and Latin America, for instance, liturgy is embedded in the indigenous cultures and is expressed realistically in a recognizable, enthusiastic ritual performance that acts as an identity-forming force throughout the celebrating community. The *drómenon* is much more important there.

In cases where *legomenon* is over-accentuated, some people are speaking of a kind of "Protestantization" that results in a purely verbal, sometimes cerebral liturgy, which evokes for some Christians deviating connotations. In the case where *drómenon* is over-accentuated, the central curial authority in Rome greets these enthusiastic celebrations with a certain hesitation and transparent accents of constraint. Lively, beautiful liturgy is going on in countries where the Catholic faithful often intertwine their animated and playful festive celebrations with still-archaic and outdated religious images of God.

A truly harmonious combination of *legomenon* and *drómenon,* or of word and gesture, is not easily achieved. To my mind, that is understandable after so many centuries of stagnation of open (albeit disciplined) liturgical creativity, which had been curbed in Catholic churches since the Council of Trent until some new inaugurations during the last years of Pope Pius XII and the great liturgical constitution *Sacrosanctum concilium,* the first accepted conciliar document of the Council. Thanks to the Second Vatican Council the liturgy is liberated from its fixation on rigid adherence to formulas and gestures. The Council brought some flexibility.

The scope this opened up unleashed a fervor that led, in some ways, to an impetuous approach that was hardly justifiable, either liturgically or theologically, by the modest innovations of the Council. Nonetheless, no one can be blamed for the fact that a harmonious balance in the current sacramental, liturgical praxis is not self-evident at this stage of searching for both the human and liturgical dimensions of vividly beautiful Christian celebrations. Accusations in this regard, particularly if directed to our best pioneers in the field of liturgical innovations, I consider plainly unfair and ungrateful (even when there have been some failures).

While Christianity may be a school of wisdom, it is not a philosophical institution. Besides the dogmatic tradition, which transmits the substance of the Christian faith through reflective documents, authoritative traditions, academic theological traditions, and popularizing theological traditions, there are other ways in which the Christian Gospel fans out in all sorts of traditions. The first that comes to my mind are the biblical stories depicted in mosaics, sculptures and paintings in ancient primitive little house churches, and later on in patristic basilicas and medieval cathedrals. They familiarized the faithful with the stories of the Old and the New Testaments. Secondly, one should not forget the mystagogy from the time of the Church fathers, a practice that remained firmly focused on knowledge, instruction in the practice and a mystical, intensified experience of the sacraments of initiation: Baptism, anointing or confirmation, and the Eucharist. Third, there are the vitally important experiential and religious practices that come on the tides of the church's liturgical seasons.

The ritual, liturgical expressions of religious belief are what the Christian sacraments are about, expressing and passing on a shared religious identity. But to many believers these expressions are now in crisis, a crisis so acute that many have turned their backs on sacramental practice.

## What Council teaching was most difficult to implement in the local churches?

To my opinion, it is not the teachings of the Council that are difficult to implement in the local churches, but merely the formulation—and therefore the interpretation—of the teachings. The teachings of the Council have a general and universal formulation, which implies that more (sometimes contradictory) interpretations can be given for one and the same statement. That is why it has been possible in Africa and Asia to adjust the teachings of the church to their own situations.

Finally, in view of the multicultural, multireligious situation in our world, in my opinion the church stands in need of an interreligious dialogue. Today, such dialogue and interreligious collaboration on some levels must have urgent priority on our agendas.

On the other hand, I remain thankful for the Second Vatican Council. In all its ups and downs, in its effervescences and its moments of human shortcomings, this Council—from the beginning to the end—happened not without the sensitive and active gift of God's Holy Spirit and not without our human powerlessness, disability and failures. I believe in the Pentecostal leading of the divine Spirit, knowing that ecclesial activities are a very human enterprise as well.

Dr. Edward Schillebeeckx OP was born in Antwerp, Belgium in 1914 and studied philosophy in Ghent, theology at the Catholic University of Louvain, and at and the Collège de France in Paris. In 1952 he defended his doctoral thesis in theology at Le Saulchoir in Paris. During that same period he was appointed a lecturer in dogmatic theology and spiritual director at Louvain. In 1958 he accepted the chair of dogmatic and historical theology in Nijmegen (The Netherlands). During the Second Vatican Council and at the Pastoral Council in Noordwijkerhout (1966–1970), he was advisor to the Dutch bishops. Since that time, Schillebeeckx played and is still playing a major role in ecclesiastic and theological renewal. He received several honorary doctoral degrees and was honored with the prestigious *Praemium Erasmianum* in 1982. A full bibliography of Schillebeeckx's work can be found at www.kun.nl/Schillebeeckx. At present he is working on a book about the sacraments.

# PART 4

# Media/Observers

# Edmond Bliven

## Interviewer: Geraldine Ethen

**How did you, a diocesan priest from Portland, Oregon, get to attend one of the sessions of Vatican II in Rome?**

After the first sessions of the Second Vatican Council, I spoke with Monsignor Thomas Tobin, vicar general of the archdiocese (whose assistant I had been at All Saints parish), of my interest in studying at the Ecumenical Institute at the Chateau de Bossey, outside of Geneva, Switerzland. I had read an article in *America* magazine about a winter semester at Bossey that brought people of various faiths together to study theology in an ecumenical atmosphere. No Catholic priest had yet studied there but the *America* article suggested it would be an excellent opportunity for the right person. Monsignor Tobin said that if Archbishop [Edward] Howard [1877–1983] gave his permission, funds for such study had been made available from a benefactor who was interested in continuing education for the clergy.

Archbishop Howard gave me the permission and I reported back to Monsignor Tobin. He said there was "a small problem." At that time it was forbidden for priests to study theology at a non-Catholic institution without permission from the Holy Office (now known as the Congregation for the Doctrine of the Faith). Cardinal [Alfredo] Ottaviani [1890–1979], secretary of the Holy Office had let it be known that he would not give such a permission.

I replied that it seemed like more than a small problem. "Don't worry," said the monsignor. "We'll have an audience with the pope and get his permission." I knew that Tobin had many connections in Rome, so I trusted that it would work out all right.

Archbishop Howard had attended the first session of Vatican II with Monsignor Tobin as his *peritus* (theological advisor). But the Council schedule and the Italian meal pattern did not suit him, so he suggested that Monsignor Tobin, who loved Rome, attend the rest of the Council without him.

Monsignor Tobin invited me to come to Rome with him and his two sisters, Mrs. David Powers of Cincinnati and Mrs. Simeon Winch of Portland, and spend a week with them in an apartment they had rented. We agreed on a fair price for my share of the rent and the other expenses of the apartment. (There was a cook and a housekeeper to help with the entertaining of guests.)

After we arrived in Rome, the first item on the agenda was a papal audience. Pope John XXIII had died after the first session and we were eager to meet his successor, Paul VI. We dressed in formal attire. The monsignor wore a purple *ferraiola* (full-length cloak) over his cassock. Since I was a simple priest, my *ferraiola* was black. His sisters wore black dresses and black lace veils. After the general audience, the pope walked from room to room and visited with invited guests. He spent about a half-hour with us. Monsignor Tobin introduced his sisters and me and spoke about my interest in studying at the Ecumenical Institute. Pope Paul smiled and gladly gave me permission to attend.

Monsignor Tobin had a lot of history in Rome. He had studied there before ordination, earning two doctorates (philosophy and theology). After a few years in parish work in Portland, he was sent back to Rome to study canon law so he could set up a Chancery Office in Portland. During both of these Roman periods he made many friends. Some of them came to dinner at the apartment during my week in Rome; one of them made it possible for me to attend an actual session of the Second Vatican Council.

Another "small problem" threatened to keep me out of the Council session. Archbishop [Pericle] Felice, who was in charge of protocol, had tightened the restrictions on attendance at the sessions. He would give permission for individuals who had a legitimate interest in the Council to attend the Mass that preceded each session, but after the Mass, everyone had to leave except the Council fathers: bishops and certain religious superiors, accredited non-Catholic observers, and the *periti*.

One evening we had as a dinner guest a monsignor who worked for Cardinal Ottaviani in the Holy Office. Although he had little enthusiasm for my ecumenical interests, he had a good heart and wanted to help me get into the Council session to be held the next morning. It was especially appropriate because the Council fathers were going to discuss the Catholic church's relations with other Christian bodies. Monsignor Tobin had secured a ticket for me to attend the Mass before the session. The Holy Office monsignor asked me if I had a spare passport picture. I said I did. "Bring it along," he replied.

The next morning I stood in line to attend the Mass. I was a little disappointed because it was a Roman Mass. One of the innovations of the Council was to have a celebration of each of the many non-Roman eucharistic liturgies, which was quite an education for most of the Council fathers. Most of them were quite intrigued with the Ethiopian liturgy, which features drums and dancing along with chants accompanied by the sistrum, a musical instrument pictured in ancient Egyptian tombs. (The Ethiopians were evangelized by missionaries from Egypt.)

But I was happy enough with the more sober Roman Mass.

After the Mass, a beadle walked through St. Peter's announcing to the non-participants, "*Exeant omnes*! (Everybody out!)" When he came to me, following the monsignor's instructions of the night before, I joined him at the presidents' table set up in front of the *confessio*, the stairway that leads down to St. Peter's tomb beneath the high altar.

The beadle came up and asked him who I was. "Show him your passport picture," said the monsignor. The beadle noted that it was indeed my picture and went away satisfied. A Latin will immediately understand this exchange. The rest of us must just acknowledge that is how these things are done.

I found the discussion during the session fascinating. The difference in accents among the Italians, the French, the Germans and the Americans, as they all spoke in Latin, was a treat to my ears. One of the speakers, the Melkite patriarch Maximos [IV] Saigh [1878–1967], from Lebanon, departed from protocol, because, as he said, "Our church has never used Latin; therefore I will speak in a language more universally understood—French."

The document under discussion had included the Jewish religion along with Christianity, because Judaism is the parent of Christianity. The patriarch would have none of it. "It is an insult to our Orthodox brothers of the venerable Eastern churches to put them in the same document with the Jews." Because of the patriarch's objections, which many of his Arab brothers shared, the final Council statement on relations with the Jews was issued in a separate document.

The speech I enjoyed the most was by Cardinal [Joseph Elmer] Ritter [1892–1967] of St. Louis in his flat Midwestern Latin. He commented on the difficulty that theologians were having classifying different Christian bodies. They conceded that the Eastern Orthodox bodies were certainly churches with the sacramental structures of early Christianity, but what about the groups dating from the Reformation that claimed only two sacraments or even, like the Quakers, none at all? He gave a response that I thought was typical of the American mentality at its best: "Why not refer to Christian groups as churches or ecclesial communities and let them decide which name fits them best?" His view prevailed in the final document.

## What was your impression of other American contributions to the Council?

The American bishops went to Vatican II thinking that they were conservative; however, once they got there, they discovered that they weren't. As an example, we could look at the concept of separation of church and state. The American solution was not prompted by any enmity between church and state; it was a pragmatic acceptance that, because the founding colonies had different religions, there was no way to impose one of them on everybody. So they agreed that there would be no official religion; all would be free to follow their own conscience. The American bishops arrived in Rome convinced that church-state separation was good for both the church and the state.

Cardinal [Francis] Spellman [1889–1967] of New York, both a strong theological conservative and a patriotic American, championed church-state separation. He brought with him the Jesuit John Courtney Murray as his official *peritus*. Previously, the Roman authorities had frowned on Murray's writings and cautioned his Jesuit superiors to rein him in. The final Council statement on church-state relations was a vindication for Murray and the Americans who backed him up.

## What other memories do you have of the Council?

I was impressed with Pope John XXIII's concern that the Council's decisions be arrived at by as close to consensus as possible. Pope John knew that the Council decisions were not like civil laws that must be obeyed. If the Council passed documents that many bishops did not agree with, they could go home and ignore them. The resulting compromises and adjustments made for hard work, but the results were much more harmonious than the politics of our [U.S.]

Congress. As a result, the documents of Vatican II passed by large majorities and, for the most part, are being carried out.

The introduction of vernacular languages into the Roman liturgy is an example. The majority of the Council fathers were supportive of the vernacular in the sacraments and the Liturgy of the Hours, but not in favor of a completely vernacular Mass.

The first new missal following Vatican II [1966] still had the collect, the prayer over the gifts, the preface, eucharistic prayer, and the prayer after Communion all in Latin. The second step was that all the prayers of the priest could be said in English except the eucharistic prayer, which was to be said in Latin. The third step was allowing the eucharistic prayer to be said in the vernacular, and the addition of three new eucharistic prayers in addition to the Roman Canon.

I was editor of *Today's Missal* during the various stages of revision of the liturgy. In addition to changing the presider's prayers to the vernacular, there was the introduction of the new three-year cycle of Sunday readings. I received some interesting letters from people who obviously had not read much of the Bible; however, we have been greatly enriched by the revised cycle of readings from the Council.

For the first time, a Catholic going to Sunday Mass could hear often more of Scripture than many Protestants who are dependent on hearing their pastor's favorite readings. As a matter of fact, many other churches have now adopted the three-year cycle recommended by Vatican II, or one based on the same principles.

What a change!

Father Edmond Bliven is a retired priest of the Archdiocese of Portland in Oregon. He was born in Salem, Oregon in December, 1925, and attended the Benedictine-run Mt. Angel Preparatory School and Seminary College from 1939–1946. His theology training was at St. Edward's Seminary in Kenmore, Washington. He was ordained by Archbishop Edward Howard on March 25, 1950.

In 1963 and 1964 he attended the University of Geneva and received a certificate in ecumenical studies. Since then he has studied in Jerusalem, Poland, Belgium and China. Besides numerous parish appointments, he has maintained an active role in the archdiocesan publications. For many years he was editorial page editor of the *Catholic Sentinel*, the diocesan weekly newspaper, and he was editor of *Today's Missal* for over twenty years. He is a member of the Board of Directors of Oregon Catholic Press. He continues to minister at Sunday liturgies and teaches classes in Scripture and church history.

# Robert Blair Kaiser

## Interviewer: John Flaherty

**Tell me about yourself.**

After spending ten years in the Jesuits, I worked as a reporter at the *Arizona Republic* in Phoenix. In three years there, I covered everything—police beat, courts, education beat and labor beat, and I did a long series on the Navajo Indians that won a Pulitzer nomination. One day I was sent out to the home of Clare Boothe Luce to interview one of her houseguests—a Jesuit named Martin D'Arcy. Both had just written a book called *The Mind and Heart of Love*, a very abstruse work that no one could understand. In the Luce living room, with Mrs. Luce sitting in and listening, I interviewed him; we had a nice conversation about his work. When the interview was over she turned to me and said, "I have been reading your stuff in the *Republic* and have been wondering who you were and what you wanted to do with your life." I said, "I think I'd like to work for *Time*." And she said, "I think I can be of some assistance."

Very shortly, I got a call from Dick Clurman, *Time*'s chief of correspondents, who said, "Can you come see me in L.A.?" We had an interview, and he said, "Your clips are impressive; you can do anything, but I'm not going to hire you." I asked him why not. He said, "I'd like to be known as my own man—I don't want to be a tool of the Luces—so I'm not going to hire you." He was playing "bad cop," but there was a good cop sitting next to him named T. George Harris, who was *Time*'s bureau chief in San Francisco. Harris said, "Why don't you come up to San Francisco and try out for two weeks?"

So that's what I did. I tried out for two weeks and did very well, and hit a home run my first time up in the major leagues. I broke into the magazine with a big story on the Jesuit Institute of Lay Theology in San Francisco; it was a new idea then. It ran more than a full page in *Time*.

### What year was that?

1961; before the Council. Then Clurman said, "Can you go to L.A. and try out there?" I put in a full summer in L.A.; he called me and said, "How would you like to work for *Time* magazine?" I said, "Of course, yeah." He said, "There's only one thing, I'll never send you to Rome. I'm afraid of your Jesuit background." Well, I got hired; I spent the fall in L.A. and the winter in Boston. He called; I went to New York, and he said, "How'd you like to go to Rome?" Apparently, the six months that I spent working for *Time* and doing Catholic stories, he realized that I was only an asset, that my Jesuit background only helped me be a better reporter. He sent me to Rome in March of 1962, before the Council. I started to immerse myself in the preparation for the Council—I did a bunch of stories; got some of them in the magazine.

In August 1962 we were working on a cover story on Pope John XXIII. I got an exclusive interview with John XXIII before the Council. It happened like this: Henry Luce was a friend of Cardinal [Francis] Spellman [1889–1967], who told Luce, "I'd like to use *Time*'s pictures of the Sistine Chapel so we can recreate the Sistine Chapel at my Vatican pavilion in the New York World's Fair." Luce said "Of course, but I have a favor to ask of you; I've got this correspondent in Rome who would like to talk to the pope."

Popes don't give interviews.

So they arranged that accidentally on purpose I would go out to his summer residence, talk to the pope's secretary, and the pope would saunter up the hallway after his Wednesday morning audience and just say, "Oh, what a nice surprise meeting you here." I thought it was going to be a pro forma interview; you know, maybe two or three minutes, he'd give me a blessing, and I'd be off. But no, he really wanted to talk to me; he had important things he wanted to tell me about his hopes for the Council.

## At that point did you have any idea how big the Council would be?

I was one of the few who had an optimistic view that the Council would help the pope bring the church up to date. The pope used the Italian word *aggiornamento*, and I figured he wouldn't have used it on a whim—he was serious about updating the church. I thought, "The last Council was a hundred years ago and the world has undergone more changes in the last hundred years than it has in the previous nineteen centuries. If they're serious they ought to be moving the church ahead." My friend Gus [Gustave] Weigel, a Jesuit theologian, said after the second session, "Well, the Council has moved the church ahead centuries, from the sixteenth to the eighteenth." But in fact I was surprised, as almost everyone was, at the radical changes that occurred at Vatican II—changes in spirit, more than in the letter. The charter written at Vatican II helped make the church more human, more at the service of the people, more humble in the face of history, less a church of laws and more a church of love. That is the spirit that came over the church.

## And that was the prevailing spirit that permeated everything?

The main thing at the Council was free speech. For the first time in their lives, these 2,200 bishops sat there and they listened to other bishops saying things that were rather radical, things they had been thinking all their lives but never dared say because they didn't think they could. So when Bishop Emiel-Jozef De Smedt [1909–1995] of Bruges, Belgium, got up there and inveighed against the Roman Curia and their juridicism and their clericalism and their triumphalism, he got the hugest applause during that first session of the Council. People knew this was an all-out assault on *Romanitá*—De Smedt was saying that the church is not Rome and Rome is not the church. Gradually, as all of this began to be implemented and put into texts that they would vote on and vote on and vote on, and amend and amend and amend, it became clear what they were up to. They were trying to write a charter to change the church, to give the church back to the people. That is not the normal "take" on Vatican II that you get in the Associated Press, or in any popular journal. The general press has tended to trivialize Vatican II; the Council, it says, turned the altar around and put the Mass in the vernacular. But that's just on the surface. The really radical thing about this Council was that when they were writing the Constitution on the Church (*Lumen gentiun*), they took the people of God and put them in first place. The people are the church, they said, and the bishops are there to serve the people of God. Authority, they said, is not for domination but for service; any authority we have, if we are bishops, is to serve. And that's embodied throughout all the rest of the documents of Vatican II.

**Within that context, tell me about some of your conversations with the Council fathers and the one interview with the pope.**

The most interesting thing the pope told me was that he wanted to end the Cold War, that he considered the Cold War a crusade just like the ancient crusades, and that Christianity had been around long enough not to need any more crusades. He wanted to make friends with Moscow, to bring the patriarch of Moscow to the Council so he and other Orthodox observers could see his intentions, to bring all Christians back together.

**So really, the fall of the Berlin Wall—**

That was way before the fall of the Berlin Wall. It goes all the way back to John XXIII.

**It's just not well known.**

That's right. In the spring of 1963 (he would die a few months later, in June) John XXIII had a very important visit with Nikita Khrushchev's son-in-law, Alexei Adzhubei, and Khrushchev's daughter [Rada]. He made it very clear to them how much he loved the Russian people. That meeting started to break down barriers. I tell this story in my memoir, *Clerical Error* [New York: Continuum Publishing Group, 2002]; most of the book is about my adventures at Vatican II.

As you know, or maybe you don't, the Council was closed [to the press]. Members of the press were not allowed inside the Council, so we had to rely on press releases from the official Vatican press office, which were terrible. Early press releases would say, "We had a debate on the liturgy this morning, and twelve bishops spoke in favor of the *schema* and thirteen bishops spoke against the *schema* and here were their names." That was it. You couldn't make a news story out of that. The trick was to develop your own sources inside the Council who would come out and tell you what had happened there. At noon the bishops would all come tumbling down the steps of St. Peter's; it looked like a waterfall of purple and red and black.

## Would the press be out there?

We would be out there in St. Peter's Square, ready to collar our favorite guys and take them off to lunch and interview them. We'd find out who gave the most brilliant speeches that morning; they'd tell us and then we would split and go off and get the speeches. One guy would get one speech, and another guy would get another speech, and we'd share them. We pooled our resources.

## Were you pooling with correspondents from the American press primarily or from the international press?

Both. We made friends with the French, the Belgians, the Dutch, the Spanish, as well as the guys from Asia, Latin America, and so forth, and a few Americans as well. My major breakthrough came early in the Council. I looked at the list of bishops and I saw the name Archbishop T.D. Roberts, S.J. [1893–1976]. He was the retired archbishop of Bombay. I had read some of his books and I was really a fan of his. He was staying at some nuns' *pensione.* I called him; he asked to meet at the Foyer Unitas, where some Dutch sisters had an ecumenical center near the Piazza Navona. I saw him at three o'clock and we talked for a couple of hours. I drove him home, where he was living was really bleak; there wasn't a tree around. I said, "How'd you like to come home for dinner?" He said, "Oh, yeah!" So I took him home and after dinner I said to my wife, "You know, he's staying out there, and we've got an extra bedroom. Why don't we let him stay here?" So we did, and he did. I had my own Council father in residence, who would come home every afternoon with the secret documents and give them to me. They were all in Latin, but I was fluent in Latin: I took eleven years of Latin. When I was in the Jesuit novitiate, we used Latin as a living language. We played baseball in Latin!

## So that answers the question, "Did you have any personal contacts in the Council?"

Sort of. Archbishop Roberts had a lot of friends who were missionary bishops, mainly from India and Africa and Latin America. He would invite them over for dinner, so I began to meet more and more of the missionary bishops—Denis Hurley [b. 1915] of Durban, South Africa, for example. And Joseph Blomjous [1908–1992] from Tanganyika. And Gerard van Velsen [1910–1996] from Kroonstad, South Africa. Those were three of my favorites. And some Jesuits would come from the Gregorian University. One Sunday night, Jesuit Father

Thurston Davis, the editor of *America*, came with about five other Jesuits. We didn't have enough places at the table, so we had a buffet supper. A light bulb went on over my head and I said, "Why don't we just have a buffet supper every Sunday night? Come back next Sunday night and bring your friends." Very quickly we had about seventy-five Council fathers there every Sunday night. Some foreign journalists, too, but few Americans. Michael Novak and John Cogley were regulars, and so was Bennett Bolton of the Associated Press.

## Michael Novak was with?

*Harper's Magazine* sent Michael to Rome to do a piece on the second session. But in the first session, there were no American journalists at my party because I didn't want to share. These were my sources, right? There were maybe half a dozen American bishops, of the liberal wing.

## Who were they?

[Paul] John Hallinan [1911–1968] of Atlanta; Robert Tracy [1909–1980] of Baton Rouge; [Peter] Bartholome [1893–1982] of St. Cloud, Minnesota. Leonard Cowley [1913–1973], the auxiliary bishop of Minneapolis-St. Paul, was a fabulous storyteller and mimic; he would tell funny stories in dialect. Hallinan liked to play the piano, so we rented a piano and started singing Irish songs during the parties.

## These bishops were from all over the world?

From all over the world, yeah. Hans Küng, the Swiss theologian from Tübingen, was a regular. He had written a book called *The Council: Reform and Reunion* [Sheed and Ward], a huge bestseller that anticipated what many liberals wanted to see happen at Vatican II. Every Sunday night he would be the last one to leave. We became close friends. I still see him; we exchange emails.

## The conversation would always gravitate toward what happened during that day or that week?

Right, right. In fact, I didn't do any work at those parties; I just took in by osmosis what was happening and what was going on with this conversation in this corner of the room, and another conversation over there, and another one over there. I would encourage my theologian friends to go back into one of the back bedrooms and write speeches for this or that bishop at the party. The Paulist Tom Stransky would work with a bishop on his speech, and some Protestant observers there helped the bishops write speeches. Robert MacAfee Brown, a Presbyterian observer; Albert Outler, a Methodist observer, George Lindbeck; a Lutheran observer—they were all there. This was the place to be on Sunday night in Rome; it was a real jamboree. I knew how the chess game was being played at the Council so I was really tapped in.

### Were you present for the closing ceremony at St. Peter's? And what was your reaction to that event?

It was a great sense of victory that we had gotten through it; there were a lot of battles fought, and finally the war was over. The side in favor of updating the church won, quite clearly; most of the votes would be two thousand to two hundred. The no-change party, whom I called the *semperidems* [always the same], were always outvoted ten to one. After the Council, people sometimes accused me of not being objective because most of my stories and my interpretations reflected the liberal side. Well, I had to say in my own defense that I was reflecting the winning side. That was the story. In fact, the other side always insisted that there was no story. "Don't expect any change at this Council," they told me repeatedly before the Council began. The famous TV personality Archbishop Fulton J. Sheen [1895–1979] told me that. He didn't even want to talk about the Council, wouldn't give me an interview. He said, "The Holy Spirit is in charge. He will take care of it all." For him, the Council was a supernatural event. But I had eyes. I could see that this gathering was a parliament of the world's bishops. All the things that happened in any parliament happened at the Council.

### But the momentum for change was overwhelming and headed in that one direction?

Oh, yeah.

### What was your impression of the interfaith and ecumenical strides that were made in the church during the Council?

You have to know what the church was before the Council to appreciate what changes really occurred at the Council. Before the Council, Catholics in America couldn't even go to a Protestant wedding. We were not allowed to go to a Protestant church. We were told not to associate with Protestants. We lived in something like a Catholic ghetto. But at Vatican II we were led by Pope John XXIII, the most non-sectarian of popes, who said it doesn't matter what religion you are as long as you are trying to make a difference in the world; that's the only thing that counts. He even said this to Communists in Bologna and Venice, where he was the archbishop before he became pope. He set a whole new tone. Before the Council, the no-change party, led by Cardinal Alfredo Ottaviani [1890–1979], did not want any observers at the Council—Protestants or Orthodox or anybody. There was a huge fight to get them there. But John XXIII wanted them there. He charged Cardinal Augustin Bea [1881–1968], a Jesuit biblical scholar and head of the Secretariat for Promoting Christian Unity, and his sidekick Jan Willebrands [1909–1983—archbishop of Utrecht] to make it very clear to the Protestant and Orthodox world that they were really, really, really welcome. When these observers finally got to the Council, they were given seats way in the back, but when the pope saw the seating arrangements he said, "No, no, no, you bring them up front!"

## The Protestant observers?

Right. They had better seats than any of the bishops, because the bishops were relegated to the bleachers and the Protestant and Orthodox observers were now in the box seats. They didn't have simultaneous translation—all the speeches were given in Latin—but the observers were each given a mentor to sit close and whisper simultaneous translations from the Latin to the English or German or French, or whatever they needed. My friend Gus Weigel [Gustave Weigel SJ] was there with George Lindbeck, the Lutheran observer, listening to the speeches and translating them for Lindbeck, whispering in his ear through the whole thing. Soon the observers weren't Protestants any longer. All of a sudden, the term of choice was "separated brethren."

## That's when that phrase was coined?

Right. The separated brethren became celebrities around Rome. You'd see them at every reception. You'd see them at my Sunday night parties. I had Jewish observers at those Sunday night parties, too, one from the American Jewish Committee and another from the World Jewish Congress.

## They got a good reception from the Council fathers?

Very warm, very warm. This was in some contrast to Vatican I, a hundred years before. The best bishop-theologian at Vatican I was a man named Joseph Strossmayer [1815–1905], from Bosnia-Herzegovina. He was way ahead of his time; he was saying good things about the Protestants, and the old guard actually hooted him off the floor. If you read any history of Vatican I you'll read about Joseph Strossmayer and how shamefully they treated him for saying good things about the Protestants.

I could go on and on. I could tell you shocking stories about the rocky history of ecumenism in the church. In the early 1920s, there was a very ecumenically-minded cardinal in Belgium, Cardinal [Desiré] Mercier [1851–1926]. After World War I, he launched conversations between the Anglicans and the Roman Catholics. They were called the Malines Conversations (after the primatial see in the ancient town of Malines in Belgium). In 1925, Cardinal Mercier made a very famous speech, actually ghosted for him by a Benedictine monk, Dom Lambert Beauduin [1873–1960]. The speech was called, "United, Not Absorbed." In that speech, the cardinal proposed that the entire Anglican Communion be brought into communion with Rome, whole and entire, with their own patriarch (the archbishop of Canterbury), their own married clergy and their own English language liturgy; and the Anglican Communion would be part of the Catholic Church, just like the autochthonous churches of the Middle East, the Maronites, the Melkites, the Byzantines, the Copts and so forth.

### Full communion?

Full communion with Rome. That's what Mercier proposed. But the pope at the time, Pius XI, hated this idea so much that he closed down the Malines Conversations and wrote an encyclical, *Mortalium animos* (1928), which said, "No more of this ecumenical nonsense." That's the way things pretty much stood until Vatican II. Rome considered ecumenical contacts suspect. Vatican II represented a huge change.

### Who helped John XXIII come to his landmark decision not to only invite our separated brethren but to give them a place of such prominence at Vatican II?

Well, maybe we ought to give some credit to the Holy Spirit. But, humanly speaking (which is the only way I can speak—I didn't have a chance to interview the Holy Spirit), I'd say Cardinal Bea had the most major influence. His contacts with solid Protestant biblical scholars had taught him the church had nothing to fear from solid biblical theologians, even if they were Protestants. They were Christians, after all—some of them reforming Christians who were way ahead of

Catholic reformers. I can't leave out Dom Lambert Beauduin, who died before the Council began; he knew Archbishop Roncalli as papal nuncio in Paris before he became cardinal patriarch of Venice and then Pope John XXIII. It was Beauduin who planted the idea of calling a Council in the mind of Roncalli, way back in 1946. This story just came out recently in a 1,612-page work, *Un Pionnier Dom Lambert Beauduin (1873–1960) Liturgie et Unité des chretiens*, by Raymond Loonbeck and Jacques Mortiau, professors on the faculty at the University of Louvain-Leuven.

## So the seeds of the Council were planted way back in 1946?

Dominican Sister Maureen Sullivan, a theologian from St. Anselm's College in New Hampshire, is doing a book for the Paulist Press on the seeds of Vatican II. She's writing about Beauduin and theologians like Yves Congar, M.D. Chenu, Henri de Lubac, Edward Schillebeeckx, John Courtney Murray and other theologians who were on the Curia's enemies list before Vatican II. They couldn't even publish in the years between 1946 and 1962. They were *personae non gratae* to the Vatican because they were interested in the *aggiornamento*. Pope John didn't just think this up by himself; he put his blessing on an *aggiornamento* that had already been begun by these great theologians.

## Most of this work was done prior to 1946?

No, they did their work from 1946 until 1962. Some early stuff, like the work of Cardinal Mercier, began in the twenties, but World War II was the thing that really made everybody sit up and take notice. They said, "Look, the church of the nineteenth century pretty much withdrew from the world, and it became an embattled church." In fact, Pius IX, who was pope from 1848 to 1892, forbade Italian Catholics from even voting in Italy's civil elections—they were excommunicated for voting! In effect, the hierarchical church tried to take Catholics out of public life. And how did that public life play out? Very poorly. The world was soon plunged into a great world war, World War I, without this leavening influence of Christianity—and then plunged into World War II as well. That was the compelling idea for the post-WWII Catholics in Europe, especially in Northern Europe, especially in France, Belgium, Holland

## The reaction was to be fully immersed....

That's right; that's one of the great upshots of Vatican II. *Gaudium et spes,* the crowning document of Vatican II, really lays out the whole plan. In *Gaudium et spes,* they quoted with approval the great optimist Pierre Teilhard de Chardin [1881–1955], the Jesuit paleontologist-philosopher, whose work had been condemned by Cardinal [Alfredo] Ottaviani in December 1962, during the Council's first session. Even as late as 1962, Teilhard was *persona non grata* inside some circles in the Vatican, for his writings about the future of the world. The point I am trying to make is this: that the fathers of Vatican II put their blessing on the world as something good and not evil, because the whole world is redeemed by Christ.

## Can you speak to the role of the church, as you see the work of the Council continuing? There are those who will say that the Council has failed, or that it's stalled, or at the same time that the spirit and the documents of the Second Vatican Council haven't been implemented, or have been ignored. Can you speak to all of those?

A lot of the people who criticize the Council are using a criterion that is basically institutional. They're looking at the number of priests in the world today as compared to before; they're looking at the number of sisters, the priestless parishes, the Catholic schools that have closed—and all of these are institutional criteria. Maybe those aren't the criteria that we should use.

The question before the house is, "Was the Council good or bad? Did it help make us better or worse as a people, as a church?" We're fighting about this now, the right wing and the left wing of the church, fighting all the time. I say if you're going to use institutional criteria, I'll agree with you. Maybe the Council struck a deathblow to the church—if you identify the church with clerics and clericalism. Is that bad? It's clericalism that's been behind the priest sex abuse crisis in the United States, which we saw come to full blossom in 2002. Priests were covering up for priests, even bishops were covering up for bishops, for wayward priests— that was all because they were in the same buddy system. That's clericalism.

## Looking back at your time in Rome and reflecting on the work of the church now in terms of the global village...

Well, the major change that's been effected is that we have a whole new attitude toward other religions—toward Islam, toward Buddhism, toward Hinduism, toward Confucianism, toward all the other great mainstream religions.

That we see the goodness in all of these religions. Jacques Dupuis [b. 1923], a Belgian Jesuit who spent twenty-five years in India before he came to teach at the Gregorian University in Rome, was in trouble for two years recently because he was writing some marvelous things about interreligious dialogue between Catholics and the other religions. The Holy Office did not like what he was writing, but he won that battle. They found that he wasn't a heretic. He even had the pope [John Paul II] on his side. Although the pope didn't say the right things, he certainly did the right things; he brought a whole bunch of people from all different religions to Assisi—in 1998, I believe—and the heads of all the world's great religions prayed together. The Holy Office went bonkers over that. They thought that was terrible—how dare they pray together!

But by his actions, at least, John Paul II was putting his blessing on the idea that we are after all worshiping the same God, we are all brothers and sisters under heaven. That's a huge change and it was begun at Vatican II. Cardinal [Franz] König [b. 1905] of Vienna was the first man in charge of the dialogue between the so-called non-Christian religions, the Eastern religions. Of course, this dialogue has to go on. We have a lot in common with the mainstream of Islam but the extremists in Islam are as crazy as the extremists in Catholicism; they would put us all into nuclear war if they had their druthers, which is really crazy. The future of the planet, really, rests on more dialogue among the members of all these mainstream religions. We have to find a way of marginalizing the fanatics. Every religion has its fanatics, both left and right wing. I think the Council was very timely in that regard—in fact, a little ahead of its time.

**Connecting the seeds for the Council all the way back to World War I and the withdrawal of the church from the secular world—if I can hear you clearly, the work of the Council is all the more important in this post-September 11 world.**

Absolutely! The Council's relevance is much clearer now than it was twenty-five years ago. The spirit of the Council is still alive and has to go on living. I know that some considered Cardinal [Joseph] Ratzinger [[b. 1927] and the pope to be rather hard on liberation theology. However, liberation theology is continuing to take root all around the world.

## Including Poland?

Right. Liberation theology began after Vatican II with the theologians in Latin America, who redefined salvation: Salvation is not "pie in the sky when you die"—"'Salvation is now,' sayeth the Lord." Salvation is being all we can be not only in the next life, but also in this life. We are not going to sit back and let the oligarchy continue to suppress us. We want bread and justice now; we're not going to wait until we die and go to heaven before we get justice. That's what liberation theology was all about.

Because it had kind of an air of Marxism about it, John Paul II—coming from Poland, where the Communists had been in charge—hated the idea of liberation theology, and helped suppress it. But it's going on anyway, not only in Latin America, but also in Asia. I spent a week in Sri Lanka last year with a Jesuit named Aloysius Pieris, who is preaching and writing books about liberation theology for Asians. Catholic feminists are using the same liberation theology. What does liberation mean? It means being all we can be. For my money, the greatest moment in the preaching of Jesus comes when Jesus says, "I have come that you may have life and have it more abundantly."

## What are one or two things that you feel that we still haven't begun to crack open yet in terms of the work of the Council as you saw it imagined in 1962, 1963? What have we not gotten to yet?

The church is still too clerical. The Council said the church is all of us; clerics are really there to serve us. The Council erred, however, when it left the implementation of that project in the hands of the clerics.

In a restaurant, we have to be able to tell the waiter what we want. If the waiter says, "We know what's good for you; we're going to give you macaroni and cheese," and we don't like macaroni and cheese, we're not being very well served.

The most radical thing about Vatican II was the idea that we are the church, that the church belongs to us, and that we ought to be able to make the call. Those in the church—popes and bishops and priests—who are supposedly "in charge" are not like presidents or kings in charge. Their authority comes by reason of the fact that they are called to serve us. (cf. *Lumen gentium*, 18, 28; *Optutum totius*, 16; *Presbyterorum ordinis*, 15)

I'm not saying we don't need bishops. We've had bishops from almost the beginning—not quite the very beginning, but bishops began to come along about the second century—and we kind of got used to them. We love our bishops, but we love bishops who are at our service, not bishops who are scoundrels. Even popes have been scoundrels. We've got to kind of reverse that whole idea of authority. What John XXIII kept drumming in all the time during the first session of the Council was that authority is not for domination, but for service.

**Given how much the world has changed, even within the last century, do you perceive a need for a third council at this point? Or is the work to fully implement what was done at the Second Vatican Council?**

I don't see a need so much for an Ecumenical Council of the whole church; I see a need for provincial councils in every country. Every country is different. The bishops of Indonesia have asked for an autochthonous church in Indonesia. Autochthonous doesn't mean independent or autonomous; it means homegrown. The Maronites, and the Copts, the Melkites and the Byzantines and so forth are an ancient model.

What we need in the United States is an autochthonous church, which would allow us to implement the Council according to our own cultural norms. Then we can be Catholic and American. I'm not talking about changing doctrines; I'm talking about discipline and governance—rules and regulations.

The Vatican is probably one of the last monarchies left in the world. The world does not much like monarchy, especially the idea the divine right of kings. Officially, we still hold to the divine right of kings in the Roman Catholic Church. The pope is the executive branch, he's the legislative branch, and he's the judicial branch. There's no appeal on anything he decides.

**Could the Council have happened at any other time in this century?**

It was really the right time.

**Is [the clergy sex abuse scandal] part of the growing pains in a critical moment in terms of the authority of the church?**

If you want to take a long view of this sex abuse crisis, it's probably going to put us in a better place. The crisis will be over when our bishops can work out a way of becoming accountable to the people. So far, I'm not sure how many bishops really understand that yet.

That's the way the church was in the early years, right? It was a church of the people, and the Eucharist was presided over by people named Priscilla and Prisca and Phoebe, and so forth—I think they were women, women in charge of what they called "household churches." They were like our small faith communities. We're going to see some radical changes in those small faith communities very soon, or else get used to a long eucharistic famine.

Robert Blair Kaiser spent ten years in the Society of Jesus; three years shy of ordination, he left the Jesuits to pursue a career in journalism. He covered Vatican II for *Time*, worked on the religion beat for *The New York Times*, and served as journalism chairman at the University of Nevada, Reno. Two of his ten published books deal with Vatican II: *Pope, Council and World* [McMillan 1963] and *The Politics of S-e-x and Religion* [Sheed and Ward 1985].

Kaiser won the Overseas Press Club Award in 1963 for the "best magazine reporting of foreign affairs" for his reporting on the Second Vatican Council. Editors at three newspapers have nominated him for Pulitzer prizes, and the book publisher E.P. Dutton nominated him for another Pulitzer for his exhaustive 634-page work on the assassination of Robert F. Kennedy, a work that will be republished in 2005.

Since 1999, Kaiser has been a contributing editor in Rome for *Newsweek* magazine. He is also writing a book there on the future of the church. He has a contract with CBS Television News to provide color commentary for that network's coverage of the next conclave.

# Columba Kelly, OSB

## Interviewer: Michael P. Mernagh

At the time of the Council I was a student, both at San Anselmo and at the School of Sacred Music, of some of the leading *periti* (experts) at the Council: Camaldolese Benedictine Cyprian Vagaggini [1909–1999]; Eugeneo Anglaise, for the music school; Dom Eugene Cardine, OSB [1905–1988], who was on the staff; and Archbishop Annibale Bugnini, CM [1912–1982], for liturgy. These were the key people with whom I had either seminars or full-blown classes.

From 1956 to 1959 I studied the theology of the liturgy under Cyprian Vagaggini at San Anselmo. Many of the ideas in that course then appeared in the liturgy document at Vatican II.

Among my other teachers between 1959 and 1963 were Bugnini, who taught liturgy and *musica sacra* and later became head of the *postconciliar* commission for implementing the document on the liturgy; Eugeneo Anglaise, who was president of the school, and Eugene Cardine, a monk of Solesmes and founder of semiology studies in chant.

### Did you attend any of the Council sessions?

No. I got feedback at the seminar by Bugnini. We had a weekly seminar in the spring semester of 1963. In that seminar Bugnini would describe what had happened in the previous week in [the Council's] discussions on how they were to arrange the paragraphs and how to word the paragraphs in the document on the sacred liturgy. We [students] got an analysis of how the document was being put together and why the paragraphs were being worded and placed in the fashion they were.

I remember clearly the smile on Bugnini's face as he said, "Now, you may consider this a contradiction, but the paragraph on preserving the Latin chant in the heritage of the church will be only a few paragraphs ahead of one in which the vernacular in the churches will be not only be allowed but be promoted. We want both of those in there so that history will take care of how to balance the two." That was his comment to us in class. This was directly from the man who was in charge of the *postconciliar* commission until 1975.

## What was the most significant moment at the Council for you?

Let me give you the story. It was before the Council, at the coronation of John XXIII. According to the old rite, the Gospel was first proclaimed, officially, by a Greek-speaking deacon who sang it beautifully in Greek; as soon as he had finished and descended from the ambo, another deacon came up and immediately proclaimed it in the vernacular—*Latin.* That needs to be emphasized. That was one of the most illuminating moments in my life. This occurred in 1958 when John was crowned in St. Peter's. I was within a few feet of the deacon; I was in the schola singing the Latin chants. All of that registered in me right there. Later, when the Council started and our professors started speaking of how the church has used different languages and the importance of the people responding to that—all that made perfect sense.

The most significant moment of the Council itself was probably when Paul VI announced that the Council would continue, because after the death of John XXIII there was a moment when they weren't sure whether the Council would continue. The students in Rome were laying odds as to whether the Council would continue its work or simply disband. So much work had already been done on the liturgy document; however, it needed some fine-tuning and finishing, otherwise the work was all going to be wasted. I remember the announcement shortly after Paul VI was elected that the Council would go forward. The document on the liturgy would be completed. Sure enough, in the fall of 1963, it was the first document approved.

Some of my teachers were on the opposite side of this issue. Eugeneo Anglaise, the Spanish president of *Musica sacra*, was adamant against what the document was going to present—namely the use of the vernacular. He fought tooth and nail against inserting anything about including the vernacular in that document. He was the one who helped get that thing polished about preserving the tradition of the Latin rite and Gregorian chant. He was well aware that once you put the vernacular in, then these would no longer have pride of place necessarily. Once you sing the liturgy in the vernacular, you would no longer be singing in Latin—maybe never.

Latin was the first vernacular of the West. That is literally what it was. We are not going to have this as the unique form of music.

Singing the liturgy—that's going to be one of my theme songs. We need to return to sing the liturgy itself, its prayer texts, not things tacked on or paraphrased, but singing the liturgy. That's what the Council intended.

On the other side, Bugnini was trying to hold the whole thing together. It's not a question of either/or, it is both/and.

## Of all the documents of the Council, which is most significant for you and why?

*Lumen gentium* is a core document that defines what the church is. It's a foundational document. However, I think in the long run the one that has had the most influence is *Sacrosanctum concilium,* the document on the liturgy. The liturgy document dealt with how we express and communicate faith. A famous church father said, *"Lex orandi lex credendi"* [the law of prayer is the law of belief]. There is a dialogue between receiving faith and shaping it. *Lumen gentium* is the underpinning for all of that. Theologically, *Lumen gentium* is a key document; *Sacrosanctum concilium* is historically more influential.

John XXIII was asked why he put liturgy first. "Because I wanted all these bishops to speak and I knew that since they felt—knew—they were experts on the liturgy, they would feel more like speaking at the Council." He wanted to get them dialoguing. When they got to *Lumen gentium,* they were all busy making interventions, interjecting and emoting, no problem; they all got up and said something. But if they hadn't done that before, it was because they had gotten their feet wet with *Sacrosanctum concilium.* I got these stories from Benedictine Father Guy Ferrari [monk of St. Meinrad and curator of the Borgia Apartments in the Vatican Museum], who worked under Cardinal [Eugène] Tiesserant [1884–1972] at the Vatican Library, and shared these over coffee breaks in the morning, swapping stories. These stories come straight out of the Vatican.

## What's the most important teaching that came out of the Council?

Going back to the theological foundation of faith and how that should be expressed in contemporary cultures. Return to the roots of the church and bring them to life in a contemporary setting. Bring that life present in the root to life in the church.

We had frozen history at the Council of Trent; somehow it seemed that nothing happened before Trent, and history only started with the Missal of 1570. Paul VI made a point of promulgating his Missal in 1970—it is tied in, 1570–1970—all of which is symbolic.

## Whom do you feel was the most significant figure at the Council?

Ultimately it is going to be Paul VI; he was behind all that stuff. John XXIII made the Council possible. He knew how to get things done, how to work around the conservatives. He was very pious.

Before Vatican II, Pius XII wanted a reform of the liturgy. He was talked out of having a council; they said it was an inappropriate time and too expensive and too dangerous to happen. Instead, Pius XII got the Jesuits together and they revised the Easter Vigil. Before then, the Easter Vigil was on Saturday morning and finished before noon. I feel very blessed that I experienced all of this—the entire Tridentine rite, including the Easter Vigil being done at eight a.m. on Holy Saturday; we were all done with alleluias and everything, and ready to eat a big meal before noon. That whole thing of singing the *Exsultet* in blazing sunlight made no sense. You talk about darkness—*what* darkness? It didn't make much difference because it was all in Latin anyway.

Once the Easter Vigil was revised, the Tridentine rite was no longer rock solid; we got a break in it. John XXIII inserted the name of Joseph in the Roman Canon; there was much consternation because that was tampering with the Eucharistic Prayer, the Roman Canon of the Missal of 1570. It was the first time it had been tampered with since 1570.

Paul VI (then Cardinal Montini) and another cardinal were in charge of the Secretariat of State. Paul was known as a liberal and not entirely trusted. A compromise was worked out that there would be two cardinals in charge—one conservative and the other...Montini was the one who was not quite trustworthy. Montini was removed from the office and made Archbishop of Milan. He was exiled to Milan, according to the Italian press; they had a picture of him getting off the train in Milan with very few people there to welcome him. One of the first things John XXIII did was to make Montini a cardinal; otherwise he would never have been in the conclave.

Montini did behind-the-scenes work. There were three chairmen; they decided who spoke. They saw to it that the first document on the liturgy was trashed; they decided, "No, we need to start from scratch." They did the same with *Lumen gentium*. Montini was influential with this group who were in charge of the sessions. Bugnini is also important.

### What was the most significant statement of the Council and why?

In his most publicly known statement, John XXIII said, "Open the windows and let some fresh air into the church." It had gotten stale. We needed to return to the sources of our faith, in order to reestablish the vitality of the early church and to respond to the needs of the current church.

### We had a Christology but we didn't have a sense that the Spirit was continuing to work.

Nor did we have the dynamism of the sacrament of the Eucharist. It is not a frozen aspect to be adored. It is a motion of the Father through the Son in the Spirit to us, then we in the Spirit through Christ to the Father. It is a *perichoresis*. Father Cyprian Vaggagini, professor of dogmatic theology at the Pontifical Atheneum at San Anselmo, condemned what happened in the Middle Ages when we reified the Trinity—made a "thing" of it. This is exemplified in the texts of the Feast of the Holy Trinity. Father Cyprian taught us that we celebrate the Trinity at every Eucharist. The eucharistic prayer is Trinitarian. Those are fundamental principles. When we wandered into the Christological motifs, we got bogged down with our battle over the real presence and the terms. "Transubstantiation"—the term is now meaningless.

There is currently a return to practices that emphasize the reification—namely, kneeling, which is a posture of getting people to adore the static presence. It has nothing to do with action of giving thanks, of *Eucharistia*. In fact, if we return to sources, kneeling has nothing to do with the eucharistic prayer. We have betrayed Vatican II by not going back to our roots.

Ironically, standing is part of the Tridentine Rite and part of the early church. That tradition is implied in the Missal of 1570: "We give thanks for all of us standing around here *(et omnes circumstantes)*." That is to say: standing around the altar. By that phrase, *et omnes circumstantes*, I don't think they just meant the priest and the deacons.

I am distracted every day when I see people kneeling. They didn't even do that in Rome under Pope Pius XII for the Tridentine Canon.

## What has happened that you never imagined would happen?

The use of a vernacular language for the entire rite—that the entire rite would be in our native language. We thought at best we would have a bilingual liturgy. We had our missals; Father would say it in Latin and we would read it in English.

Chant had always followed the language that it was composed for.

## What hasn't happened?

In 1975 Bugnini was still in charge. Before 1975, Bugnini had been granting permissions to what was submitted. He said that he was waiting for bishops' committees to make reasonable proposals for adaptations of the liturgy to local needs. He realized that these adaptations needed to meet local conditions, and that the bishops were the only ones who could say what was needed for their cultural situations. "We wait for you to make reasonable proposals." He wanted us to tell them what worked.

But conservatives said, "Stop all of this granting permissions." Due to the post-1975 takeover of the Congregation of Divine Worship, these kinds of petitions from various conferences for local needs were no longer respected for what they were. Bugnini was exiled to Iran. So what was happening between 1963 and 1975 had ceased to happen. It began to shut down when Bugnini was pushed out. This movement has resulted in the present problems of not getting texts translated and approved.

So the same kind of movement forward has not continued since 1975. That was the beginning of retrenchment, and the pope brought in a very conservative cardinal to run it [the Congregation of Divine Worship]. We are in the process of moving backwards, resulting in kneeling for only *part* of the eucharistic prayer, at the consecration—not for the preface and its introduction, or for the Holy, but only for the consecration. Why don't we kneel for the whole prayer?

If Christ is present in the word, in the presence of the priest presider, the assembly, and the body and blood, why is it we stand for the proclamation of the Gospel and not kneel?

Why don't you genuflect before the celebrant when he walks in? It is mostly subconscious, and that makes it dangerous. We are not totally aware of what we are up to—perpetuating the fight over the real presence—namely, is Jesus present? I am going to prove to you that he is present by doing these gestures like kneeling.

**Would you call this an accurate statement: It seems that this particular movement away from really understanding Christ's presence in the priest presider and in people of God is a movement of fear. It is much easier to look at the host and reverence the host, but it is much more difficult to look at you and see the body of Christ.**

It is much less threatening to go stare at the host than it is to stare at a fellow member of the body of Christ. If we are one body and one spirit, how come we are not genuflecting to each person present?

**Is there any issue you regret that the Council did not address?**

We did not resolve the issue of the vernacular. They have left that issue in history, and therefore it has come back to haunt us. Due to fear we have had this regression. The problem with adaptation is that "we've never done it like that before"—which is the great cry of someone in fear. We have no proof that it will work well.

We need to trust the Spirit to guide us through the adaptations needed in our current time and space. The answer in Mexico will be different from the answer in New York.

*Ecclesia semper reformanda est* [The church needs always to be reformed]. This was a Council battle cry. We have not addressed that. We can retrench or adapt to current needs. There are two responses to that. We have opted for the fear factor instead of trusting the guidance of the Spirit.

**Some people think the Spirit is telling us that we are going in the wrong direction—that we bought into a Protestant model. How are we distinctly Catholic?**

The church needs to go back to its original charism. If we go back to Hippolytus, that looks like a Protestant service. Going back to the sources became identified with Protestantism because that is precisely what they did with the Scriptures; they went back to the original texts. They went back to the early church. The conservatives, in a way, are cheating us of part of our heritage.

**What has been the most significant liturgical achievement? What do we yet need to do to implement full, conscious and active participation?**

The vernacular—getting people to use their vernacular out loud in church in approved rites. It was used for devotions, the rosary, et cetera, but you didn't do it for the official liturgy. For example, many of Irish descent associate singing with being Protestant. Singing is a major achievement—getting people to sing, period; getting people to sing anything other than devotional practices, Benediction and novenas. But when it came to Mass, how many Catholics sang at Mass?

We need to get them to sing the liturgy instead of just singing at it!

Sing the rite itself: the text of the liturgy—sing the prayers, the responsorial psalm, the *Sanctus*. Sing a post-Communion hymn of praise. Reintroduce the hymn of praise as one of the gems of the Missal of Paul VI.

**In your opinion, should there be a third Vatican Council, and what topics would you bring to the table?**

It is probably too soon, but we will probably need a third Vatican Council and it will need to continue to reintroduce the implementation of the return to sources called for by the Second Vatican Council. That affects the organization of ministry in the church, including the hierarchy, and the church's prayer life. There needs to be further implementation of what the church ministry structure implies in liturgy. For example, the role of cantor should be a ministry in the church; I don't see that being emphasized as a truly ministerial role in the church.

**What Council teaching was most difficult to implement in the local churches?**

The distinction of ministries at the local level—and the baptized community taking on the responsibility of fulfilling those ministries. We just ticked off a whole list of these: You've got people who visit the sick, you've got people who take care of the poor, you've got people who do book work—gosh, all of those people got to be recognized in the early church. They were called deacons—they ran the finances of the diocese of Rome. There are people who take care of finances, your financial officers in the parish— that's a ministry in the church. I don't hear that!—but that would be in line with Vatican II.

The challenge is our involvement in the ministry of the church and our identification with a local parish community.

**Is there any special historical or cultural significance that Vatican II occurred in the 1960s? Could it have happened earlier, later, in your opinion?**

It couldn't have happened earlier. Pius XII tried it and he could only get a revision of the Easter Vigil by a private crew of scholars. The 1960s allowed it to happen.

**What about the sixties allowed it to happen?**

The questioning of unreflective authority. Some of it was off the wall, but some of it needed questioning.

It ties in with John XXIII's "reading the signs of the times." That's the key. He read the signs of times: We have to have a Council. Many said no, but he said, "Oh yeah, the signs are there." From politics and family, he read the signs of the times. We, too, have to continue to read the signs of the times. That's the challenge.

The Council couldn't have happened later, because it would have been during a period of reaction against this openness; it would have been too late.

It was the Holy Spirit's window of opportunity. John XXIII kept insisting, "It's the Holy Spirit; don't blame me."

Columba Kelly, OSB [b. 1930], is a Benedictine monk of Saint Meinrad Archabbey, St. Meinrad, Indiana. A native of Williamsburg, Iowa, he earned a Licentiate in Sacred Theology (STL) degree from San Anselmo in 1959. He then studied at the Pontifical Institute of Sacred Music, earning a doctorate in 1963. In 1964, he was appointed choirmaster for Saint Meinrad Archabbey, where he began his work of composing English-language chants based on the principles used to create the original Gregorian Chant repertory. That same year, he also began teaching at Saint Meinrad College and Saint Meinrad School of Theology. For twelve years, he taught summer session courses at the Liturgical Music Program of St. Joseph College, Rensselaer, Indiana. He has led numerous workshops on chant throughout the United States, at the Abbey of Solesmes in France, and for Benedictine communities in Australia. In recent years, he has directed Saint Meinrad's chant schola in a program of Latin and English chants produced for CDs and has also assisted in a number of special projects and compositions regarding Gregorian chant.

# Irving R. Levine

## Interviewers: Elaine Rendler and Hank McQueeney

**Were you assigned the Council story, or did you volunteer?**

I was the Rome correspondent, so it was my area to cover.

**What was your role during the Second Vatican Council?**

The Second Vatican Council began during my time as NBC bureau chief and TV/radio news correspondent to Rome, Italy, and the Middle East. My responsibility as a news reporter was objectivity, not commentary. Prior to my being in Rome to cover the Council, I covered the U.S.S.R. for four years. The two were not entirely dissimilar: Both the Vatican and the Soviet Union kept a tight lid on the news. But the Vatican [Council] would open up the church as *glasnost* would open up the Soviet Union. Also, Rome was a marvelous setting. Rome had just hosted the 1960 Olympics with visitors from all over the world; that had changed the face of Rome. Now Rome was the site of the Council; it, too, changed the face of the city, which was flooded with scarlet capes—a setting of great pageantry.

## What were your observations of the assignment?

There is no question that the Second Vatican Council was an event of dramatic and historical impact. First, it had all the elements of a good story, one that would appeal to a wide general TV audience, not just a religious or parochial one. And it had all the elements of history-making, spanning months, years and even centuries. Like every good story, it had two sides—a controversy between those wanting change and those not—and especially in the massively impressive figure of Pope John XXIII. There were observers from many faiths. There were many news conferences representing liberal and conservative views. The Vatican itself held its own news conferences and had its own spokesperson. Many religious orders had a presence in Rome. I worked closely with the Paulist fathers out of Santa Susanna, the American church; Fathers Thomas Stransky and Robert O'Donnell were most helpful. Monsignor Paul Marcinkus, the American, was close to Pope John XXIII and was most helpful. I met Xavier Rynne [Redemptorist Father Francis X. Murphy 1914–2002]; however, I didn't know him. I had read his pieces for *The New Yorker*.

## What significant events, if any, do you remember?

In general, the Council began as a platitudinous event, but I remember one very dramatic time. That was when Pope John XIII fell ill. After a long deathwatch with vigiling, he died. The big question was whether the Council would continue. There was a conclave, with the burning of the ballots and the white smoke, and the election of [Giovanni Battista] Montini, who became Pope Paul VI. It is interesting that Pope John XXIII was said to have advised Montini (who was handpicked by John to be his successor) not to make enemies and not to play a dominant role in the Council. He did not.

## What significant visual images struck you from that time?

As a correspondent in the Far East and Africa, I had witnessed many ceremonials. But to be in St. Peter's in Rome, and see the pope being carried in, in sight of all those works of art—past Michelangelo's *Pietà* and the Bernini columns—you knew that you were seeing a momentous event with an overwhelming quality to it.

## Did covering the Council end up being a bigger responsibility than you first thought?

I did daily reports on radio and television. Here I was, dealing with a whole new vocabulary. I was very careful, as I should be in covering any other special event, that I was using the right vocabulary and language. We had a lot of help. The Paulists assisted us here as well. There were news conferences every day. One had a sense of the story and allocated resources to what was important. I had a little radio studio in my office. I had a film crew and we shipped the film home every day. There was a day's lag between the filming of the event and its being broadcast.

Satellites were in very early form. The first satellite capable of carrying a TV signal was launched in 1963; it was called "Early Bird." We had a limited window of time—ten minutes—to access the satellite in order to transmit live back to the United States. We had arranged for Pope Paul VI to do a live appearance on the *Today Show*. We had our staff assembled. The pope was seated and ready to speak. The control room, with great anxiety, waited to see if they had acquisition. The words "cue the pope" came out. His first words? "Peace on earth...." Even the pope had to accede to the demands of television.

## Were you surprised that they were doing a document on ecumenism?

No, that was a stated proposal. It did serve a purpose. At the time, there was a rather negative element in the relationship between the Jews and the [Roman Catholic] church. Some held that the Jews were responsible for the crucifixion of Jesus. This had created a longstanding barrier between the two faiths. The document served to ease the enmity between groups; it attempted to remove an impediment in relations between Catholics and Jews. There was also the Holocaust, which was a recent exhibition in the minds of some regarding persecuted people. So there were hundreds of years of anti-Jewish sentiment and the more recent Nazi era.

## Were a lot of women there?

There were some nuns there. But the absence of women in large numbers, at least compared to today, is noteworthy.

## What do you think were the accomplishments of the Vatican Council?

The church then was losing people. It had not kept pace with modern times. Some said it was an uncaring church. The real purpose of the Council was to open it up—to bring it up to date. A fulfillment of what the Council was about was the liturgy in the vernacular—some Catholics I know don't like that—but my own opinion is that it is good to retain the original language but to make it understandable to a wider audience, using current language and inclusiveness. This was an accomplishment of the Council. Another positive result was the Mass facing the people.

## Do you think these were good changes?

As a reporter, [I thought] the Council accomplished what it set out to do.

## Did you have any opportunities to interview either Pope John XXIII or Pope Paul VI?

Paul VI was the first pope to fly internationally. He eventually took many flights. I traveled with him on three flights: to the United Nations, to Bombay and to the Holy Land. On these trips he would occasionally come back to speak with the reporters, asking questions such as "How is your work going?" He spoke mostly in Italian. Then he would give us a blessing. The only time I felt safe in a plane was when I was flying with the pope.

## Were you in Rome when John F. Kennedy was killed?

Yes. The phone rang in my apartment; a colleague told me that the president was dead. I asked, "A plane crash?" "No, he was shot." I remember at the time drawing some similarities between Pope John and John F. Kennedy. They were vastly different in age and their deaths occurred under different circumstances, but both were men of great magnetism, charisma and vision. JFK sent a man to the moon. Pope John XXIII would shake the foundations of the church. Their deaths cast a pall over wide areas of humanity.

## Do you have any souvenirs or mementos from the Council?

I have a leather billet for passports, et cetera with the papal seal, which was given to correspondents. There are some pictures of me with Pope Paul VI on one of the plane trips and I have a medallion of Telstar. All of these can be found in the Irving R. Levine collection at the Library of Congress along with my scripts.

Irving R. Levine [b. 1922] was an NBC correspondent for more than thirty-five years—including four years in Moscow, ten years in Rome (during which time he covered the Second Vatican Council), two years in Tokyo, and a year in London. His insightful reports and commentaries were regular features on *NBC Nightly News, Today* and NBC news special broadcasts.

His work as a foreign correspondent included coverage of the Berlin airlift, the Soviet invasion of Czechoslovakia, the Eisenhower-Khrushchev summit meeting in Paris, and the Kennedy-Khrushchev summit meeting in Vienna. He served as an officer in the Signal Corps during World War II in the Philippines and Japan.

Photo courtesy of AEI Speakers Bureau. Used with permission

Levine is the author of four books: *Main Street, U.S.S.R.* [1959], which was on the national nonfiction best-seller lists and has been used as a university textbook; *Travel Guide to Russia* [1960], described by *Life* magazine as the one essential book for anyone traveling to the Soviet Union; *The New Worker in Soviet Russia* [MacMillan Publishing Company] and *Main Street, Italy* [1963].

A native of Pawtucket, Rhode Island, Levine graduated Phi Beta Kappa from Brown University. He received his master's degree from Columbia University Graduate School of Journalism and has been awarded honorary degrees from Brown University, Bryant College, Roger Williams College and the University of Rhode Island. In 1988, he received Brown University's highest alumni honor, the William Rogers Award for "outstanding professional achievement and extraordinary service to humanity."

# Dr. Martin Marty

## Interviewer: Bryan Cones

**What was your experience of Roman Catholicism before the Second Vatican Council?**

I grew up in a small Nebraska town in which everyone was Czech Catholic or German Lutheran in background. There were rivalries on the basketball floor and friendly snowball fights; but in general the two communities were on separate tracks, yet not hostile. It did not occur to me until I grew up that while our closest friends were Catholic and we played on the playground with them every day, we were never in their houses nor they in ours. Everyone feared intimacy, romance, intermarriage, and the conflict over marital laws and rites. Still, there was no ugliness between us.

In my high school years at a Lutheran prep school in Milwaukee, we Lutherans became good friends of Catholic prep debaters and athletes. Again, no hostility, no intimacy. At seminary in St. Louis I had my first profound contacts, and profound they were. My first mentor and friend was Jesuit Father Walter Ong [1912–2003], an intellectual giant and a warm human being, who helped introduce me around St. Louis University.

When I was a pastor before Vatican II, starting a Lutheran church in a planned community next door to the Catholic parish, Father Morrison—of the old school theologically but with a warm heart—could now and then be spied praying in one of our pews. My sons saw to it that he had greeting cards from this Lutheran house. But by then at the University of Chicago I'd had many intellectual encounters—for example, with my friend-for-her-life, Dominican Sister Candida Lund of Rosary College (now Dominican University). Dan Herr of the Thomas More Association also helped build bridges.

*Christian Century* magazine, which signed me on in 1956 as a part-time editor, was known for anti-Catholicism, and it kept its suspicions up until the election of Pope John XXIII. By then, I not only did not share such positions but openly opposed groups like Protestants and Other Americans United for Separation of Church and State back in its anti-Catholic phase.

We all pushed the limits. The year before the Council, the University of Notre Dame was one of two places where Catholics and Protestants could formally talk theology in what became annual ten-on-ten meetings. With the permission of the bishop, the provincial general and the university president, we could even end the meeting with a lit candle as we said the Lord's Prayer—so long as we didn't tell anyone we had prayed together. A dam was ready to burst; ecumenical energies were so strong.

## How did you become involved in the Council? What was your capacity there?

I became involved in the Council as a member of the press, a gadfly, an informal Protestant consultant and a not-quite-legal attendee at the third session. A different *Christian Century* editor would go each session; my turn came in 1964. I was then a cleric in the Lutheran Church–Missouri Synod, a maverick who would not have been chosen as a delegated visitor, and a member of a body that was not part of the Lutheran World Federation, a credentialed invitee agency. I began at noon press briefings and the exciting afternoon press gatherings.

Then I met Bishop Peter Bartholomew [1893–1982] of the diocese of St. Cloud, Minnesota. We chatted about the coincidence of my name with that of the first bishop of that diocese, the Benedictine Martin Marty [1834–1896]. Was there anything the bishop now could do for me? Yes, a little blue pass-book [that allowed entrance into Council sessions]. He provided it, and I had a chance to brush up on my Latin during long sessions.

## How many sessions of the Council did you attend?

I attended only the second half of the third session.

## What was the most significant moment during the Council for you?

The most significant moment during my time at the Council was when the declaration on religious freedom was ready to go. We American Protestants had the heaviest investment in it, but "on higher authority" it was withdrawn. God? Pope Paul VI? High hierarchs? At the afternoon press conference someone asked Jesuit Father John Courtney Murray, a principal drafter, if he was disappointed. Disappointed? No, very angry. (He may have even used a more explosive adjective.) Cardinal Albert Meyer [1903–1965] of Chicago, Father Murray and others worked through the night to keep the *schema* alive, and it passed the next year.

## Is there an anecdote that embodies for you the spirit of the Council?

My anecdote has not to do with what went on inside at the Council but on the streets. When mental gangrene set in after three hours of Latin, I would go to an outdoor cafe in the Via della Conciliazione and have coffee with Joseph Lichten, an American Jewish official observer. One day the bishops came out for lunch and siesta; as they boarded buses, he asked, "Marty, if you were a Jew, would you want 'you' [Protestants] to win?" He translated: He knew I was very ecumenically committed and hoped for much. But as long as Catholics fought Protestants, they would not gang up on Jews. I told him that this time it was different: The positive tone set by the two popes of the Council and the spirit of the Council fathers and visitors was not "against" other religions.

## What is the most important statement or teaching that came out of the Council?

The most significant statement had to do with collegiality, shared consultancy and authority among the bishops and the pope. I do not think Pope John Paul II has paid much attention to this most important achievement. Maybe a future pope will. The most important teaching of the Council can probably be codified in some terms that became near-mantras. The church is not the hierarchy surrounded by the faithful laity. It is "the people of God," a "pilgrim church," a "servant church." These concepts enabled great change.

## Who do you feel was the most significant figure at the Council?

The most significant figure at the Council from my perspective was the German Cardinal Augustin Bea [1881–1968], advocate of Christian unity. Cardinal Bea was certainly among the five or ten most influential cardinals at the

Council, and was well-beloved by the moderates, progressives, guests and press. He was the point-maker on Christian unity endeavors, and treated the extra-Roman ecumenical cause with a generous spirit and theological depth. I think he arranged for a memorial service for Jesuit Father Gustave Weigel, at which Albert Outler [a Protestant] preached; it was to our knowledge the first (possibly only) time that a pope attended a Protestant-based service and took no part except humbly to share a pew.

An aside: I like to tell people that Cardinal Bea saved my life. The last night of the third session I received a packet of materials supporting the late Norman Cousins for a Nobel Prize, for which he had been credibly nominated. The urgent word was that I was to put this into the hands of the cardinal, who was on the Nobel Committee or was consulted by them. That was hard to do, since the packet came at six p.m., and I was to leave on a very early morning plane. I went out to dinner with journalists, etc., and it got very late. I was still sitting on that envelope. A cab driver misunderstood our directions; it took a *long* time to get to Bea's house. I woke his housekeeper; she was understandably miffed, but I emptied my Italian coins and currency on her, and got a big hug and a blessing.

By then my friend and I decided it was too late to get to sleep and up for that early plane and booked a later one. The one on which we had been booked skidded off the Fiumicino Airport runway and wrecked, killing (I believe the number was) thirty-four people, including the bishop of Des Moines. Thanks to the complexity of the night before, I was spared. Naturally, I felt close to the cardinal, whom I had only just met.

## What has happened that you never imagined would happen? What hasn't happened?

I never imagined that the Catholic Church would officially speak so warmly of Protestants, Orthodox, Jews, Muslims, even Buddhists and Hindus, as it did in *Nostra aetate* [the declaration on the church's relations with non-Christian religions]. The Council fathers showed how the church can adhere to its truth and yet be generous in seeing the light of some kinds of divine truth in circles far beyond it.

## What hasn't happened?

Not enough expression of collegiality.

## Is there any issue you regret that the Council did not address?

I regret that it did not deal more systematically and positively with the ecclesial status of bodies not of the Roman obedience. The Council and the present pope know how to recognize individuals as faithful to Christ but have a hard time seeing the body of Christ, even in broken form, in the Orthodox, Anglican, Lutheran and other bodies *as* bodies. Even more, my ecumenical dream is shared Eucharist, full communion; and nothing but barriers remain, even though there is wide agreement on the meanings of the presence of Christ in the Eucharist.

## How have the reforms in the Roman Catholic Church initiated by the Council affected the Lutheran and other Christian churches?

The reforms in the Catholic Church have affected Lutherans and other Christians in innumerable ways. We are now welcomed in each other's sanctuaries, if not at the table. We rejoice in the liturgical changes, the embrace of the Bible, the encouragement of common theological and practical activities, and so forth.

## How has the Roman Catholic liturgical reform affected the liturgical reforms of other Christian churches, in particular your own Lutheran church?

I think that Catholic and Lutheran liturgical changes had been in the making for a couple of decades before the Council, but the Council gave encouragement to these. Many Catholics who are guests at our own parish, for example, say that they have difficulties seeing or hearing any differences. I think a few elements of "the canon of the Mass" [eucharistic prayer] are still differentiating.

## In your opinion, should there be a third Vatican Council? If so, what topics would you bring to the table?

A third Vatican Council would be futile right now, I think, but I thought the second one would be, too. Right now the Roman Catholic Church has been busy turning more exclusive. The boundaries are higher, the impulse to listen is dulled, and the internal divisions in the church are so drastic that it might be opening an ecclesiastical can of worms to discuss them. The gap between most of the bishops appointed by this pope and huge percentages of the faithful is large; voting would hardly represent what Cardinal John Newman called "consulting the faithful."

Topics that I'd want to hear discussed but would not [advise doing so] yet include ordination of women and optional clerical celibacy. To me, the Catholic church is the Mass, and the Mass is the Catholic church. Head-in-the-sand officials hide themselves from the reality of what is emerging: an almost priestless church. Relying on Poor World clerics to fill in the "northern world" will not work. Expecting a sudden vocational turnaround on present terms is folly. If I were a young Catholic observing this strong, smart, courageous pope in action, I'd entertain entering the priesthood. The pope draws hundreds of thousands of youth to his processions and Masses and rallies—but almost no one is drawn to the priesthood. They may love the church and like to be in its ministries, but in the unordained form. Having a circuit-riding eighty-five-year-old priest come by every six weeks to bless the bread is a poor substitute for regular Masses. We've seen wonderful compensatory liveliness among laity, but they can't do it alone.

## What Conciliar teaching was easiest to implement in the local churches?

Realizing that the members are the people of God, that they are taught and free to act that way.

## Is there any special historical or cultural significance that Vatican II occurred in the 1960s? Could it have happened earlier or later, in your opinion?

Historians are reluctant to ask, "what would have been if..?" I think it occurred because the Holy Spirit whispered to a very aged, cancer-wracked pope, and that could have happened in the 1930s or the 1990s. I didn't see much "sixties-ish" in the calling of the Council or its enactments. The "underground church" and other faddish brief experiments in North American and Western European cultures may have been products of the 1960s, but most Catholics don't live there and were untouched by the local fervor and chaos.

Here's an image to illustrate: You can have so much water behind a dam that the dam can burst unless one opens the sluice gates. Vatican II was such an opening.

Dr. Martin E. Marty [b. 1928], a Lutheran pastor ordained in 1952, is the Fairfax M. Cone Distinguished Service Professor Emeritus at the University of Chicago, where he taught for thirty-five years. He attended the Second Vatican Council during a portion of its third session in 1964. Dr. Marty is also the author of over fifty books, and currently writes the "M.E.M.O." column for the biweekly *Christian Century* magazine. Dr. Marty and his wife, Harriet, reside in Riverside, Illinois.

# Cardinal Adrianus Johannes Simonis

## Interviewer: James Hansen

**What was your role at the Council?**

I was a student at the Biblicum in Rome, and the announcement of the Council was a big surprise to all of us. The initial movement was signaled by the appointment of the preparatory commission. A member of that commission was Cardinal [Bernard Jan] Alfrink [1900–1987], a predecessor of mine. The students began to hear what would be discussed, and also that a *schema* would be prepared. The cardinal was silent about most of this; he didn't speak much about the proceedings of the commission, but I heard from other sources that the documents being prepared were rather traditional.

The students of the Dutch College in Rome had to move out to make room for the Dutch bishops who would occupy their rooms during their stay in Rome. About 70 Dutch bishops came from mission dioceses along with eight bishops from Holland. Cardinal Alfrink was the Cardinal Archbishop of Utrecht, but along with Cardinal [Franz] König [b. 1905] and Cardinal [Alfredo] Ottaviani [1890–1979], he was very influential at the Council. As I was the *capo di studenti*, the head of the student body, I was allowed to remain at the college; consequently, throughout the sessions of the Council, I heard the continuing discussions. During the meals and into the evenings the conversations continued endlessly. Different theologians were present; of course, [Edward] Schillebeeckx [b. 1914] was present at the Dutch College and we noticed the tensions that accompanied some of the ideas.

I remember especially the *Nota previa*, a statement of Pope Paul VI, found in the documents of the Council before *Lumen gentium*, the document on the church. It was in this talk the pope felt obliged to make some corrections— addenda for the interpretation of *Lumen gentium*. There was much discussion about this *Nota previa* because it stressed that the pope is the pope, and that when one speaks of collegiality it is in light of the pope being the first of the other bish- ops, much more than the phrase *"primus inter pares"* might indicate, as he is also shepherd of the shepherds. From the one side the pope is with the bishops, but from the other side he is head of the bishops. This, I would say, was the most sig- nificant moment for me during the Council, for while it instigated much turmoil at the time, it has become an important influence on the way many ideas from the Council are interpreted and understood. Its importance lies in the action of the pope not against the Council but to correct, more or less, certain interpreta- tions that he foresaw could be problematic. While many bishops were somewhat upset, in time they accepted this statement and its meaning.

As I was a bystander, my presence was somewhat limited to affairs at the college and I was able to follow all the discussions. However, I was able to attend one of the Council sessions as a guest, the session at which the document on ecumenism was passed. This was also the famous session during which Pope Paul VI embraced the Patriarch Athenagoras I [1886–1972]; patriarch of Constantinople, a very emotional moment indeed.

## What would you consider the most significant document from this time?

The most significant document, in my opinion, is *Lumen gentium*, the doc- ument about the church. Others would insist on the primacy of the liturgy doc- ument, and this is, of course, a writing of high moment. But for me, theologi- cally speaking, my support lies with *Lumen gentium*. There for the first time was a teaching about the church, and the mystery of church, which created profound changes from what had gone before.

Before that time, the primary illustration of relationships in the church was one of a pyramidal structure, with pope and bishops at the top, and priests, religious and faithful in layers from top to bottom. But Vatican II says, "No, the church is *communio*." It is communion. All belong together; all have baptism and confirma- tion. In that communion each person has his or her own role so that as priests and bishops are a part, they are not above the communion. Baptism is the firm foun- dation of membership for all in the communion, including pope and bishops.

**The next point concerns the most significant figure at the Council.**

Without a doubt I consider the pope to have been the strongest figure—both Pope John XXIII at the first session and Pope Paul VI during the remainder of the sessions. The person of the pope and the position of the pope were for me the most significant presence at the Council.

**As a student, did you develop an admiration for any particular Council figure—a sort of hero?**

I am not a person to put stock in heroes. But if you mean an admiration of intelligence, acuity or for brilliant ideas, several of us recognized such in Father [Joseph] Ratzinger [b. 1927]. He was at that time a priest, an assistant to Cardinal [Joseph] Frings [1887–1978], and was thought of as the deepest thinker. I also had frequent contact with Father Schillebeeckx; as a student I had tremendous discussions with him. I realized he was a famous theologian and was greatly admired. We often went out into the city at night, eating and talking into the late hours. But I didn't agree with Schillebeeckx.

**As we previewed the questions earlier, you said you found the next question very interesting: what has happened since the Council that you never imagined might happen?**

I can think of two things that were very surprising to me. After the Council many, many people (priests and people alike) did not read the documents of the Council, and at the same time everyone was speaking about the "spirit of the Vatican Council." What was that "spirit of the Vatican Council" they referred to? In their opinion, openness and permissiveness; all is well and all is possible. I never would have believed that likely. In addition, I was disturbed by the role adopted by the media, which chose to stress and exaggerate the so-called differences that existed between certain of the bishops, and to portray them as a struggle between two camps.

**Have you any regret over issues that were not covered at the Council?**

My initial response is no—what truly needed to be attended to was covered. But then I know there are people who would ask, "Why was the issue of contraception not treated in the full Council? Why was not the question of celibacy in the western church dealt with in full session?" And my answer would be connected again to *Nota previa*, with respect to the Holy Father, who, in reserving these questions to himself, was setting some boundaries, as it were.

**The next area of our concern is the matter of the liturgy and the movements stirred by the liturgy documents.**

I would suggest the greatest achievement in this field has been the soberness of the liturgy.

**You used the word "soberness"?**

Soberness. Throughout the preceding centuries there were so many elements which conspired to alienate liturgy from the people. As a result of work at the Council, liturgy came nearer to the people. For me that was the most significant achievement. In the past the liturgy was practically only a question of the priest and the bishop. Now priest and faithful are praying together in the communion of liturgy.

**What must we do to implement full, conscious and active participation?**

There is a simple answer to this question. Reading and studying the documents of the Second Vatican Council is the first thing.

I speak now of the church in Holland: Liturgy is, first and foremost, honor to God, and not honor to people. Here it has become, in a large part, honor to people. One of our primary needs is for good biblical songs: songs based on Scripture and on the Roman Missal. The songs we have are, for the great part, humanistic. There are some good songs in the Dutch language but we need more.

**There is more and more talk about the possibility of a third Vatican Council.**

I say, "Yes," but in the far future—after one or two more centuries, but not now. The Council we have just witnessed deserves much more study. It took the Council of Trent fifty years to begin to have an influence. It is a like situation with this Council; we need to study it and implement its documents. After forty years we are just starting with some of its aspects.

There is another side to this issue. I sometimes think that it will not be possible to have a Council again as we have in the past because of sheer numbers. It was a miracle that the last Council was so well structured after such a short period of preparation. There were 2,900 bishops present then, and now we have 4,500.

Now we can treat one of the most difficult teachings brought forward by the

Council. In my opinion, it surely is that we as faithful people have to be obedient to pope and bishops. Number 25 of *Lumen gentium* states in plain language that the faithful have to be obedient to the doctrine put forward by the pope and bishops. This is certainly difficult to put into practice on any level.

## And finally, regarding the historical and cultural significance of the time of the sixties in relation to the Council.

Surely it was the person and the figure of [President John F.] Kennedy. In the sixties, there was Kennedy, young, energetic, dynamic. We were coming into a new world. Here, in Europe after the war, we were rebuilding our countries and our economies. The world was filled with growth and dynamism. This was very important as a background to the Council. Then Pope John XXIII, who was old, but presented himself as an energetic and renewing man. These factors, speaking historically, were all contributory to the energy of the Council.

Soon after, Cardinal [Godfried] Daneels [b. 1933] of Belgium referred to *Gaudium et spes*, the famous last document from the Council, as simply too optimistic. We need to be more realistic about people and our condition in the world. This Council was different from every other council in its optimism. Another historical element to shape the Council was the death of Pope John XXIII. I am convinced that if Pope John XXIII had lived through the Council, there would have been more attention to the texts of the documents and stricter adherence to them. Pope John XXIII was a person of great authority, charism and authenticity. In the second part, after his death, there came divisions, tensions, and Pope Paul VI had the difficult task to complete the Council in the line of Pope John XIII, but not yet with his particular kind of authority as the old man and the old father of the Council.

## As Cardinal Simonis prepared to leave he had a final word.

I'd like to tell you a little story.

"Do you know the difference between being involved and being committed?" I put the question once to the late Cardinal [Basil] Hume [1923–1999] as we were sitting together one evening drinking a glass of wine. "It is an interesting question," he said. "I will think on it during the night."

The next morning we had Eucharist and breakfast. During breakfast I went to his table. "Oh, yes," he said, "the question. I slept more than I thought."

We were having an "English" breakfast with ham and eggs, and I said to him, "But now I know the answer. Look at your table. The chicken is involved but the pig is committed."

Hume looked at me and said, "That is exactly the difference."

Adrianus Johannes Simonis was born November 26, 1931, in Lisse, in the diocese of Rotterdam, Holland. He was educated at the seminary of Hageveld; the major seminary of Warmond; the Pontifical University of St. Thomas, Rome; and the Pontifical Biblical Institute in Rome, where he earned a doctorate in Sacred Scripture.

Ordained to the priesthood June 15, 1957, he did pastoral work for two years in the diocese of Rotterdam. He went on to further studies in Rome, 1959–1966. From 1966–1970, he was pastor in The Hague and chaplain at the Red Cross Hospital, and cathedral canon of Rotterdam and member of its diocesan pastoral council.

He was elected bishop of Rotterdam on December 29, 1970, and consecrated March 20, 1971 by Cardinal Bernard Jan Alfrink, archbishop of Utrecht. On June 27, 1983, he became archbishop coadjutor of Utrecht, with right of succession, and succeeded to the metropolitan see of Utrecht on December 3, 1983. He became a cardinal on May 25, 1985.

He attended the Second Extraordinary Assembly of the World Synod of Bishops in Vatican City, November 24–December 8, 1985, and was President of the Episcopal Conference of Holland. He attended the Eighth Ordinary Assembly of the World Synod of Bishops, Vatican City, September 30–October 28, 1990; the Special Assembly of the World Synod of Bishops for Europe, Vatican City, November 28–December 14, 1991, and the Tenth Ordinary Assembly of the World Synod of Bishops, Vatican City, September 30 to October 27, 2001.

# Brother Roger of Taizé

## Interviewer: Brother John of Taizé

**How did you come to participate in the Second Vatican Council?**

From the very beginnings of Taizé, Cardinal [Pierre-Marie] Gerlier [1880–1965], the archbishop of Lyons, had been very close to us. It was he who encouraged us to go to Rome in 1949 and 1950 for meetings with Pius XII and his collaborator, Monsignor Montini, the future Pope Paul VI. In 1958, wishing to place in his heart the question of the reconciliation of Christians, the cardinal asked the newly elected John XXIII to receive Taizé at one of his first audiences. Why so quickly? The pope was elderly, the cardinal explained, and very soon he would hear a great many words, so it was important that he should remember well what we had to say to him.

John XXIII accepted, "provided that they don't ask any questions that are too difficult." He received us immediately after the inauguration of his ministry, on the first morning when private audiences were held. He was very attentive to the question of reconciliation and ended the conversation by asking us to return. From the very first meeting, the pope transmitted to us a kind of unexpected surge of new life.

At the beginning of 1959, John XXIII announced the Council. Brother Max and I were filled with gratefulness when we realized that he wished us to be present as observers. I remember well the day when the letter arrived: To be invited to take part in that search made our hearts overflow.

## How many sessions of the Council did you attend?

Almost all of them. It seems to me that in the entire four years I only missed two sessions. During the early days of the Council, I used to read texts by St. Teresa of Avila during the night; she gave me the courage to continue.

## What were your days in Rome like during the Council?

We found a four-room apartment right in the center of Rome. In those days, unlike today, there were many such apartments for rent at a modest price. Our windows opened onto an inner courtyard with no sun. Brothers took turns coming from Taizé to help with hospitality.

Early in the morning, we would meet for prayer; then we left for the Council. For the entire four years, as we went to St. Peter's each morning, approaching the basilica filled me with the same happiness. As we came close to the Tiber, the sky would open up—a soft sky, filled with light.

As soon as we reached the basilica, before entering the section for the observers, we used to spend a moment in silent prayer with many bishops before the reserved Eucharist in a side chapel, long before the time of the daily assembly.

At the end of the morning, on our way out of St. Peter's, we looked for the bishops with whom we had made an appointment and we brought them to our apartment for the midday meal.

We had set up a tiny chapel there and we began with a sung prayer. Around the circular table for the meal, the topics of conversation were quite varied, depending on whether we were hosting Asians, Americans or Africans. It was good to hear their concerns, to discover how they lived in faraway lands. The fourth year, when women were invited to the Council as auditors, they sometimes came to eat with us. Around that table we also got to know Karol Wojtyla, the future Pope John Paul II, who was a young bishop at the time.

The meals were simple, and sometimes quite joyful. We had so few resources that the food was frugal. We found out that some people used to say, "It's better to have something to eat before going to dine with the Taizé brothers!" There was usually rice and tomato sauce, a little wine, and we always found flowers to put on the table.

During the afternoon, people of the most varied sort came to visit us, particularly young people. At the end of the afternoon, quite often we replied to an invitation from a seminary to go and meet students. Then we returned quickly through the crowded streets to come home for evening prayer and to welcome other bishops for a meal.

When there were letters to write, texts to compose, notes to prepare in order to express our viewpoint if it was asked for, it was only possible to spend time doing this at the end of the evening or late at night.

## What was the most significant moment at the Council for you?

There were many significant moments, but I especially remember Pope John's discourse on the day the Council opened in 1962. The Pope could have used traditional language. Instead, in clear terms, John XXIII was able to find expressions that encouraged people to go forward, without losing any time listening to prophets of doom. On that day he said, "In the current situation of society, the only thing these prophets of doom see is ruin and calamity; they say that things have become much worse in our day, as if everything were perfect before; they announce catastrophes, as if the world were close to its end."

Another thing he said that same day is astonishing because of its intuitive power and remains relevant today: "The Church prefers to make use of the medicine of mercy rather than to wield the weapons of severity."

## What was the most important teaching that came out of the Council?

Great intuitions remain from the Council. They are Gospel treasures to respond to urgent needs at the beginning of the third millennium. There is one luminous Gospel insight that the Council brought to light; it had previously remained for a long time hidden under the dust of the ages. It is found in *Gaudium et spes*: "Christ is united to every human being without exception." Later on, Pope John Paul II, in his first encyclical, quoted those words and added, "...even if they are unaware of it." Multitudes of human beings do not know that Christ is united to them and are unaware of the way he looks at every person with love. They know nothing about God, not even God's name. And yet God remains in communion with everyone. This striking intuition can open up a new understanding of faith on earth. Yes, for every human being, the invisible God is a kind of influx of light, peace and love.

## Whom do you feel was the most significant figure at the Council?

Again, for us, it was Pope John XXIII, who opened unexpected ways of rec-onciliation. Already in 1959, when he announced the Council, he spoke some words that were among the most crystal clear possible; they are able to make totally transparent that communion of love that is called the church. "We do not want to put history on trial," he said. "We will not try to determine who was wrong or who was right; both sides bear responsibility. We will only say: let us be reconciled!" The pope had that intuition that a council could open ways for Christians to live in communion.

After a meeting we had with him on October 13, 1962, we learned that he had said about us, "We did not negotiate; we spoke together. We did not argue; we loved each other."

Our last meeting took place on February 25, 1963. There were three of us— I was with my brothers Max and Alain. Suffering from an advanced stage of can-cer, at the age of 82, the Holy Father knew his death was approaching and we had been warned of this. We were told that our audience would be fixed for a day when John XXIII was not in pain; a day when he would be rested and we would be his only visitors. That audience lasted an unusually long time. Aware that we would never see him again, we wanted to hear a kind of spiritual testament from his lips. John XXIII was concerned that we not be worried about the future of our community. Making circular gestures again and again with his hands, he emphasized, "The Catholic Church is made up of concentric circles that are larger and larger, always larger." During that last meeting with him, we saw tears in his eyes because, he told us, some of his intentions had recently been deliberately misinterpreted.

His successor, Pope Paul VI, continued the trust shown to us by John XXIII. He had a great ability to listen, and in him could be discerned signs of the holi-ness of Christ. Some words he spoke at the closing of the Council have always remained with me: "Human beings are sacred by the wounded innocence of their childhood." At least, that is what I remember hearing him say.

During the Council we became close to many Latin American bishops, in particular Cardinal [Raúl] Silva Henriquez [1907–1979] and Bishop Manuel Larraín [1900–1966, bishop of Talca] from Chile, and Dom Antonio Fragoso and Dom Hélder Câmara from Brazil, to name just a few. I think it can be said that Dom Hélder first tried out many of the talks he gave during the Council at our dinner table! And Bishop Larraín's premature death in a car accident was a true tragedy for the church. Before unexpectedly leaving the Council for his mother's death, in a spontaneous gesture of affection he took off his episcopal ring and gave it to me as a sign of friendship. I returned the ring to his successor on a trip to Chile in 1974.

Countless bishops from across the world impressed us by their pastoral attentiveness. During the daily assemblies, our attention was particularly awakened when, under the dome of St. Peter's, we heard a bishop affirm what would open new ways forward for the future and corresponded to our own basic concerns: the presence of Christians in the contemporary world.

## Do you have any regrets about what the Council did or did not accomplish?

At the beginning of the Council, the ecumenical dynamism was such that it seemed as if a concrete reconciliation among Christians would come to pass. John XXIII had called people "not to try and find out who had been wrong and who had been right." In his turn, as universal pastor, Paul VI had asked non-Catholics for forgiveness "if a wrong could be attributed to the Catholic Church regarding the causes of separation."

But were the denominations capable of seizing that historical moment? The weight of the past created irrational refusals, and after the Council some people wondered whether an hour of ecumenism had been missed.

In Taizé, we have always been deeply marked by one of Christ's sayings in the Gospel: "First go and be reconciled." "First go!"—not "Put it off till later!" The ecumenical vocation has led to remarkable dialogues and discussions, but it comes to a standstill when it creates parallel roads that cannot meet and on which, in the end, cause living energies to be used up. Reconciliation cannot be put off until the end of time. The ecumenical vocation leads nowhere when it is not made tangible in a communion.

In the history of Christians down through the ages multitudes have discovered that they were divided without even knowing why. Today it is essential for a reversal to take place, so that multitudes of Christians can discover that they are in communion. And this implies that there be no humiliation for anyone.

Is not every baptized person who disposes himself or herself, day after day, to trust the mystery of the faith already in the communion of Christ?

For forty years now we have been welcoming a great many young adults to Taizé week after week, and we remain hopeful that the spirit of the Council will bear unexpected fruit in the lives of the younger generations.

Born on May 12, 1915, Brother Roger of Taizé is prior of the ecumenical community of Taizé, which he founded in 1940 in France. Brother Roger tried to open ways to heal the divisions between Christians and among human beings in general. The Taizé community is made up of more than 100 brothers from Catholic as well as different Protestant backgrounds; they come from more than 25 different countries and work for reconciliation and peace. The brothers make a lifelong commitment to celibacy, life together and a great simplicity of life. Some brothers live in small groups that share the life of the poor across the world. Week after week, thousands of young adults from every continent go to Taizé to pray and to prepare themselves to work for peace, reconciliation and trust among human beings. At the end of each year, a meeting brings together 70,000 to 100,000 young adults in a large European city. Gatherings are also held on other continents.

photo © S. Lentonegger, CH-will. Used with permission.

Brother Roger was present at all four sessions of the Second Vatican Council as an observer, the guest of Cardinal [Augustin] Bea's Secretariat for Christian Unity.

Brother Roger has written many books, including *The Sources of Taizé* [Continuum International Publishing Group], *Living Today for God* [Harper Collins], *Festival Without End* [Continuum International Publishing Group], *Struggle and Contemplation* [Seabury Press], *A Life We Never Dared Hope For* [Harper San Francisco], *The Wonder of a Love* [Continuum International Publishing Group], *His Love is a Fire* [The Liturgical Press], *Peace of Heart in All Things* [GIA Publications] and, together with Mother Teresa, *Seeking the Heart of God: Reflections on Prayer* [Harper Collins].

He has received many awards, including the Templeton Prize, London 1974; Peace Prize, Frankfurt 1974; UNESCO Prize for Peace Education, Paris 1988; Karlspreis, Aachen 1989; Robert Schuman Prize, Strasbourg 1992; Award for International Humanitarian Service, Notre Dame University 1997; Dignitas Humana Award, St. John's University, Collegeville, Minnesota 2003.

# Sister Mary Luke Tobin, SL

## Interviewer: Michael P. Mernagh

I was working for the Leadership Conference of Women Religious as president. I wanted to find out what this [Second Vatican] Council was about and how sisters in the United States would benefit from it; so they asked me to go over and listen and find out whatever I could. I was on a ship going to Rome when I got a telephone call—I didn't know that you could get a telephone call on a ship, but you can—and two or three telephone calls came in at one time from the United States. They wanted to know how I felt about being invited to be an auditor at Vatican II.

### Who invited you to the Council?

The invitation came from an authentic and authoritative source.

### How did you feel about that?

Wonderful. I was delighted to have an official invitation. See, I was going anyway and I was going to report on it for the heads of the orders of women religious. I was going to come back from Rome and tell the sisters of all the United States groups what I found out about Vatican II. I think it was a great step. They were wise enough to get ready for it, to prepare for it and to invite the people who should have been invited—namely, women!

I attended the last two sessions. There were four sessions of the Council all together.

## What was the most significant moment at the Council for you?

Now, that's one I haven't been asked! Well, I suppose it was important for me to hear everything that was said and to try and understand it. I'll tell you a little story. At the end of the Council, when everything was being finalized, there was a ceremony. The pope [Paul VI] was sitting in front of this huge audience in St. Peter's big square outside. There were thousands of people. They were honoring people who had done something for the Council. First they honored four artists, then four musicians, and finally they honored four women.

I protested and said that isn't something that you honor somebody for. I said women *and* men make up the church! So why do you want to honor somebody who is already in the church? I don't think they ever thought of it.

To me that was a significant moment because I saw right there that they were getting that wrong. Women *and* men make up the church so you don't honor one; I said, "Then you should honor the men, too!" You see my point.

Benedictine Father Godfrey [Diekmann] was surprised, but I think he understood what I was saying. I've always felt he did. Men *and* women make up the church. I think that that is the point of Vatican II: all are the people of God. That's the church! It took us a long time to realize that, but that is what it is.

## Which of all the documents of the Council is the most significant for you, and why?

I would say *Gaudium et spes* (The Church in the Modern World), because we are in the modern world. We need to see how our faith is compatible with the modern world. That's why that is a very important document.

## What do you consider the most important teaching that came out of the Council?

Face the world and incorporate the world. We had too much division. We still have it between the official church and the people; I think the incorporation into the church as one, the hierarchy and the people together, is a very important concept. The church in the modern world, in the fast world or the medieval world—the church is the people; the people are the church. That was emphasized in Vatican II.

## But they struggled with it, didn't they?

Yes, they did. They are still struggling with it.

## Who do you feel was the most significant figure at the Council?

I am an advocate and follower of the German theologian and Jesuit Father Karl Rahner, who was a *peritus* [expert] at the Second Vatican Council. I feel that what he said in his theology is so important that I would put him as number one. The theology that he wrote, what he proposed, what he gave us, backs what we are saying: that the church is the people of God.

## What was the most significant statement from the Council?

I don't know that I would put it as statement. The whole message that we are talking about—the connection of the church in the modern world itself—is a statement. I don't know that you can pin it on to a particular sentence.

## What has happened that you never imagined?

Well, I would say the church becoming unified—a sort of common theology that does exist. We have a unity in Catholic belief and practice that we never had before. I don't think we ever had that before. It isn't perfect, of course. It has some place to go, but it is a unity of thinking and practice that we never had before. And I think that is due to Vatican II.

There's a new movement today by the bishops with the new *General Instruction on the Roman Missal* [GIRM] that pays much attention to reverence for the Blessed Sacrament and unity of posture. What we are hearing is that, for example, everybody has to be doing the same thing at the same time; this shows our unity. I think that there can be some merit to that.

## What hasn't happened?

If we don't get the social justice question right—too bad! That goes right back to the Gospel. The social justice question is rooted in the Gospel or it is nothing. I think that the social justice question comes out of the Gospel, and you can find any number of illustrations of justice. If you don't have it there, where do you have it? This hasn't taken root as it should have. It needs to be there; it is, but not universally.

Every social question needs to be faced by the Gospel. You say, how does this fit in? How does the war in Iraq [2003] fit in with the Gospel? Every public address to every question of the day ought to fit in with the Gospel. How does our soldiers' going into Iraq fit in with the Gospels? That's the way you can make it modern. That's the way you can bring the church up to date. Every Christian, every day, has to ask himself or herself, "How does the world situation fit in with the Gospel?"

## Is there any issue you regret that the Council did not address?

They could have done better on the question of women. They haven't faced that question yet—to see that women *and* men are the church. It is a question for the whole society, of course. And it has to come. It has to be faced eventually. Men *and* women are the church.

## What has been the most significant liturgical achievement? What do we yet need to do to implement full, conscious and active participation?

Helping the people of God to understand that the liturgical act is theirs. They are the ones who celebrate their unity in the act of worship.

## Before, it was like two different things going on: one thing going on in the front of the church and everybody else sitting in the back...

Saying their rosaries.

## What was that all about?

It was a lack of understanding. And I do think Vatican II helped bring the correct understanding of liturgy into greater prominence. We haven't got it right, but we can work at it all our lives to see the unity that exists in that very act of worship.

Of course, there are all kinds of work we can do. The understanding has to go deeper than it has so far. People have to be educated and then brought into the action. You can do that only when you can get the people to understand that it is *their* work that brings about the action in the Mass.

## Should there be a third Vatican Council? What topics would you bring to the table?

I would debate that; you could have the same kind of go-round. Vatican II did it well, but we really haven't absorbed Vatican II. We haven't brought to life the action and the inspiration of Vatican II; we haven't brought it into the life of the people of the church. Until the people begin to understand what Vatican II was about, we haven't done our work.

So I wouldn't say let's have a third Vatican Council but, rather, let's bring the second one into livelihood and into the life of the people and get the people to see what it is about. We said it, but it needs to be in the action of the people.

## What Council teaching was most difficult to implement in the local churches?

That is a hard one. How do we get the people to see that *they are church*? It doesn't mean that you don't have bishops or authority. It just means that the people have to stand behind every act and every issue that is brought up regarding the church, or you won't have any church at all. So the people have to incorporate and be able to speak for the people in taking on Vatican II or the decrees that were made and so on. The people have to absorb those. When they do, and speak to those issues, then I think you have a coming together of the people in the church.

## Is there any special historical or cultural significance that Vatican II occurred in the 1960s?

The world scene—we were not at war. Increasing studies, great theologians—[Karl] Rahner [1904–1984] and [Edward] Schillebeeckx [b. 1964], in particular—and seminaries were using their teachings. We were in a good place for this kind of teaching to grow.

You have to integrate into everyday life that what Jesus taught is what the church is about. What one has learned through one's studies and one's life needs to be expressed freely.

The theological teachers, Schillebeeckx and Rahner, were the right people at the right time. For them to be at Vatican II was important—their writings are still invaluable.

## Is there anything you would like to add?

I guess I would like to be heard on the virtue of hope. I believe that unless we incorporate the virtue of hope into our lives, we are not going to get through the modern period. We won't carry on and go forward. It's hope that gives us the courage to go forward. Only if we go forward can we meet the Christians of the next age.

Mary Luke Tobin, S.L., entered the Loretto community in 1927 at age 19; she celebrated the seventy-fifth anniversary of her profession on December 8, 2002. Sister Tobin was president of the Leadership Council for Women Religious (LCWR) from 1964–1967 and member of the International Union of Superiors General, 1967–1971. Tobin was one of fifteen women (and the only American woman auditor) invited to attend the third session of the Second Vatican Council. At the time of this interview Sister Mary Luke was 95 years of age. In 2003 she received the LCWR's first Outstanding Leadership Award.

# PART 5

# Appendix

# People of Note

**Antonelli, Cardinal Ferdinando, OFM** (1896–1993)—secretary to the Congregation of Rites, titular archbishop of Idicra, active participant in planning. Served as secretary for the conciliar commission on the liturgy during the Council. In 1966 appointed secretary to the Roman Curia's Causes of Saints.

**Bea, Cardinal Augustin** (1881–1968)—president of the Pontifical Commission, and president of the Secretariat for Christian Unity (founded in 1960 in preparation for the Council), member of the commission for liturgical reform established by Pope Pius XII. Member of the *Consilium.*

**Beauduin, Dom Lambert, OSB** (1873–1960)—monk of the Benedictine abbey of Mont-César, where he started the organized liturgical movement in 1909.

**Botte, Bernard** (1893–1980)—Benedictine monk of Mont César and director of the Institut de Liturgie, Paris, 1956–1964. He inspired the insistence found in the *Sacrosanctum concilium* that efforts of the liturgical renewal would be futile without the proper liturgical formation of priests.

**Brown, Robert McAfee** (1920–2001)—American Presbyterian minister. Leading figure in the ecumenical movement and observer at the Second Vatican Council.

**Bugnini, Annibale** (1912–1982)—secretary of the Commission for Liturgical Reform under Pius XII (1948–1960), secretary to the preparatory commission (1960–1962), *peritus* of the Second Vatican Council and its commission on the liturgy (1962–1964), secretary of the *Consilium* for the implementation of the Constitution on the Liturgy (1964–1969), secretary of the Congregation for Divine Worship (1969–1975).

**Cardine, Dom Eugene, OSB** (1905–1988)—monk of Solesmes; consultor of the preparatory commission, subcommission on sacred music; taught at the Pontifical Institute of Sacred Music in Rome.

**Congar, Cardinal Yves-Marie-Joseph** (1904–1995)—French Dominican. Theologian at the Second Vatican Council, elevated to cardinal in 1994 at the age of 90.

**Diekmann, Godfrey, OSB** (1908–2002)—monk of St. John Abbey, Collegeville, Minnesota. Editor of *Orate Fratres/Worship*, organizer and participant in the national and international liturgical weeks, Consultant to the Pontifical Liturgical Commission that prepared for the Second Vatican Council. *Peritus* from 1963–1965, founding member of the International Commission on English in the Liturgy (ICEL). Consultor to the *Consilium* for the Implementation of *Sancrosanctum concilium*. From 1964–1970 head of the *coetus* (working group) entrusted with the reform of the initiation rites of baptism of adults and infant baptism.

**Felici, Archbishop Pericle** (1911–1982)—secretary general of the Second Vatican Council, who announced the results of the vote on the Constitution of the Sacred Liturgy. Member of the Sacred Congregation for Divine Worship; prefect of the Apostolic Signature (1977–1982).

**Fischer, Balthasar** (1912–2001)—relator to the preparatory commission, professor, consultor for the preparatory conciliar commission; from the Liturgical Institute in Trier, Germany.

**Frings, Cardinal Joseph** (1887–1978)—archbishop of Cologne, Germany; addressed the Council on the "Painful Point in the Ecumenical Dialogue" on November 29, 1963.

**Hallinan, Bishop Paul** (1911–1968)—of Atlanta, a relator at the Council and only American bishop to be a member of the conciliar commission on the liturgy and a member of the *Consilium*.

**Haring, Bernard, CSsR** (1912–1998)—German Redemptorist and moral theologian who was looked upon with suspicion during the pontificate of Pius XII, but John XXIII praised his moral theology and named him to the prepatory commission of the Second Vatican Council.

**John XXIII** (1881–1963)—born Angelo Giuseppe Roncalli. Ordained bishop in 1925 while a Vatican official in Bulgaria. Apostolic delegate to Bulgaria, Turkey, Greece and France. He was elevated to cardinal in 1953 and several days later was made patriarch of Venice. On Oct. 28, 1958, he was elected pope and was installed on Nov. 4, 1958. Beatified September 3, 2000.

**Jungmann, Josef Andreas, SJ** (1889–1975)—Jesuit, from the University of Innsbruck; a *peritus* to the conciliar commission on the liturgy and consultor for the *Consilium*. Author of numerous books including *The Mass of the Roman Rite* [Christian Classics] and *The Place of Christ in Liturgical Prayer* [The Liturgical Press].

**Küng, Hans** (b. 1928) Swiss Roman Catholic theologian and author. Ordained in 1954, he became, in 1960 professor of theology at Tübingen and served as a papal theologian and adviser to the Second Vatican Council.

**Lefebvre, Archbishop Marcel** (1905–1991)—archconservative bishop who rejected the teachings of the Second Vatican Council. Appointed archbishop of Tulle, France, January 23, 1962 and resigned as bishop on August 11, 1962.

**Lercaro, Cardinal Giacomo** (1891–1976)—president of the conciliar commission, member of the Sacred Congregation for Divine Worship, Archbishop of Bologna 1964–1968. Gave the address "The Declaration on the Jews is the Result of the Church's Self-awareness" on September 28, 1964.

**de Lubac, Henri, SJ** (1896–1991)—French theological expert at the Second Vatican Council. Elevated to cardinal in 1983 at the age of 87.

**Martimort, Canon Aimé-Georges** (1911–2000)—consultor for the preparatory commission and *peritus* for the conciliar commission for the liturgy; from the Catholic Institute for Toulouse, France.

**Murray, John Courtney, SJ** (1904–1967)—Jesuit theologian whose work was instrumental during the Second Vatican Council reform of Catholic teaching on religious liberty.

**Ottaviani, Cardinal Alfredo** (1890–1979)—secretary to the Holy Office 1959–1966. Pro-prefect of the Congregation for the Doctrine of the Faith 1966–1968.

**Outler, Albert** (1908–1989)—Methodist observer who served as a delegate-observer in all four sessions of the Second Vatican Council 1962–1965, after which the University of Notre Dame conferred an honorary doctorate upon him and he was elected president of the American Catholic Historical Association.

**Paul VI** (1897–1978)—born Giovanni Battista Enrico Antonio Maria Montini, archbishop of Milan 1954–1963; Elected pope in 1963.

**Philips, Monsignor Gerard** (1899–1972)—Belgian theologian from Louvain (1942–1969) who was especially prominent in the deliberations which led to the formulation of the dogmatic constitution *Lumen gentium.* Member of the prepatory theological commission and undersecretary for the Commission on the Faith.

**Pius X** (1835–1914)—born Giuseppe Sarto; elected pope in 1903; strongly opposed to religious modernism.

**Pius XII** (1876–1958)—born Eugenio Pacelli; elected pope in 1939. Led the way of the liturgical renewal at the Second Vatican Council by restoring the rites of Holy Week in 1955.

**Prou, Dom Jean, OSB** (1911–1999)—Abbot of Solesmes, France (1952–1992); member of the *Consilium* commission on the liturgy (appointed by the pope).

**Rahner, Karl, SJ** (1904–1984)—German theologian and Jesuit priest, regarded as one of the foremost theologians of the twentieth century. Served at the Second Vatican Council as a *peritus* and advisor to the members and consultors of the organizations for liturgical reform.

**Ratzinger, Cardinal Joseph** (b.1927)—German theologian; served as *peritus* for Cardinal Joseph Frings at the Second Vatican Council (1962–1965). Since 1981 has been Prefect of the Congregation for the Doctrine of the Faith.

**Rynne, Xavier (Rev. Francis X. Murphy CSsR)** (1914–2002)—As the Second Vatican Council opened in October 1962, *The New Yorker* published "Letter from Vatican City," the first of thirteen pseudonymous articles spread over the next four years of the Council. All were written by Xavier Rynne, whose identity was a secret, but not a particularly well-kept one.

**Saigh, Cardinal Patriarch Maximos IV** (1878–1967)—of the Melkite Church of Antioch in Syria. The only Council father not to address the assembly in Latin, he used French to point out that Latin cannot be considered *the* language of the church. He addressed the Council on November 6, 1963, "On the Reform of the Curia."

**Suenens, Cardinal Leo Joseph** (1904–1996)—archbishop of Mechelen and Brussels. Member of the Central Commission for the Second Vatican Council and appointed as one of four moderators who guided the Council proceedings.

**Teilhard de Chardin, Pierre, SJ** (1881–1955)—Visionary French Jesuit, paleontologist, biologist and philosopher, who spent the bulk of his life trying to integrate religious experience with natural science, most specifically Christian theology with theories of evolution.

**Tillard, Jean-Marie, OP** (1927–2000)—author, ecumenist, specialist in sacraments and papacy; from Canada; advisor to members and consultors of the organizations for liturgical reform. Theological advisor to the Canadian bishops during the Council.

**Vagaggini, Cyprian, OSB Cam.** (1909–1999)—Italian consultor for the preparatory conciliar commission; *peritus* for the conciliar commission on the liturgy. Author of several books, including *Theological Dimensions of the Liturgy* [The Liturgical Press].

**Vagnozzi, Cardinal Egidio** (1906–1980)—apostolic delegate to the Philippines in 1949, apostolic nuncio to the Philippines in 1951, apostolic delegate to the United States in 1958; became cardinal in 1967; appointed Prefect for Prefecture for the Economic Affairs of the Holy See in 1968.

**von Balthasar, Hans Urs** (1905–1988)—Swiss theologian whose theology drew much attention in Europe during the Second Vatican Council. He received the Paul VI Prize in theology and was named a cardinal by Pope John Paul II but died two days before his elevation in June of 1988.

**Wagner, Monsignor Johannes** (1908–1992) consultor for the preparatory conciliar commission, *peritus* for the conciliar commission on the liturgy, director of the liturgical institute in Trier, Austria.

**Willebrands, Cardinal Johannes** (b. 1909)—Archbishop Emeritus of Utrecht. During the Council he was president of the Secretariat for Christian Unity; member of the Sacred Congregation for Divine Worship.

# Interviewers

**Nihal Abeyasingha, CSsR**, was born in 1939, entered the Redemptorists in 1957 and was ordained a priest in 1962. Since then, he has served in a parish, preached missions and retreats, and taught in the Redemptorist seminary in Bangalore (1976–1986). Because long-term residence in India became difficult due to civil restrictions, he continued as a visiting lecturer in Bangalore while working as Senior Lecturer in Christian Culture at the University of Kelaniya from 1986 to the present.

He has degrees from Sri Lanka in civil law and Buddhist philosophy. He received a doctorate in theology with specialization in sacramental theology in 1976; Dom Cipriano Vagaggini at San Anselmo in Rome supervised his research. Fr. Abeyasingha has published books and articles mainly dealing with the relation of religion to culture and analyzing the changes required in the institutional dimension of religion by the present world context. In 1994, he obtained a D.Litt. from the University of Somerset in the United Kingdom.

**Bryan Cones** holds an M.A. in theology from Catholic Theological Union at Chicago, Illinois. A former editor at Liturgy Training Publications in Chicago, he currently teaches and writes on various topics touching Roman Catholic worship and theology. He is the author of *Daily Prayer 2004*, an annual prayer resource published by Liturgy Training Publications.

**Michael S. Driscoll**, a presbyter of the diocese of Helena, Montana, is associate professor of theology at the University of Notre Dame and was president of the North American Academy of Liturgy (NAAL) in 2002. In August 2001 he was elected to the Council of *Societas Liturgica*, an international and ecumenical society of liturgists. He has also served as a liturgical advisor to the Bishops' Committee on the Liturgy (BCL), a standing committee of the United States Conference of Catholic Bishops (USCCB). He holds the following academic degrees: S.T.B., Gregorian University (Rome), 1977; S.T.L., San Anselmo (Rome), 1980; S.T.D., Institut Catholique (Paris), 1986; Ph.D., University of Paris Sorbonne, 1986.

**Geraldine Ethen** is a Portland-based writer/organist who has worked at Oregon Catholic Press for thirteen years. Born in 1944, she attended Catholic schools and completed her undergraduate degree and a year of graduate studies in English at the University of Portland. She has been an organist at various Catholic parishes in the Portland area for more than forty years and accompanies choral groups and instrumentalists.

**John Flaherty** has been involved in music and educational ministry for 25 years as an educator, elementary school principal, music director, liturgy director and composer. He has taught on the elementary, secondary and college levels and is presently on the Campus Ministry Team at Loyola Marymount University in Los Angeles, where he serves as the Director of Liturgy and Music and teaches in the Center for Religion and Spirituality.

Mr. Flaherty has served as the chairperson of the liturgy committee and music director for the Los Angeles Religious Education Congress since 1991. He is also a contributing writer for *Modern Liturgy, Pastoral Music, Our Family* and *Hosanna* magazines. He has served on the editorial boards of *Table, Hosanna* and *Modern Liturgy.* World Library Publications and GIA Publications publish his compositions and recordings. His credits include scoring motion picture soundtracks for Lorimar and ABC-TV. He has worked extensively with the United States Catholic Conference of Bishops and has served as music director for *Encuentro* 2000 and Jubilee Justice. Mr. Flaherty and his wife Kathleen have five children.

**John B. Foley, SJ**, is a liturgical and classical composer, theologian, liturgist, author and teacher. He has master's degrees in philosophy and fundamental theology and a doctorate in liturgical theology from the Graduate Theological Union in Berkeley, California. He has been director of the Center for Liturgy at Saint Louis University since 1993.

For ten years, **Bernadette Gasslein** has been the editor of Canada's award-winning liturgy magazine *Celebrate!* For the past 30 years she has been engaged in various liturgical and catechetical ministries, including four years as a project specialist with the National Office of Religious Education of the Canadian Conference of Catholic Bishops. She now leads workshops in parishes and dioceses around Canada and is coordinator of liturgical life at St. Charles Parish, Edmonton, Alberta, where she and her husband live. She holds a license in sacred theology with specialization in pastoral catechetics from the Institut Catholique de Paris, and an associateship diploma in performance in piano from the Royal Conservatory of Toronto.

**Jerome Hall, SJ**, is a liturgical musician and former professor of liturgical theology at the Gregorian University, who now serves on the formation faculty at Theological College and as adjunct professor at Catholic University in Washington, D.C.

**James Hansen**, longtime coordinator and master teacher for the NPM Cantor and Lector Schools, has been instrumental in forming an entire generation of cantors. His collections of liturgical music compositions include *Litany: When the Church Gathers, Carried by the Ark, The Advent of Our God* and *Requiem and Remembrance* [all published by Oregon Catholic Press]. He is the author of the books *Cantor Basics* [Pastoral Press] and *The Ministry of the Cantor* [The Liturgical Press]. He lives in Michigan with his wife, the cantor Melanie Coddington.

**Russell Hugh Hardiman**, a priest of the Bunbury diocese in Western Australia, was the first Australian to receive a doctorate in liturgy from San Anselmo (Rome) in 1970. He is currently senior lecturer in liturgy at the University of Notre Dame, Australia. In addition to twenty-five years of full time parish ministry, he has lectured on liturgy in Western Australia for eighteen years and has been publishing editor of *Pastoral Liturgy* since 1970.

**Paul Inwood** is a *summa cum laude* graduate of the Royal Academy of Music in London; for more than four decades as a liturgical musician, composer and international workshop presenter, he has served in a wide variety of posts from parish churches to cathedral and diocesan positions. From 1981–1986, he was organist at Clifton Cathedral, Bristol, and from 1986–1991, diocesan director of music for the diocese of Arundel and Brighton. Mr. Inwood worked fourteen years for the St. Thomas More Center for Pastoral Liturgy in London as an editor, presenter and music specialist; he founded what became known as the St. Thomas More Group of composers. He introduced the music of Taizé in the 1970s into the United Kingdom and the music of the Iona community into the United States in the 1980s. From 1986–1998, he was the English-language president of *Universa Laus*, and remains an active member. From 1995–1999 Mr. Inwood was director of music for the Roman Catholic cathedral and diocese of Portsmouth, England; he continues as diocesan director of music; since 2000, he has been head of that diocese's department for liturgical formation—the only lay person to hold such a position in England. He is a member of the subcommittee for liturgical formation of the Department for Christian Life and Worship of the Bishops' Conference of England and Wales, and an associate member of the Federation of Diocesan Liturgical Commissions (FDLC). He is perhaps best known as a composer whose music has been published by Oregon Catholic Press, World Library Publications, GIA Publications and a number of publishing houses in the British Isles. He lives in England with his wife, the accomplished organist and choir director Catherine Christmas.

**Conrad Kraus**, a presbyter of the diocese of Erie, Pennsylvania, is director of the Office of Worship. His seminary training was at St. Mary's, Roland Park, Baltimore. He has served in campus ministry, parish ministry and worship coordination. He holds an M.A. in Religious Education and Liturgical Studies, has served on the Board of Directors of the FDLC, and is a member of the North American Academy of Liturgy. Monsignor Kraus is currently pastor of St. Michael the Archangel parish in Emlenton, Pennsylvania.

**Christa Pongratz-Lippitt** has been Vienna correspondent of the London *Tablet* for the past fifteen years, and is a close collaborator of Cardinal König.

**Daniel McCarthy, OSB**, is a monk of St. Benedict's Abbey, Atchison, Kansas, stationed at San Anselmo, Rome, where he is working toward a doctorate in liturgy at the Pontifical Institute of Liturgy. Fr. McCarthy holds a master of divinity degree from St. John's Seminary, Collegeville, Minnesota, and a master's in theology (liturgy) from the University of Notre Dame.

**Sean M. McCarthy** is a presbyter of the archdiocese of Boston, ordained in 1991. He has served as chair of the Boston Liturgical Commission and served on the board of directors for the FDLC. He presently serves as parochial vicar at St. Elizabeth of Hungary parish in Acton, Massachusetts, and continues to work in liturgy within the archdiocese of Boston.

**Hank McQueeney** was born in Boston. He holds an A.B. (liberal arts) from Boston College and a Master of Hospital Administration degree from the University of Michigan. He served in the Navy as an intelligence officer and spent thirty years as a hospital administrator, much of that time at Georgetown University Hospital. Mr. McQueeney has long been an admirer of Irving R. Levine and, like Mr. Levine, occasionally wears a bow tie. He currently lives in West Virginia with his wife, Elaine Rendler.

**Michael P. Mernagh**, a native of Canada, is director of liturgical music at St. Meinrad School of Theology in southern Indiana. He holds an M.A. in Theology with a concentration in liturgy from St. John's University in Collegeville, Minnesota.

**Dr. John R. Page** served on the staff of the International Commission on English in the Liturgy (ICEL) from 1972–2002. In 1997 he was the recipient of the McManus award from the Federation of Diocesan Liturgical Commissions (FDLC). In 2003 Dr. Page was the recipient of the *Pax Christi* Award from St. John's Abbey in Collegeville, MN.

**Aurelio Porfiri** was born in Rome in 1968. Mr. Porfiri is a graduate in choral music from the Conservatorio of San Pietro a Maiella of Naples. In 1993, he joined the *Vicariato* of the Vatican City and serves as one of the organists at St. Peter's Basilica. He is the organist in charge for the weekly audience of the Holy Father in the *Aula Paolo VI* or in the *Piazza San Pietro*. He is also employed as the music director at the Church of St. Susanna, the English-speaking church in Rome, where he conducts the Santa Susanna singers, a professional choir. His compositional forms include oratories, Masses, motets and hymns in Italian and English, some commissioned and broadcast by Vatican Radio during liturgical celebrations and other programs. He contributes music and articles frequently to the journals *La Vita in Cristo e nella Chiesa*, *Liturgia* and *Rogate ergo*. He has also collaborated with various publishers, including Edizioni San Paolo, Città Nuova and Hortus Conclusus.

**Michael R. Prendergast** has more than thirty years' experience as a musician and liturgist at the parish, cathedral and diocesan levels. Currently, he is OCP's liturgy specialist and editor of *Today's Liturgy*. A native of the diocese of Helena, Montana, he served as the cathedral musician at St. Mary's Cathedral in Fargo, North Dakota. Before coming to Portland in the fall of 2000, he was Director of the Office of Worship and Christian Initiation for the Diocese of Great Falls-Billings in eastern Montana.

Mr. Prendergast edited the Pastoral Press book *Full, Conscious and Active Participation: Celebrating Twenty-Five Years of Today's Liturgy*. He is the author of *Music in the Liturgy for Small Parishes*, published by the Liturgical Press. He has written on topics related to music and liturgy in *Pastoral Music* and *Church*. He served on the task force of the Bishops' Committee on the Liturgy for the revision of the ritual book *Sunday Celebrations in the Absence of a Priest*. He holds a master's degree in theological studies from Mount Angel Seminary, St. Benedict, Oregon, and a master's degree in liturgical studies from St. John's University in Collegeville, Minnesota. He is a member of the board of directors of Partners in Preaching, a national ministry of consultation, training and formation for the church's ministry of liturgical preaching.

**Elaine Rendler** is a teacher, author, choir director, composer and pastoral liturgist. She works with parishes and dioceses throughout the country to further the cause of liturgical renewal. Her weekly column appears in *Today's Liturgy*. She is on the music faculty of George Mason University in Fairfax, Virginia, and is director of the Georgetown Chorale, a 90-member singing group that combines community service with music while performing the classics of choral literature. She lives in West Virginia with her husband, Hank McQueeney.

Ms. Rendler holds a bachelor's degree in music education, a master's degree and doctorate of musical arts in organ performance from the Catholic University of America in Washington, D.C. She is the author of two books, *In the Midst of the Assembly* and *This Is the Day*, and the two volumes of *Keyboard Praise*, musical settings on hymn tunes all published by OCP Publications.

**M.D. Ridge** is a composer of liturgical music, journalist, author and editor. Her music collections include *In Every Age*; *By Cross and Water Signed*, and *A Light in Darkness*, all published by OCP, and *Awake, O Sleeper!* (GIA). She is the author, with Mark Purtill, of the OCP book *Good Guitar Stuff*, and is editorial coordinator of OCP's *Liturgical Music News*.

Her articles have appeared in *Rite*, *Pastoral Music*, *Music and Liturgy* (U.K.), *Modern Liturgy*, *Today's Liturgy*, *Liturgia y Canción*, *Liturgical Music News* and *The Hymnology Annual*, as well as several secular publications. A native of New York City, Ms. Ridge holds a B.S. (Humanities) from Le Moyne College, Syracuse, New York. She lives in Norfolk, Virginia.

**Christina Ronzio** is director of the liturgy office for the diocese of London, Ontario, Canada. She earned a master's degree in liturgical studies from St. John's University in Collegeville, Minnesota.

**Pedro Rubalcava** is a composer, clinician, recording artist, performer and pastoral minister. He is director of Hispanic Ministries at Oregon Catholic Press and serves on the board of the *Instituto Nacional de Liturgia Hispana*, representing the Northwest region. He has served in various leadership roles in the areas of Hispanic ministry, liturgy and music, catechesis, evangelization, RCIA, and youth and young adult ministry on both parish and diocesan levels. He holds a B.A. in Religious Studies from the University of San Diego in San Diego, California. He resides in Boring, Oregon with his wife and two children.

**Philip J. Sandstrom, S.T.D.**, is vicar for the English-speaking people of St. Michel and St. Gudule's Cathedral in Brussels, Belgium. Born in 1936, he is a presbyter of the archdiocese of New York, where he has served as a parish vicar and administrator, and taught for fifteen years at Cardinal Spellman High School. Among other publications he has edited the liturgy bulletin *Focus* for the archdiocese of New York, edited for several years the *Ordo* published by Paulist Press, and prepared the Bulletin Notes for *Today's Liturgy*. He is a member of the North American Academy of Liturgy and *Societas Liturgica*, an international and ecumenical society of liturgical scholars. He taught in the Summer Master's Program of Church Music and Liturgy at St. Joseph's College, Rensselaer, Indiana (1978–1990). He was on the faculty of the Deacon Training Program in the diocese of Bridgeport, Connecticut (1979–1985) and was a member of the staff at The American College at the University of Louvain, Belgium. Among his academic degrees are: B.A. (1957) Manhattan College (New York); M.A. (1962) Saint Joseph's College and Seminary (New York); M.A. (1965) Notre Dame University (liturgy and sacramental theology); doctorate in theology (1987) Institut Catholique (Paris, France).

**Dr. Carl Sterkens** graduated from the high school of the De La Salle Christian Brothers in Ekeren, Antwerp, studied philosophy and religious studies at the Catholic University of Louvain, and received his doctoral degree in 2001 from the Catholic University of Nijmegen. He works as an assistant professor in practical theology and a pastoral supervisor at the Faculty of Theology in Nijmegen [Radboud University Nijmegen], where he is director of the Institute of Pastoral Studies.

**Brother John of Taizé** was born in Philadelphia in 1950 and joined the Taizé community in 1974. He spends much of his time in Taizé helping the young adults who take part in the international meetings, there to learn how to read the Bible as a source of meaning for their own lives. In the 1980s he was part of a small group of Taizé brothers who lived in Hell's Kitchen on Manhattan's West Side. He continues to travel in the United States and Italy for meetings and retreats for young adults. Brother John has written seven books on biblical topics discussed in the meetings in Taizé; they have been translated into a dozen languages: *The Pilgrim God: A Biblical Journey* [Pastoral Press] (1985); *The Way of the Lord: A New Testament Pilgrimage* [Pastoral Press](1990); *Praying the Our Father Today* [Pastoral Press](1992); *The Adventure of Holiness: Biblical Foundations and Present-Day Perspectives* [Alba House](1999); *At the Wellspring: Jesus and the Samaritan Woman* [Alba House](2001); and *Reading the Ten Commandments Anew: Towards a Land of Freedom* [Alba House] (2003).